FARTHER

EIGHT MONTHS ON AMERICA'S TRIPLE CROWN TRAILS

HEATHER ANDERSON

MOUNTAINEERS BOOKS

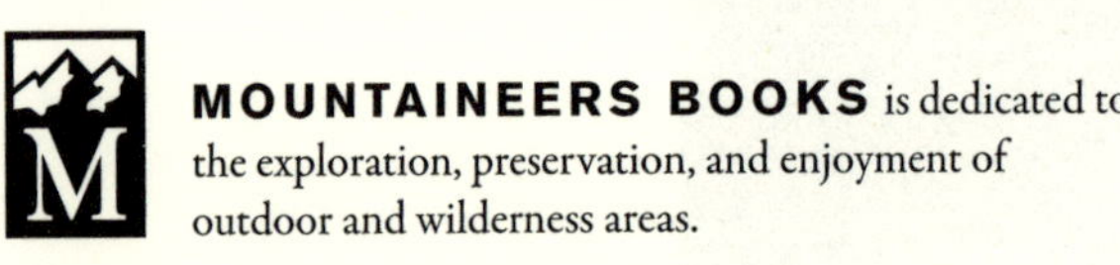

MOUNTAINEERS BOOKS is dedicated to the exploration, preservation, and enjoyment of outdoor and wilderness areas.

1001 SW Klickitat Way, Suite 201, Seattle, WA 98134
800-553-4453, www.mountaineersbooks.org

Printed in China

29 28 27 26   1 2 3 4 5

Design and layout: Jen Grable
Cartographer: Martha Bostwick
Cover and part opener photographs: *Hiking through a meadow on the Pacific Crest Trail* (davelmorgan/iStock); *flaming azaleas on the Appalachian Trail* (WendyOlsen-Photography/iStock); *Colorado's Collegiate Peaks Wilderness on the Continental Divide Trail* (Douglas Rissing/iStock)

Library of Congress Cataloging-in-Publication Data is on file for this title.

Mountaineers Books titles may be purchased for corporate, educational, or other promotional sales, and our authors are available for a wide range of events. For information on special discounts or booking an author, contact our customer service at 800-553-4453 or mbooks@mountaineersbooks.org.

Printed on FSC®-certified materials

ISBN (paperback): 978-1-68051-814-6
ISBN (ebook): 978-1-68051-815-3

An independent nonprofit publisher since 1960

PRAISE FOR HEATHER ANDERSON AND HER PREVIOUS BOOKS

"*Mud, Rocks, Blazes* is beautifully written, intense, and exhilarating—a no holds barred, one-woman show."

—Barney Scout Mann, author of *Journeys North*

"Anish's story is an incredible reminder of the power of determination to accomplish great things."

—Elsye "Chardonnay" Walker, first African American to complete the Triple Crown

"I couldn't put this book down!"

—Sirena Rana, author of *Urban Trails: Tucson*

"In *Farther*, Heather Anderson reveals the mental and emotional depth it takes to live in constant motion across America's three great trails. Her writing pulls you into the perseverance, solitude, and triumph of chasing something bigger than limits, while carrying the memory and lessons of her father as both compass and fuel. *Farther* is a meditation on endurance, courage, and choosing to keep moving forward."

—Derick Lugo, author of *A Fabulous Thru-Hike*

"*Mud, Rocks, Blazes* is a story of perseverance, overcoming self-doubt, and believing that we can achieve anything if we want it enough."

—Joe "Stringbean" McConaughy, record-setting thru-hiker

"*Thirst* is a testament to human endurance, inspiring to hikers and non-hikers alike."

—Shelf Awareness

"Beautiful and deftly written and intimate and searing in its honesty, Anish's is a quest to conquer the trail and her own inner darkness."

—*Foreword Reviews*, starred review

"With humility and vulnerability, Heather 'Anish' Anderson reminds us that the most impressive feats of strength and endurance are entirely human endeavors, achieved one step at a time."

—Ben Montgomery, author of *Grandma Gatewood's Walk*

"Heather Anderson's book is much like her extraordinary trail accomplishments: extremely personal yet universally inspiring."

—Jennifer Pharr Davis, author of *The Pursuit of Endurance*

"*Thirst* is the kind of book that sits in your bones. It gives you hope and courage by showing that no matter who you are or where you are at now, you can do more."

—Liz "Snorkel" Thomas, author of *Long Trails*

"In no uncertain terms, Heather 'Anish' Anderson is a legend in the long-distance hiking community."

—Zach Davis, editor in chief of The Trek

FOR MY FATHER
AND MY SISTER

CONTENTS

TRIPLE CROWN TRAILS
Manning Park
Snoqualmie Pass
Holden Village
Goat Rocks Wilderness
WA
Waterton Lakes National Park
Glacier National Park
C A
MT
ND
Butte
Crater Lake
OR
Yellowstone National Park
ID
PACIFIC CREST TRAIL
Bridger-Teton Wilderness
WY
SD
Wind River Range
halfway point
Sierra City
NE
NV
Steamboat Springs
CONTINENTAL DIVIDE TRAIL
Denver
CA
Mount Whitney
CO
Kennedy Meadows
UT
Salida
KS
Cumbres Pass
Chamas
The Saufleys
Grants
AZ
Albuquerque
NM
Campo
Doc Campbell's
Mimbres
Columbus/ Palomas
TX
Pacific Ocean
MEXICO

ADA
Lake Superior
Lake Michigan
Lake Huron
L. Ontario
Lake Erie
Mount Katahdin
ME
VT
NH
Hanover
Killington Peak
MA
NY
CT
RI
Delaware Water Gap
PA
NJ
halfway point
DE
MD
MN
WI
MI
IA
IL
IN
OH
WV
DC
VA
APPALACHIAN TRAIL
MO
KY
Grayson Highlands State Park
Roan High Knob
NC
TN
Great Smoky Mountains
Springer Mountain
AR
SC
MS
AL
GA
LA
FL
Atlantic Ocean
0
250
500 mi
0
250
500 km

AUTHOR'S NOTE

A journey of this magnitude is difficult to put into words. My hiking of the Calendar Year Triple Crown, and all that dominoed from that year, significantly altered my relationship to myself, to my loved ones, and to hiking itself. Nothing has been, or will be, the same.

The events and conversations chronicled in *Farther* are accurate to the best of my memory; however, slight adjustments to the timeline of flashbacks have been made for better narrative flow. Some names have also been changed.

PROLOGUE

JANUARY 23, 2017

A thin line of pale yellow demarcated the flat horizon, so different from the mountainous one I'd left behind the evening before. The plane banked wide over southern Michigan as the lights of Wayne County became visible—people awakening after another frigid January night. Somewhere down there my father's body, once wiry and strong, was now breathless and cold, waiting at the crematorium.

My collar was soaked from a night of crying, prior to boarding and throughout the red-eye, but I still couldn't stop. From midnight in Seattle to a midwestern dawn, I'd wrestled with new realizations. Every achievement in my life—my straight-A grades, my college education, my attempts at marriage and career, every top-five-female finish in hundred-mile ultramarathons, and becoming a world-class athlete who set records on three National Scenic Trails—had been fueled by one desire: to get him to say one simple phrase. *I'm proud of you.*

Yet, he never had, and I had been too afraid to ask. Now, I would never know. A lifetime of smoking and the ensuing COPD had drowned him, extinguishing any chance of finding the answer.

The plane touched down with enough force to slam my head forward and then back into the headrest. My eyes blurred with tears again. I felt my drive to push my limits ebb, leaving me engulfed in an ocean of emptiness.

Without rudder or sail, I drifted off the plane.

PART I

WALKING WITH WINTER

CHAPTER 1

SPRINGER MOUNTAIN

The two-wheel-drive pickup bounced up the dirt road. Adam—my partner on trail and off for fourteen months—had been largely silent the past five hours as he'd driven us northward from Florida, where we'd been living next door to my sister Marie, into the Appalachian Mountains of north Georgia. I could sense the honey-thick tension between us as well as his dejection as we drew ever closer to the inevitable parting. He gunned the engine and we fishtailed through a muddy hairpin.

"I don't remember this road being so rough," I commented, staring down the long drop through dense trees covering the mountainside.

He mumbled something I didn't quite hear.

I'd been on this narrow, steep, potholed road to Springer Mountain twice before, but I had no real recollection of it. Both times I'd been too preoccupied by the journey that lay ahead of, or behind, me. Yet, for some reason, today—March 1, 2018—each detail stood out in stark relief.

The first time I'd been here, fifteen years earlier, two of my best friends from college had driven me up this road to the beginning of the Appalachian Trail. Unbeknownst to any of us, it was also the beginning of my future as a repeat thru-hiker. The steps I took away from them were the first of millions walked on trails all over the world. At the time I had no idea what I was getting myself into, but the Appalachian Trail had become my instructor. Over the next four months I'd learned much of what it meant to backpack—and how to live.

A dozen years after that first thru-hike, I completed the Appalachian Trail for a second time, in the opposite direction, ending on Springer Mountain in the early evening. My record-setting traverse of the entire trail—almost two thousand miles in fifty-four days—was a beautiful culmination of what I had begun there on my first thru-hike.

As Adam pulled the truck into the dirt parking lot at the end of the road, I wondered: *So why am I here again?* It was only five p.m. but already almost dark. We got out without saying anything. The wind was shaking the bare trees and biting our bare skin. I pulled on a sweatshirt and a rain jacket as mixed precipitation sputtered against us, dotting his wild, dark hair with white pellets.

"We're not in Florida anymore," I muttered.

Adam nodded and zipped up his warm charcoal coat over his lean torso. A few cars down, my hiking friends Apple Pie and her husband, Greenleaf—trail nicknames they had earned while thru-hiking—were also throwing jackets on. They headed our way and we huddled in a cold cluster.

"So, do you want to do the mile out and back tonight or in the morning?" Apple Pie asked in her bright Dutch accent.

"Um," I looked questioningly into Adam's brown eyes.

"It's your hike—it's up to you."

It *was* my hike. Adam did not want me to go, and he had not pretended otherwise through the months of preparation. Yet, I appreciated his begrudging support of my decision. His disappointment that I was embarking on a seven-thousand-plus-mile journey to rehike the Appalachian, Pacific Crest, and Continental Divide Trails made me question whether I even wanted to. When he drove away, I wouldn't see him for months.

Do I want that? Can I handle being apart for so long? Can we *handle it?*

"Okay, well, yeah—let's go do this mile tonight."

We headed south on the AT to reach its southern terminus at the summit of Springer Mountain. Only the northbound mile I walked back to the parking lot would count, but this lot was the closest you could drive to the official start of the trail.

As we climbed, the wind increased and the rain intensified, making the rocks underfoot slick. The hem of my cotton yoga pants dragged in the mud, and water wicked upward to my knees. *I probably should have changed into actual hiking clothes before heading out.*

It grew completely dark, and I turned on my headlamp. Raindrops sparkled in the beam of light.

The familiar Springer summit rocks came into view, illuminated by my light. I stepped out from the protection of the forest canopy into the full brunt of the pouring rain and violent wind, with Adam following a few steps behind. Dots of light from Apple Pie's and Greenleaf's headlamps bobbed toward us from a quarter mile away. I reached for the summit plaque, letting my fingertips graze it briefly before turning to get down off the mountain.

I nearly tripped over Adam as he slid toward me on the rocks and landed on one knee. I reached to help him up—realizing, as I did, that he hadn't fallen. In his outstretched hand was a ring.

"Will you marry me?" His eyes brimmed with tears.

Those were the last words I ever expected to hear in a tempest on a mountain in the southern Appalachians. I grabbed the plaque and held on tightly to the summit that had now witnessed three of the most pivotal moments of my life—starting and finishing prior hikes and now a marriage proposal.

"Yes."

DESPITE THE HOWLING WIND, I slept well in the back of the pickup. Just before first light, the alarm jarred us out of sleep. Adam clambered out and began prepping coffee on the tailgate. I joined him, hopping lightly back and forth to stay warm. We got into the cab and gulped our hot drinks, barely controlling our shivering bodies enough to keep from slopping liquid everywhere. Dawn appeared out the windshield as a vibrant raspberry streak across layers of pale violet and lavender marred by skeletal black trees.

Coffee finished, I got out, squinting into the bright sun that was now bathing the back of the truck. Adam kissed me goodbye.

"Drive safe."

With my loaded backpack, I made my way over to where the first of the many white blazes that marked the entire length of the Appalachian Trail was painted on a tree, and I headed downhill, away from the powerful winds that sped across the mountaintop. It was hard to believe I had ever thought it never got cold in Georgia.

The forested trail was devoid of people, but it was not silent. The wind clacked tree branches together—castanets in the gale. My footfalls were lost in their raucous rhythm as I followed the AT along the rippling terrain of the southern Blue Ridge Mountains, the Appalachian subrange I would traverse for the next twelve hundred miles or so to their northern terminus in Pennsylvania. From there I'd cross into the ridges and valleys, making my way across South Mountain and northward to far-flung places like Sunfish Pond in New Jersey and Mount Katahdin in Maine that were etched into my memory.

Like scent, nature has a way about it that evokes vivid memories. While I might struggle to recall the color of a room, I can easily remember the half dozen shades of green that painted the forest of New Jersey when I saw my first bear up close. The hum of mosquitoes that ceased to exist when I made eye contact with the dark eyes above a hickory snout flaring in an attempt to smell me more fully. The way the glossy blue-black fur rippled as the animal rose up onto its haunches to tower above the berry-heavy bushes drooping across the trail. Nature inscribes stories in my mind next to important dates and phone numbers, to-do lists, and the names of coworkers. The intensity of living close to the land is a mnemonic that can never be erased.

Back in the Chattahoochee National Forest, my hands and feet began to thaw. The wind diminished to a gentle breeze that occasionally caused a snag to groan in displeasure at being disturbed. My legs swung in a comfortable tempo as I climbed, descended, traversed, and repeated. I relished the return of quiet and the retreat of sluggishness. A sparkle caught my eye as I pushed off my trekking poles, and I paused to inspect the fleeting glimmer. With surprise I realized it was the new ring I wore on my left hand.

"I'm engaged," I told the trees.

With a sudden gust, the castanets cheered.

CHAPTER 2

CARTER GAP

Why do I want to hike these trails for the third time? Why all in one year? I pondered the questions I'd cycled through for months. I kept coming back to the fact that 2018 was the fiftieth anniversary of the National Trails Act, which created the Appalachian and Pacific Crest Trails, with the Continental Divide Trail added a few years later. Yes, I'd hiked each of these trails twice already—setting fastest known times on both the AT and the PCT. I could think of no greater celebration of places that had been so incredibly meaningful in my life than to hike them all for a third time. If I did so between now and December 31, I would be the first woman to complete the so-called Calendar Year Triple Crown (CYTC), a feat only a handful of men had accomplished. My FKTs would fall someday, but being the first to do something could never be taken away.

Walking through the still-dormant Georgia woods, I ruminated on my previous thru-hikes. Each represented an era in my life and my growth as a human. My life journey was interwoven with thousands of miles of rocks, roots, trees, and mud. At more than two thousand miles each, these trails would never provide the same experience twice, even if I were the same person on each hike—which I most definitely wasn't.

When I completed the Triple Crown the first time between 2003 and 2006, each trail was a new and exciting adventure, almost entirely through terrain I had never seen and in many states where I'd never set foot. I was in my early twenties, and as I discovered the trails, I also discovered myself. I found connection, grounding, and new capacities.

Those treks were as much an introduction to the mountains as they were to who I was.

My second Triple Crown between 2013 and 2017 saw me become a record setter, learning to find comfort in the miles and mountains I had walked before even as I discovered a new understanding of my physical and mental abilities. Those journeys had helped me find an intimacy with both the footpaths and the deepest parts of myself.

Now, on my third Triple Crown I was once again venturing into the unknown of the known. Who I would be afterward would only be revealed by the walking. This time I would compress three thru-hikes that each typically took an entire summer into one season, bending them around my decision to thru-hike the PCT with Adam as he completed the final leg of his own Triple Crown, begun with his AT thru-hike in 2015.

RAPID BEEPING ROUSED ME from the depths of sleep on the third morning of my hike, and I thrust my hand into the frigid air outside my sleeping bag to silence it. I fumbled the watch, cursing the multiple tries it took to find the tiny button. *If the alarm doesn't wake me, the frustration of shutting it up will.*

Sitting up in the darkness, I yawned and dug my phone and water filter out of the bottom of my sleeping bag, where I'd protected both of them from freezing with the warmth of my body. I filtered water into my pot and set it on the meager flame of a partial Esbit solid fuel tablet. A few minutes later I added instant coffee and pulled the hot beverage into my cocoon. I scrolled through yesterday's messages on my phone while sipping and dawdling in avoidance of the inevitable parting from Adam.

"I found a camp at the base of Standing Indian," I had typed to him the night before. "Right where I slept on my FKT when the owls serenaded me. I hear them again right now. I wonder if they're the same ones."

"I'm glad you have a spot. I made it to the truck. Sleeping here tonight."

"Okay. Where will I see you tomorrow?"

"Deep Gap Parking Lot. I'll have coffee and breakfast for you."

"Great! I miss you."

There was a long pause between the texts then, and I finished my coffee wincing. *Had it been a slow cell tower, or second thoughts on his part?*

"I miss you too. Love you."

I closed the screen on the phone.

Why was he out here meeting me along the way?

Instead of leaving from Springer, Adam had met me at road crossings multiple times each day over the past few days. I had returned to the trail each night and slept under rhododendrons on recently thawed ground while he slept in his truck at nearby trailheads. He hadn't wanted me to embark on this hike, but now he was immersed in it with me. After we thru-hiked the CDT and the Oregon Desert Trail together the previous year, it seemed natural to plan to hike the PCT together. However, his ultrarunning race schedule and job at a running store in Washington were supposed to occupy our time apart. I'd chosen to break up my CYTC in order to accommodate his request to hike the PCT with me. Now his inserting himself into this first part of the journey even though he had claimed he didn't want to be here had me feeling conflicted and tense.

Why am I out here walking? We've just decided to spend our lives together. Should I quit and do this some other time? After we've gotten married and cemented our relationship?

It kept my backpack lighter to see Adam frequently, making the hiking a bit easier. I was sometimes able to leave my tent, sleeping bag, and other overnight gear with him for the day. But saying goodbye every evening was getting harder. He was supposed to be training for the Umstead hundred-mile race, and I knew assisting my trip was stripping away the hours he needed to be running. I wanted him to stay with me forever, but I also wished he'd leave and do something that made him as happy as thru-hiking made me.

Being crewed didn't sit well with me. Being my crewperson didn't fit Adam well either. But for some reason he was still here.

"Why don't you hike with me instead of crewing me?" I'd asked him yesterday for the third time in as many days, knowing we'd both enjoy that a lot more.

"Because I don't want to hike the AT again."

"You don't have to do all of it, but you hate crewing me and you need to log miles to train for Umstead. Why not just hike? You like hiking. We get along well when we hike. Just hike for however many days that you'd be out here anyway."

"I don't know how long I'm going to do this. Just a few days. I don't want to have to figure out where to leave the truck or deal with any of those logistics."

The closer we had gotten to my March 1 start date, the more Adam had slipped into depression over my planned adventure. I had been looking forward to hiking away from that sadness. Yet, here he was every day, reminding me that pursuing my goals was hurting him.

Adam had signed up for the race to give himself an objective to take his mind off my hike, vowing he would see me off at Springer and then go his own way until we reunited in San Diego in late May to begin our PCT hike together. Now here he was reneging on what he had said he needed and wanted. If he was going to abandon his own goals, I wished he'd just put on a pack and join me. But no matter how many times I asked, he said no. Instead he seemed intent on living in this limbo—neither following his own plan nor fully committing to crewing me.

I considered my full food bag. Without knowing when Adam would decide to leave, I was hesitant to stash too many extra supplies or too much gear with him overnight.

I drank the last sip of coffee, hurriedly exited my sleeping bag, and dressed in multiple layers to ward off the cold air. The first ray of dawn was illuminating the treetops as I finished putting my tent into my pack. *Just enough light.* I clicked off my headlamp and climbed toward the summit out of the deep notch where I'd camped. Not being a morning person, I found starting before dawn each day onerous. Even so, I chipped away at the South, willing my body to cover at least thirty miles each day, even if I had to get up early and spend two hours or more hiking by headlamp.

"I am grateful to you," I whispered to my still-sleepy legs as I climbed.

In addition to Adam, Apple Pie and Greenleaf leapfrogged and hiked with me for the first several days. They rendezvoused with Adam to meet me at road crossings, and Apple Pie hiked a few short sections with me. It felt strange to walk into a trailhead and have a mini cheering squad waiting for me there. I thought this hike would be an intimidating solo endeavor, but instead I had so far been surrounded by supporters. It left me feeling like I had deadlines to meet because people were waiting for me.

I'm grateful for them even if it's not what I expected, I reminded myself over and over as I plodded along, feeling overwhelmed by every aspect of the hike. I knew that once they all left and I was on my own, I would miss the company.

Tenacity and resilience are two of the most important traits for successful thru-hikers. The ability to stick with it when conditions are tough and you're tired is necessary to get from terminus to terminus. I knew more than most just how essential it is to be able to roll with all of the unexpected, uncontrollable, unplanned-for moments that take place during a journey across the country on foot. And yet, feeling like my journey was spiraling out of my control within hours of its beginning was testing the depths of my resilience in ways even I hadn't anticipated. I needed to trust that I could draw upon the strength of my past to fully experience the plot twists of my present.

My reflections faded as I entered a familiar-looking rhododendron grove in a broad dish of the mountains. Sure enough, a wooden sign pointed to the shelter just off trail: Carter Gap. I felt my stomach lurch slightly with remembering.

It was here I'd first chosen to go by the name Anish on trail—an attempt to select a new identity and find out who I could be were it up to me to decide. After decades of running away from myself, I had been broken apart by my FKTs and brought back together here in September 2015.

"Hello, Anish," I whispered, grateful for the woman who had been bold enough to not give up until she found contentment in who she was.

Although it was still my trail name, I seldom used it. I'd brought Anish back to this spot in 2015, feeling whole for the first time in my life. I didn't need an alter ego to propel me forward anymore, but I still honored that aspect of my identity. I knew, too, that while I could now accept myself completely, losing my father had released a fountain of questions about my motivations. *Why did I need Anish in the first place?*

"Because of Heatherjo Eugenia," I whispered.

When I was born eighteen years after my older sisters, my parents were certain I was going to be the son they'd always wanted—to be named Basil Eugene Anderson Junior. Instead, the doctor laid a third daughter into my father's strong arms.

"I wanted to name you Heatherjo Eugenia, but your dad wouldn't let me," my mom told me, explaining that they had not considered any girls' names beforehand. "They wouldn't let me leave the hospital with you until you were named, so I picked the first Scottish name I could think of."

My very genesis had been a disappointment, my naming a rush to fill out paperwork. Why did I need Anish? Because I held a deep fear that I had never been good enough—that despite my being a tomboy, I was never what my parents wanted. *No wonder I struggled to fully accept myself.* As I shuffled away from Carter Gap, a few tears slid down my cheeks.

CHAPTER 3

THE SMOKIES

I clambered up Cheoah Bald for the third—and what my gasping lungs desperately hoped would be the last—time in my hiking career, cursing the steep, relentless ascent. The views from the grassy top were, as always, reward enough to make me forget the promises just made to my body. In all directions, undulating mountains poked into the sky. Their rounded summits clad with winter-gray branches resembled a multitude of hunched porcupines prickling the sagging, snow-laden clouds.

A short distance down the other side, I set up camp in a tiny kink of terrain where a small hollow dipped away from the switchbacking tread of the Appalachian Trail. Last year's leaves, once resplendent shades of red and gold, now a uniform sepia, crackled under my feet as I set up my tent. By the time I was settled, night had fallen, although far beyond the folds of Cheoah I could see pale yellow light gracing the hilltops. I lit an Esbit tab on fire and boiled water to add to my dehydrated beans. After eating mechanically, I fell into the kind of deep sleep I find only inside the walls of my tent.

I awoke to see that overnight my breath had frozen in whorls to the ceiling of the tent. I lay there in predawn darkness with my wan headlamp illuminating the fragile lacework my exhalation and nature had cocreated. Outside, fat snowflakes were falling. Powder dusted the dreary leaves visible under the vestibule. Adam checked the weather for me religiously and hadn't mentioned snow. Likely there wasn't any a few hundred feet lower. I was once again reminded that the mountains made their own weather.

I started my morning routine, which began with heating water for coffee and ended as I forced my feet into frozen shoes, wincing in pain. Before light kissed my side of the mountain, I was moving down the trail.

It wasn't long before the foot pain started. I ignored it, expecting it to dissipate as my feet warmed and my shoes thawed, but it persisted—growing steadily more intense as the miles passed. By the time I reached the monotonous, rolling lowland forests between Cheoah and the Great Smoky Mountains, I was compensating visibly for the intense burning in the ball of my left foot.

"The road crossing through Newfound Gap is closed." Adam greeted me with the news flatly when we met near Fontana Dam several hours later. "Why are you limping?"

The trail until that point had been covered intermittently with snow even at this low elevation, so his news wasn't a shock. Yet, it threw me into a reorganization of thoughts and mental preparation as he turned around and I fell into step behind him. *Crossing the Smokies is going to be much harder without him meeting me at the road halfway.* My foot was only going to complicate things.

"I don't know. It just started hurting on the way down Cheoah. It's like an intense burning pain in the ball."

"Sounds like a neuroma. How many miles do you have on those shoes?"

"Uh, they were new when I started the AT, so about 120."

"Hmm."

He led me back to where the truck waited. Great Smoky Mountains National Park lay just ahead. Through it the Appalachian Trail snaked along the ridgelines for seventy-two miles. In that entire distance there was only one road crossing, at Newfound Gap. In clear weather with a light pack, I had traversed this distance easily in two and a half days. But now, with an unknown amount of snow—enough to close down the normally open highway—and my twice-as-heavy backpack on an injured foot, I had no way of knowing how long it would take.

Or if I can even do it.

We reached the immense paved dam complex, which was deserted. It felt odd to be all alone in a place that typically hums with recreation. Adam led me to his pickup—soon to be *our* pickup, I reminded myself—where I loaded my backpack with two and a half days' worth of food and all of my cold weather gear.

"Do you have another pair of shoes?" he asked.

"I guess. I mean, I wasn't supposed to get them until mile five hundred. I'm only a quarter of the way there."

"You should probably switch and see if that helps."

"I can't afford to waste a pair of shoes!"

"Can you afford to hike injured for more than seven thousand miles?" he countered.

I sighed and decided not to argue. Instead, I dug through the boxes in the back of the truck until I found a new pair of shoes, a model I'd hiked thousands of miles in before. I slipped them on my cold feet and pulled the laces snug. Then we hiked across the dam and up the dirt trail, animatedly debating my decision to take only enough food to cross the mountains in the same amount of time it would take me in clear weather.

"What if you run into too much snow? It could take you twice as long." Adam's forehead creased with worry and he gripped my hand tightly.

Feet of snow still covered the land above us and I knew he was right, but already my pack was full to bursting with the zero-degree sleeping bag and extra clothing. I stood belligerently firm.

"I can walk all night and all day if necessary. I've done it before. I'll see you at the end. I love you."

"I love you too."

I watched his back disappear down the semifrozen trail for only a few seconds before I turned and pushed upward. Tears filled my eyes and spilled over, leaving cold tracks on my face. I hated the continual goodbyes marred by worry and tension.

At deep dusk I reached the first campsite in the park and turned left on the short side trail. There were already two tents there with no discernible movement or noise, the inhabitants presumably asleep. I pitched my tent a short distance away, struggling to drive the stakes into the rock-hard, frozen ground. I crawled inside, shivering. My breath and the steam from boiling water for my instant refried beans crystallized onto the silnylon of my tent. I ate my dinner by headlamp under the sparkling ceiling.

My alarm went off at four a.m. I opened my eyes to complete darkness and fumbled to make coffee, which cooled so fast I had only two sips that were hot enough to burn my lips and mouth.

How cold is it? I'm going up thousands more feet. How cold will it be up there?

I felt a slight qualm in my stomach. Maybe I didn't have enough gear. I packed quickly, feeling as though I was once again in pursuit of an FKT. But this time my early morning efficiency was driven by cold and the potential for slow travel rather than speed objectives. My goal was to reach Newfound Gap and the heated bathrooms thirty-five miles away.

"You're not hiker trash until you've slept in a privy," I muttered to the dark forest.

The climb into the Smokies is one of the longest of the entire Appalachian Trail—or so it seems. No matter which direction you approach from, you ascend nearly five thousand feet to eventually reach the spine of the mountains. Along the way, you can see the rolling beauty of Southern Appalachia for countless miles in all directions. At least, you can while winter still holds the world in her grip and no leaves grace the trees. The highest landscape is viewless year-round, as it's clothed in a mixed forest of spruce and fir, dense and secretive. Today those trees were bedecked with so much snow I felt as though I were wandering through an unshaken snow globe—perhaps beneath the gaze of a bemused watcher following my struggling body as it bucked ivory drifts. I looked up at the leaden sky and hoped the watcher wouldn't shake any more snow down on me.

I plodded and postholed and fought through knee-deep snow. I climbed upward for an age before beginning to follow ridges where it became obvious there were people ahead of me—people who had broken trail, and for that I was thankful. I vented my jackets and rotated snack bars from my pack into my pockets so that they wouldn't be frozen pucks when I tried to eat them.

I kept my stops to only a few seconds at a time to maintain my body temperature. I knew I would need to move until well after dark to reach my goal. *I can't stop today. I can't stop tomorrow.* I would be at risk of experiencing a Raynaud's attack that would turn my fingers white and wooden, robbing me of the ability to use my hands. The mysterious syndrome had plagued me for more than a decade, and my decisions in the backcountry were always made with its specter in the back of my mind. In these conditions I couldn't stop except briefly until I was getting into my sleeping bag.

Spots with flowing water were few and far between. I repeatedly packed snow into the water bottle that rode in my jacket's internal chest pocket. I ate handfuls often. I knew there wasn't enough moisture in it to really quench my thirst or keep me hydrated, but I also knew that in forty-eight hours I'd be back in lower country where spring was around the corner and water had been released from its icy prison.

Near four p.m. I reached a shelter. I ducked behind the tarp hanging across the opening, and took off my pack and set it down. Six hikers were inside in various stages of unpacking their gear and cooking their dinners. None of them acknowledged me. I took off my gloves and moved fast with laser focus. I knew I had less than five minutes before my fingers would begin to lose dexterity.

"Four more snacks. New hand warmers. Trash from pockets into food bag. Change gloves."

I muttered my way through the mental checklist under my breath, stuffing fresh snacks into my pockets and swapping wet gloves for dry mittens with newly activated hand warmers inside. I shoved frozen gummies into my mouth and put my pack back on. Every muscle in my body had sighed with relief when I stopped moving. Each and every one protested as I ducked under the tarp and floundered back into the snow.

I could stop here, I told myself. *There's no record to break.*

But I have only another day of food. More bad weather is coming. And Adam is waiting.

My fingers were tingling, flirting with Raynaud's. I grasped the hand warmers inside my mitts and waited for them to revive. I touched my neck where I'd hung my headlamp right before leaving the shelter. It was going to be a couple of hours before I'd need it, but I didn't plan to stop again until I was ready to sleep.

Night settled slowly over the Smokies; charcoal shadows sifted down from treetops, deepening until it was no longer possible to see without a light. In this darkness my headlamp picked up the outline of a sign I knew well—the side trail to the summit of Clingmans Dome. I was at the high point of the AT.

"Finally," I growled into the darkness, frustrated by the diminished speed at which I'd been moving. I hustled past the trail without stopping.

The traction devices I'd slid over my shoes at the shelter bit into the packed snow with loud crunches. I was relieved to find clear tracks in the snow again. *At least people have been here too.* The tracks I'd been following had petered out after I left the shelter.

The Appalachians are ancient. Older than many ranges, they once touched the Atlas Mountains of northern Africa. Their continuance still rolls through the Scottish Highlands. These mountains have seen Pangaea and weathered the seismic transitions of millennia. They've cradled glaciers and have been scoured by an inconceivable number of storms that have stripped their soil and laid them bare to their very bones. They hold not just geologic memory but also human. Uncounted generations have been born, hunted, lived, traveled, and died in their recesses. As I walked the trail at night, I often felt the presence of those who had come before, and those who'd never left.

I scampered down icy rocks and roots through a haunted spruce forest, feeling the eyes of animals (or ghosts) watching me from the dark, outside the ring of my headlamp's light. My feet lost purchase on an ice-coated rock and I fell hard onto the frozen ground. I lay there for a few prolonged moments before I finally got back to my feet. It was nine p.m. and I'd been moving continuously through snow and cold for seventeen hours. I was still ten miles from Newfound Gap. *And miles to go before I sleep.* This line from Robert Frost, whispered internally, would become a mantra repeated nearly daily.

IN THE MORNING, I TOOK my time in the warmth of the bathrooms. The sun streaming through the windows promised a better day ahead. My wet layers draped on stall doors were now mostly dry. My innermost layers had remained dry throughout yesterday's grueling hike, meaning my layering system was working well. I leaned over one of the sinks and devoured as many calories as I could. I knew I needed to go back into the snow and cold again, but I balked at the idea of leaving a heated space. Well fed, I reluctantly began packing up.

Three young women came into the bathroom as I was putting my pack on. They looked as exhausted as I felt. I said hello and they looked over my gear: mountaineering shell, synthetic jacket, wool long sleeve base layer, synthetic tights, knee-length down skirt, knee-high waterproof gaiters, water-resistant high-top trail runners, balaclava, midweight mittens, and windproof hat.

"Wow, you are so much better prepared than we are!" one of them said.

"Well, I've done this before, so I had a pretty good idea what to expect."

"The ranger out there said he found someone to take us down to Gatlinburg, even though the road is closed. One of the guys working on clearing it. We're getting a hotel there tonight. Do you want to join us?"

"No, but thank you. I have a long way to go today."

Outside, the beauty of sun-sparkling snow made it difficult to believe that another storm was on its way. Though deeply exhausted from the day before, I knew it would take another long, sustained effort to extract myself from these mountains. The ghosts of last night's forest seemed only a bad dream now as I crunched through brilliant, snowy beauty. As long as I stayed true to my goal of all-day movement, I would reach Adam by midnight.

The spring at Icewater Shelter was gushing into an ice-rimmed pool, which flowed out onto the trail and formed a treacherous ice field. Still, I was delighted to find free-flowing water. I chugged a liter and greedily refilled my bottle. I wanted to drink more, but I knew it would be too much of a blow to my core temperature. Instead, I nestled the bottle back into its jacket pocket and carried on.

The trail was once again well tracked and I made good time. Unlike the dreariness of the day before, the world sparkled and I felt happier than I had been the whole hike. I knew it was because after two difficult days, I would see Adam—if I just kept walking.

I passed a clump of trees whose boughs sagged heavily under their load of snow while their roots clung tightly to a broad rock, their curves forming a throne with a vast view. I felt a tug on my memory and did a double take at the snow-covered feature. I turned around in a circle, taking in the panorama. *Yes, this was the spot.*

Fifteen years ago, I had sat right there gazing at what seemed to be the whole of the southern Appalachians spread out before me. I'd conquered terrain I'd never before laid eyes on and had gone from uncertain to confident in my quest to walk from Georgia to Maine. More important than that, I had fallen in love. The movement and the lifestyle of thru-hiking filled a vast hole in my soul that I hadn't thought could ever be filled. For the first time in my life, I was truly content.

Three separate parties had trudged past me that day in the muggy late May air. Each had questioned me and, upon discovering that I was a thru-hiker, admonished me to cherish the experience that every single one of them wished they'd had when they were younger.

"You're lucky you're doing this now," a woman in her fifties had said to me. "Before a career and a family get in the way."

She had moved off and I had stood up on my throne. My heart had proclaimed to the vast wilds before me, "If those things will stop me from this, then I will never have those things!"

Now I smiled at the memory. I'd been twenty-one and incredibly naive. Even so, my wild, strong-hearted words had been accurate. Those things had never kept me from the trail.

I turned northward again. The man I intended to marry was waiting. He already knew that even love could not take away my devotion to this lifestyle.

Darkness fell and I was plummeting into it. Down, down, down from the cold and haunted highlands. Down, down, down into fatigue. I was not in FKT shape, my foot ached, and snow had exacerbated the difficulty. I'd barely slept the night before. As I descended, snow gave way to bare trail.

Adam is waiting. He'll take care of you. Just keep going.

I repeated the words over and over as I willed myself into a run through the gloom.

THE SOUND OF VOICES pulled me from slumber. It was black as night, but it was not night at all. Light traced edges, sharp ninety-degree angles, around me—unnatural. I wasn't in my tent. But then, where was I? It was still achingly cold and my bed was as hard as frozen ground. I sussed out Adam's soft baritone in the stream of sound and remembered.

I'd been reliant, and I felt slightly nauseated at acknowledging it. I felt shame tinged with guilt. Unlike so many nights alone on my FKTs when—at the mental and physical end—I'd still had to set up a tent, make food, and take care of my blisters, last night I'd sunk into numb repose where the trail met a rural road on the cusp of a highway.

"I'm at the steps. I need you."

That text was all I was capable of. I waited in the black, limitless time that doesn't seem to exist at all when you've pushed yourself to the edge.

He appeared quietly, attached to the small light I'd watched draw closer. He took my pack, lifted me to my throbbing feet, and led me to the truck, where he blasted the heat. I spooned mouthfuls of congealed gluten-free pasta he had made me while staring blankly at the green numbers on the dash: 11:45. Then he'd held me to him while I shivered myself to sleep—every ounce of cold I hadn't acknowledged and residual adrenaline wringing itself from my exhausted body.

Now I was warm under the covers, though my nose felt icy. He was outside and there were other people. *What time is it?*

"Adam?"

He opened the side hatch.

"What time is it?"

"Eight a.m. Good morning. How do you feel?" He leaned in and kissed my nose, which for a moment felt warm.

"Ugh," I rolled to my side, suddenly aware of hunger . . . and the smell of bacon. "What's going on?"

"There's a trail angel here. He's been here for three days feeding hikers. He's making breakfast and everyone is excited to meet you."

"Ugh," I repeated. Food sounded amazing, but socializing didn't.

Adam helped me scramble out of the back of the pickup, and I stomped my feet into stiff, but not completely frozen, shoes. I wrapped my insulated skirt around my waist and grabbed my down jacket from where it was stuffed in the side bin. There was a clank as the assorted tools it rested on shifted.

WHERE ARE YOU GOING *with my hammer?*

I started slightly. My dad was not here. But his deep voice lived on in my memories, sometimes triggered by the tactile world around me, sometimes in my dreams. Often these were real conversations we'd had, but sometimes—in my dreams mostly—the words were those I'd wished for instead.

I smiled slightly, remembering how my fifteen-year-old self had tried to hide the hammer behind my leg as I'd turned to face my dad where he stood in the doorway of the barn.

"Nowhere," I'd mumbled. My dog had pushed against my leg, nearly causing me to lose my balance.

My dad, hands in the pockets of his Dickies work pants, had started laughing.

"You're going down in the woods, aren't you? What are you afraid of? Deer?"

"I just . . . I just want to carry it."

"What exactly do you plan to do with it?"

"Nothing!" Face red, I'd turned around and stomped back across the lawn into the house, waiting for him to return to the barn before making a beeline for the forested acres that lay behind the house—hammer in hand.

Those wild woods attracted me, despite my fear of what might befall me if I went there. Something about following the silent hallways he'd created with his tractor through the pines, maples, and beech was magical. My heart pounded in fear of the what-might-be-theres and yet I felt oddly content and peaceful as my feet made their way along the paths.

I SLIPPED MY DOWN COAT on and briefly touched the cold metal of the hammer nested next to wrenches and a screwdriver. I didn't need to carry it in the woods anymore. I wondered if my dad knew that.

The folding table set up under a canvas tent was attended by three other hikers and Adam. Fresh Grounds, as the man who was feeding thru-hikers called himself, handed me a hot cup of coffee poured from the French press in front of him.

"Good morning!" His voice was far too cheerful. I wondered how many of those French presses he'd drained before I arrived.

"Hi, I'm Heather."

"Oh, I know! I'm making pancakes. Is blueberry okay?"

I opened my mouth to object but was cut off by the wave of a spatula.

"Oh, don't worry, this batch is gluten free. Adam told me." He beamed at me and pushed down the plunger in a second French press, which he slid toward the other hikers.

Definitely at least two full presses.

After an hour of consuming more pancakes, bacon, and coffee than I thought possible, I finally stood up from the table. It didn't appear that the other hikers intended to actually hike that day, not that I could blame them. Fresh Grounds was staying there until hikers he was following online arrived. That meant the others had guaranteed free food and coffee if they just stayed put.

I loaded up my backpack while Adam scoured the map for crossroads he thought he could reach. It was only thirty-four miles to Hot Springs, but with my late start and accumulated fatigue from the hard push through the Smokies, there was no way I was going to make it that night. We decided on Lemon Gap and I bid everyone farewell.

It was a relief to find myself once again walking on bare ground. Everything was a mud brown, the leaves trampled into pulpy remnants of past glory. The forest chatted quietly to itself, surely discussing the weak yet persistent sunlight sporadically punching through the clouds. Buds on the trees were swollen, and I observed the little reminders all around me that spring was coming. The forest was ready for the warmth to stay—and so was I.

CHAPTER 4

ROAN MOUNTAIN

My world was white.

Earl Shaffer—the first person to thru-hike the Appalachian Trail—titled his memoir of the experience *Walking with Spring*. I would title mine *Walking with Winter*, I decided, as my numb-cold feet plunged over and over into deep drifts blanketing Beauty Spot. The sun reflecting off the snow was dazzling, blinding. I paused to catch my breath, pondering the polarity of the moment juxtaposed with my last time here in 2015 on my FKT.

It was then, in darkness lit only by the pregnant moon, that I'd strode across the grassy hilltop meadow with purpose, my journey almost complete. Broken in ways that only relentless questing through both physical and mental difficulty can evoke, I'd finally seen something I'd been missing my whole life. Out of the shadows had come my truest vision of self, not the ruses of worth, purpose, and beauty I'd believed.

Now in light so bright my eyes wept unchecked, I tried to summon that self-same power. This journey had barely begun, and the answers I'd found here on a warm September night seemed to have evaporated in the harshness of the solar radiation reflecting off the snow. Did I need to prove my worthiness to myself yet again?

Finally reaching a wooden fence and the protective shadows of a smattering of trees at the north end, I wiped at my eyes with the back of my mittens. Cold streaks marred the warmth of my cheeks as I rubbed. Now that I was on a road, the trail was visible—or rather the bed of the road formed a broad uniformity beneath the gelato-smooth, knee-deep snow. As long as my feet stayed within the bounds of the high banks on either side, I was "on trail."

Upward I floundered, toward the distant spruce-covered summit of Unaka Mountain. No one had been through here recently, and the higher I climbed, the deeper the snow became. I scanned the forest for the familiar two-by-six-inch vertical white blazes on the trunks, the usually stark markings rendered nearly imperceptible by the whiteness all around me.

No longer on a road, I couldn't even be sure if the snow I was treading was piled on top of the trail. Conifer boughs—heavily laden with densely packed flakes, more water than crystal—sagged low, smacking me in the face and arms. These encounters freed the branches from their burdens, which cascaded into the gap between my back and pack like mini avalanches loosed with an oomph of relief by the tree. I continued on through the dense forest drenched in snowfall, surrounded by branches springing upward as I freed them. The sun was dropping steadily from its zenith toward the horizon line behind me, yet I had miles to go before I could sleep.

From the broad summit I needed to drop down to Iron Mountain Gap and then begin the long ascent to over six thousand feet and the summit of Roan Mountain. Judging by the depth of snow here on Unaka about a thousand feet lower, I would be fighting for every inch forward indefinitely. *At least my foot doesn't hurt as badly as it did.*

Adam was somewhere, running. I briefly hoped he'd be waiting at the road crossing between Cherry Log Shelter and Roan, but he'd been clear that we wouldn't see each other until tomorrow afternoon at US 19E.

"I wish you'd just quit this hike and we could go sit on a tropical beach somewhere." Adam's words echoed inside my head and tears threatened again.

He wasn't even supposed to be here at all. This was something I wanted to do alone, remember? I crossly reminded myself.

He wasn't *supposed* to be part of this. This was supposed to be a culmination of my own skill set honed over fifteen years of backcountry travel. But he *was* part of this—and was going to be part of everything else going forward. I glanced down at the alexandrite engagement ring sparking green fire amidst the whiteness. At least he would be if my plans didn't prove to be too much. And if they were, I couldn't—wouldn't—blame him. He wouldn't be the first man I'd lost to my everlasting devotion to the trail. But I wished there were space around the constant unspoken conflict.

If he would just leave and live his own life and let me do this, we wouldn't build these layers of resentment. Or if he'd just stop trying to crew, which he didn't enjoy, and hike with me instead.

The fall happened so swiftly I didn't realize I was going down until I was there, flat on my back in the deep snow, which made the landing soft. Whether from the surprise of being there or from the joy of not walking for the first time in eight hours, I didn't move.

Overhead, deciduous trees rocked gently in the breeze, their buds still clamped tightly closed, unlikely to open for many weeks. Their forms interrupted the steady gaze of the sun, making it possible to take in the wideness of sky tinted the palest aqua. My legs throbbed slightly, electromagnetic pulses in the muscles still firing, unaware that they were no longer engaged. My breath floated visibly upward, forming the only cloud in sight. Awareness of my entire body—which bits were cold chapped and which were sweaty—rose to prominence in my suddenly silent mind.

Time passed, probably not much, but stillness erased any sense of it before I finally moved. Bilaterally sliding my arms and legs through the drift, making an angel from my spill, I giggled, then laughed my way to my feet, aware now that the trail had begun to descend. My feet knew the extent they needed to reach now, the grade below them dropping steadily away, leaving spruces, summits, and fallen angels in the past.

Leaf-covered ground protruded between icy patches as I wound my way back up toward the Roan Highlands several miles later. Night—five p.m.—was rapidly approaching. With hours of energy left in my legs, it seemed senseless to stop. However, the snow depth would only increase while the overnight lows decreased the farther I went. *Fewer leaves and more ice.*

The Appalachian Trail crossed an ancient woods road, and I followed it a short distance to a spring. Water—seemingly colder than ice—gushed from the earth, forming crystalline pillars twelve inches high. I worked my bottle in between the fragile stalagmites. Nearby the old road was free of snow and the rotting leaves of last autumn lay thick on the flat bed. It would do for the night.

The frozen, rocky ground resisted my tent stakes, each one bending slightly in recognition of the power of the earth. I piled rocks on the guy lines and deformed stakes to hold the tent secure and crawled inside. Despite the hardness of the ground, I was comfortable enough on my closed cell foam pad. I managed to eat my dinner of rehydrated refried beans before complete darkness descended. Then I lay back, listening to the melody of water defying thermodynamics.

When my father died, I dreamed of him every night—at least the nights that I could find sleep. Now, a year and a half later, the dreams had subsided to weekly. Out here on the trail they were even less frequent, my utter exhaustion scrubbing my unconscious mind clear. When they did come, they followed a set pattern: I was with him somewhere and then he was gone, lost in the fog of subconscious wandering. I would always awaken and reassure myself that it was okay and for a few seconds it would be, until I remembered he was not lost or misplaced, but truly gone.

A multisport athlete, he was definitely not a hiker. Yet, as I sank into sleep, we were hiking together and he was happy.

I woke up with a start, subjected to those same familiar waves of loss, sadness, remorse, anger, and grief. I blinked back tears in the blackness of my tent, the tinkling sound of water grounding me in the present. *He really is gone.* As the emotions subsided slowly, I felt a new feeling slide into place behind them . . . comfort. I would never walk down a trail with him, but he now hiked with me in my mind.

I snuggled deeper into my bag and relinquished consciousness again, knowing that eventually the dreams would subside and the scars would heal. If only I walked far enough.

DAWN WAS BLOOD RED. It seeped across the horizon, between gray tree trunks, starkly contrasting with the white landscape. As I climbed upward, the effort of climbing warmed me, and I was glad that my body heat ensured that the water filter in my pocket did not freeze solid. In the still air, my breath floated around my head like the thoughts in my mind, half formed before slowly dissipating.

"Living the dream, one sunrise at a time," I whispered to the sun, gratitude for the return of the light swelling through my cold toes.

Sunglasses became a necessity as I breached the tree line and gazed across the complex of balds stretching on ridgelines for twenty trail miles before me. The Roan Mountain Shelter was deserted, but tracks around it revealed that one or two brave (or foolhardy) souls had slept there the night before. The bitter wind chapping my bare face made it seem impossible that it was mid-March. If not for the footprints, I could have believed I was all alone in this frozen world.

"Dear Virginia, I hope you got the memo that it's supposed to be spring in less than a week."

Nearly blinded, even with sunglasses on, I made my way down to cross the iced-over road and then back up to cross Round Bald. Despite the weather, I could tell that the equinox was near. Each day I noticed nearly imperceptible gains in light. On the open land, when no clouds marred it, the intensity of light was nearly unbearable—especially at this altitude. Each night in my tent I gained another minute to complete mundane chores without a headlamp. And at the lower elevations water circulated beneath swirled ice—a sure sign that spring *would* eventually arrive. But would it arrive where I walked? Or would I simply continue to chase winter's tail northward with vernal ephemerals burgeoning in my wake, like Olwen, the goddess of spring?

THE APPALACHIAN TRAIL STRETCHES along the crest of the ancient mountain range like the ecdysis of a giant serpent, snagged on the ubiquitous rocks. In many ways I felt my own growth had been facilitated over and over by these same rocks. Each time I'd traversed this footpath, I'd left behind another skin—a layer that no longer fit. The woman beneath grew, stretching taut her habits and beliefs until they loosened and sloughed off as I hiked, sometimes crawled, over the exposed metamorphic slabs. Now as I followed the undulating trail through the waiting woods, still hushed by winter, I felt the corset of grief constricting my breath again. Nature had always been where I could go to draw deep lungfuls of air, expanding and cleansing my mind and body. Yet, since my father died, I had choked on them—unable to draw in enough to erase the loss.

I hoped this too-tight skin of heartache would be the next one to snag, tear, and be shed.

A dilapidated barn—a splash of red, stark against the white and gray landscape—came into view in the meadow far below me much sooner than I expected, my wandering mind having passed the time rapidly. The Overmountain Shelter, named for the militia that had come "over the mountain" to aid the Continental Army in its war against the English during the American Revolution, was a drafty, uncomfortable place to spend the night, as I had learned on my first thru-hike.

The ridges and valleys around me were steep and covered in snow. Later they would be choked with saw briar and shrubs, making travel difficult. The overmountain men had had to fight nature herself before they even got a chance with the Redcoats. And yet, people had moved through this landscape for thousands of years. The Appalachian Trail followed ancient footsteps.

As did I.

Not only was I walking where others had walked for millennia, I also was treading across a continent northward as the seasons shifted. Soon I would do the same along the Pacific Crest, following summer north. Then, as days shortened, I would move southward from Canada to Mexico through the Rockies, along the same inexorable path the sun took. I was walking in footsteps older than trails themselves . . . the migration of my species.

The ridge grew narrower and thickly forested. *Thwak. Thwak. Thwak.* The wind slapped bare tree branches together over my head, the rhythmic sound reminiscent of the way my dad's axe had split through firewood, sending cleanly severed pieces flying away from the chopping block, a box elder stump.

I STOOD TEN FEET AWAY, our agreed-upon safe distance from which an eight year old could watch until he waved me over. I stood with my forearms presented, palms up, proud to help. He laid one small stick of firewood across them, gathering ten in his own arms.

"I can carry more than this!" I insisted.

He set two more sticks on. I almost dropped them but resolutely gripped them to my chest without complaint instead.

"What are we, Dad?" I asked as he stacked the winter's warmth into the woodshed.

"Huh?"

"What are we? I mean, what are humans?"

He took the sticks out of my arms.

"We're animals."

"Oh." I followed him back toward the tall pile of unsplit wood. "What kind of animals?"

"We're descended from monkeys," he said, picking up the ax. "But don't you tell your mom that."

"Why not?"

He set a round of oak on the stump and glanced at me. He finished the cigarette he was smoking and flicked it into the grass.

"Because she thinks God made us different."

Despite his warning, I greeted my mom with my newfound knowledge when she came into the house a few hours later, laden with bags of groceries.

For my penance, I was sentenced to reading the book of Genesis. I don't know what my dad's punishment was.

Movement, as a way of being, has taught me my dad was right about our animal nature. There have been moments when it has been hard—very hard—to walk through the mountains carrying all I need to survive. Yet, it is in the very action of doing so that I have felt the most alive—the most *human.*

I have never felt human at a desk in front of a computer or sitting in traffic. I'd glimpsed this feeling amassing firewood for the winter, gathering mushrooms in the spring, or foraging berries in the heat of summer. But nothing had ever felt quite so right as simply moving across the land for months on end. Though I sought a terminus instead of herds of wild game, the essence of the movement remained.

"Why?" was the question I had heard the most ever since I'd first thru-hiked this trail fifteen years ago. My answer had always seemed weak: "It just feels right." But after setting an FKT on the PCT in 2013, I finally knew why. My DNA told me to do so. Humans had evolved through millennia of performing this very act. Our survival as a species went hand in hand with our ability to travel thousands of miles to find food, escape drought, and more. In a modern world of social media and supermarkets, there was no longer a need to fulfill my biological design as a walker of mountains. Yet, these trails offered up a substitute, the movement without the urgency. Here I could sense my humanness freely just by hiking.

AT PRESENT, I FOUND MYSELF floundering in hip-deep drifts as the Appalachian Trail departed the relatively protected forest for a glade below the looming hulk of Hump Mountain. I was acutely aware that this was why my ancestors had moved with the seasons and not just ahead of them.

"Heather!"

Adam's voice was loud in the silent landscape, and I halted, squinting against the sun. He was not far away, galloping through the snow without regard for the whereabouts of the actual trail. His legs were bare beneath his running shorts, but he wore several thick layers on his torso.

"Adam!" I joined in the charge, noticing immediately that the snow was deeper away from the edge of the trees where the trail wended.

We embraced and nearly toppled into the snow—not that it would have been much of a fall. I was grateful to see him after several days apart.

"Oh my God, there's been so much snow, and I don't think anyone has been through here yet."

"There are some tracks on Hump. Someone has been up and down from the road. It's not as deep on the ridge either." Adam was breaking trail back to his own tracks in the vicinity of the AT.

I followed, grateful to have someone punching through the snow ahead of me.

"I got us a room on the outskirts of Johnson City tonight. It was cheap."

"I can't wait," I responded, but my mind was already on the next day. "Are you still leaving tomorrow?"

"Yeah."

We didn't speak much after that as we ascended what would be a broad, grassy arm in just a couple of months. He'd never meant to stay, but now that I was faced with him leaving for real, I desperately wanted him to change his mind and keep forging northward with me. The push and pull of wanting his presence juxtaposed with wanting to feel autonomous was exhausting. Climbing Hump in the snow required all of my energy, so I temporarily banished all thoughts in order to focus.

The summit was surprisingly clear, and I was happy to see that he was correct. The trail down toward the highway was well trodden and even bare in some spots. I sat down on one of the massive summit rocks protruding from the snow, pleased at the warmth radiating from it. Adam handed me a package of gluten-free cookies and I tore into them like a starved animal.

"Are you out of food?"

"No, but I didn't really stop to eat today. It's been too cold, and everything's covered in snow so there wasn't anywhere to sit. Until now." I adjusted my position to a new sun-warmed spot.

"I still have a lot of food in the truck, and there's a grocery store near the motel so we can pick up more for dinner."

I swallowed the last cookie and drank the last of my water.

"Okay, I hope it's less snowy on the way down."

"It is. It's basically clear once we get to the Tennessee border."

The switchbacks down from Doll Flats—which straddled the line between North Carolina and Tennessee—seemed endless. By the time we finally reached the truck, I had removed every additional layer I was wearing over my base hiking outfit of shorts and a wool shirt. In addition to the warmth, here at about four hundred feet it actually smelled like spring. *Perhaps it won't be as bad north of here.*

After the sun-bleached purity of the mountain air, the motel room was stifling. It reeked of stale smoke. I gagged and went back outside.

"I can't stay here."

Adam looked at me with exasperation. "Why?"

"It stinks. It smells like smoke."

"It's supposed to be a nonsmoking room. I'll go ask." He shut the hatch of the pickup and jogged across the parking lot.

I went back into the room to wait out of the wind but left the door wide open. The scent reminded me of the massive crystal ashtray adorning our coffee table when I was a child. I could see my dad absently tapping the end of his Marlboro on the edge, orange sparks and silvery ashes tumbling into a black-flecked pile.

"Heather, take this to the kitchen to empty it. Practice your balance!"

My dad settled the heavy ashtray on top of my head very carefully, steadying it until he was certain it wouldn't crash to the floor. Slowly, I made my way from the living room, gliding across the hardwood floor of the dining room past my mom, who always sighed, "Andy . . . " when she saw me headed to the kitchen with my fragile cargo.

I couldn't remember when this had first become a game my dad and I played, but at five years old I was an expert at transporting the ashtray across the house, my posture perfect.

At the paper bag in the kitchen that served as our trash can, I grasped the faceted edges and tipped, mesmerized by the silky ashes tumbling like gray glitter before reversing my performance back to the waiting cigarette wafting its scent into the air.

"They figured we'd be smoking since I told them you're a thru-hiker." Adam's voice shocked me away from the reverie of cinders and crystal.

"What? Why? Do most hikers smoke?"

He paused and looked at me.

"Yeah, I guess they do."

"Well, did they have a different room?"

"C'mon."

Our new room was clean, newish looking, and devoid of olfactory memories. We set about unpacking and organizing the many totes of gear from the back of the truck as well as preparing resupply boxes. It took several hours, but at last we had a system and labels for what he needed to mail—and when—and I had my backpack stuffed with everything necessary to face early spring in the Appalachians alone.

We lay in bed, clinging to each other as the clock inched closer to departure.

"Where are you going again?" I rested my head on his bare chest. I was exhausted, but happy to be clean, warm, and nestled close to him for the last time in an unknown number of weeks.

"The Uwharrie National Forest. It's east of here. I found a boondocking site online that I can base out of and run. The Uwharrie Trail is forty miles and I can make loops between that and other things for three weeks until Umstead."

At the mention of his upcoming hundred-mile race, I cringed slightly. Instead of logging tempo runs, doing speedwork, and getting adequate rest and nutrition, Adam had been following me along the spine of the East. He'd spent most nights alone and freezing in the back of the truck and most days driving back roads, hiking in to meet me, and walking back to the vehicle. I hoped his time in the Uwharrie would be the dedicated training he needed—that he deserved.

"Do you think that will be enough preparation?"

Adam shrugged. "I don't know."

"If it's not, why don't you postpone it and hike with me instead?"

He was silent for a few moments.

"I don't want to hike the AT again."

In the morning, I fought waking more than normal—acutely aware that once awake, I would have to walk away from Adam for the foreseeable future. Finally, I sat up and drank the coffee he'd made me. The procrastinated parting would be no easier. We reloaded the truck and pointedly didn't talk about the imminent separation. At eleven we left the parking lot in broad sunshine.

The forest surrounding the trailhead was vibrato with the songs of a multitude of bird species. I was grateful to have their assurance that at least the immediate future would be warm. Adam stretched, and I picked at my backpack where it sat next to the front tire, pretending to ensure that everything I needed was accounted for.

"Okay, hon. This is it. I gotta go." He reached for me, pulling me close.

I latched on, suddenly unwilling to walk into the woods alone. A gnawing emotion in my stomach told me if I let go, I would never see him again.

"Can't you hike with me just a little ways?" I pleaded.

He sighed, not with frustration but with sadness—and I immediately regretted making it harder for him to go.

"Of course you can't, I know." I pushed away from him, smiling as much as I could.

"It's a long drive. As it is, I won't get there until after dark."

"Right. I always forget how big North Carolina is. Drive safely and text me when you get there if you can, okay?"

He nodded.

"I love you." I leaned in and gave him a lingering kiss.

"I love you too. I'll—I'll see you," he stammered out the farewell.

I forced another smile. "See you."

CHAPTER 5

VIRGINIA IS FOR LOVERS, PART 1

A lot of moments found me climbing to yet another viewless summit and wishing that the trail was like the CDT with alternates and options to go around pointless ups and downs (PUDs) and walk past a coffee shop instead. But previous thru-hikes had taught me, more than anything else, acceptance of what is, and to not waste mental energy on wishing things were different. I reminded myself of that daily in the face of PUDs, unpleasant weather, and the strenuousness of backpacking.

Despite my fitness and the many thousands of trail miles and summits I'd logged over the years, the climbs were still hard. However, instead of complaining, I reminded myself that they were part of the AT and of this experience as a whole.

After all, the idea of hiking three of the longest and oldest National Scenic Trails in honor of the fiftieth anniversary of the National Trails System Act was to celebrate the extensive network of trails in this country and their amazing diversity and features—like pointless ups and downs. With those, the AT reminded me over and over that many times in life it's necessary to work really hard for not much reward, and *that* is the reward: learning mental toughness, perseverance, tenacity, and patience.

Tennessee would soon be behind me, and I inhaled the scent of the mixed hardwood forest deeply. *Each of the trails brings something different to the experience. Wishing one was more like the other is like wishing carrots were corn.* Much like saying, "Eat your veggies," the AT seemed to say, "Climb your mountains, on trail and off."

The next morning, I sat in a coffee shop in Damascus, Virginia, sipping an Americano. Outside the sun was shining, although it was slated to vanish again by afternoon. The last time I'd sat here over a steaming coffee had been three years prior, near the end of my AT FKT journey. I'd been slamming my body against rocks and roots for forty-two days at that point. I'd staggered into the Friendliest Trail Town early in the morning with my sleeping bag wrapped around my shoulders. My water had frozen and the pall of winter was in the air.

Today was the reverse season, mid-March. I'd slogged through snow and the cold of lingering winter for more than five hundred miles now. My body was not yet exhausted by the effort, but I was nonetheless thrilled to sit and drink a luxurious beverage and not think about walking.

"Anish?"

It was a question, but I recognized the voice. I turned to see him, the man who'd caught up to me as I left town in 2015, pedaling his bicycle furiously up the road behind me. He'd spoken words of blessing that I'd never forgotten.

He joined me at my table and we talked. It was so strange to have a conversation here with someone from before. I felt like my life was running in circles, revolving around the same mountains, the same tread.

Perhaps it's like reincarnation. I must repeat the same trails over and over until I learn the lessons needed in each iteration of myself.

We walked outside and snapped a picture together, then I shouldered my backpack and headed out. Another winter storm was coming and I wanted to get as close to Grayson Highlands as I could, hoping to pass over the highest part of Virginia before the weather arrived the next afternoon.

I walked out of Damascus, past the gushing spring pouring from a pipe alongside the road. I climbed the steps leading up the embankment and melted into the quiet woods. I was alone again. This early in the season, hardly anyone would be out on this most popular of trails. It was simply me and my thoughts. I merged with the Virginia Creeper Trail, enjoying its flatness.

My own flatness felt validated somehow. Being on trail had always been home to me. I'd walked on them through depression and heartbreak into self-love and courage. Yet, this time I felt nothing out here in the still-sleeping hardwood forests. I simply had to trust that somewhere beneath the flatness, I would begin to feel myself again. That progress toward my goal and healing from grief would come eventually, as long as I continued one step, one blaze at a time.

By the next afternoon when I reached the worn side trail leading up to the summit of Mount Rogers, the high point of Virginia, the sunshine had finally begun to melt through the bone-deep cold I'd felt for so long. Thawed and energized by the star blazing down on me in the open meadows, I turned off the AT. *I've walked past this mountain twice and I'm not going to do it a third time.*

Fifty yards up the summit trail I waded into deep straw-colored grass leftover from the previous year's growth. I tossed my backpack on the ground and wondered if I should take my food to keep it from attracting animals. I glanced around and noted that two of the feral ponies Grayson Highlands was known for were grazing nearby, their noses rummaging in the golden remnants for fresh green shoots.

"No apples or carrots in there, you guys," I muttered, turning to jog upward. It would be a mile round-trip—hardly enough time for anything to find my pack.

I was surprised at the steepness of the trail, given that I'd been striving upward for more than an hour already. The broadness of the land above me didn't resemble a peak as much as a hulking ridgeline. That was par for the course in the Appalachians. These ancient mountains once pierced the jet stream at altitudes rivaling the Himalaya. Eons of rainfall, wind, glaciers, and gravity had peeled them to their pith: sweeping metamorphic dorsa.

The apex was not immediately apparent once I crested the plateau and entered a silent chapel of spruce. Despite the warm day outside the canopy, in here ice rimed the scattered glacial erratics. Patches of granular snow clung to tree wells and crevices beneath rocks and logs. I slipped on ice so translucent it was invisible without close inspection. Under my feet was a carpet of long since discarded needles from the towering guardians, cemented in place by frozen water, the carpet's reddish hue contrasting with the darkness of the cloister hidden from the sun.

Regaining my footing, I walked from one boulder to another looking for the USGS marker that would indicate the true summit. I found it a few feet from where I'd slipped on the ice and pulled myself up on the slippery boulder. I took a deep breath of Christmas-scented air and let it out slowly. My body convulsed with a powerful shiver. I'd gotten sweaty jogging up in the sun, and now in the dense tree shadows my body was rapidly losing its stored heat.

"And my jacket is in my pack."

I slid off of the highest point in Virginia and crept out of the spruce cathedral. Back in the sun I dashed down the mountain, the effort and solar radiation warming me again. The ponies were nowhere to be seen and my pack was untouched. I returned to the AT, noting the thin stratus clouds beginning to thicken across the sky.

"I gotta get out of here before the storm gets here," I murmured to myself, remembering the winter storm advisory I'd seen while sipping hot coffee in Damascus.

At Rhododendron Gap I turned down the old AT and followed the Pine Mountain Trail downhill to where it rejoined the newer white-blazed route. The sun was blotted out now and the wind had picked up, chilling me even as I walked. Looking back up I could see that the skies above the Highlands were dark with purple-gray clouds. Ahead of me the sun still pierced the smattering of clouds forming above the trail. I sighed in relief. Perhaps I would make it to camp before the storm began after all.

The rolling landscape went by rapidly even as the temperature steadily dropped. I was relieved to reach the side trail to Trimpi Shelter before precipitation began, although I could feel that the pregnant air would deliver imminently. I rushed down the hill to the small stone structure, my heart sinking at the sight and smell of smoke coiling out of the chimney, and rounded the front just as a light pattering of cold rain began. The shelter was full of men, possibly a group, possibly other thru- or section hikers. They looked up in surprise to see me standing there and then glanced around at their stuff strewn everywhere.

I turned around and ran at a full sprint back to the AT. It was raining harder now and I forced myself to stop and haul my rain jacket out of my pack, shoving my arms into the sleeves and taking off again before I even had it zipped. I was being pummeled now by water pellets—raindrops on the verge of a phase transition. I hurried down the trail.

There has to be a spot to camp near here. There always is. How on earth is the shelter full? I've barely seen that many people total on trail in the past two weeks!

Fueled by a desire to escape the freezing rain, I scurried through the woods, vaguely aware that I should stop to put on my waterproof gloves before Raynaud's syndrome rendered my hands unusable. However, halting in the icy deluge and losing any pent-up body heat I'd accumulated seemed equally dangerous, so I rushed onward believing I would find a place to camp soon.

At last, I spotted a flat place paralleling the trail, likely an old roadbed. I quickly tried to set up, finding that my tent stakes could not penetrate the ground.

"Shit!" I cursed at the situation, stuffing my now wet tent back into my pack and yanking out my gloves. I was shaking as I hurried to try and rekindle my thermogenesis through movement.

Another twenty minutes passed and the temperature dropped to the verge of freezing. My hands were wooden and white from the tips of my fingers to the midpalm. I could barely flex them. I threw my tent down on the trail and set it up as best I could. I crawled inside and tried to calm myself down, tucking my hands into my skirt, crying at the intense shooting pain as my meager body heat began to thaw them.

That's when a rivulet of water streamed across the floor of the tent. Frantically I spun around to see what was happening. The bank above the trail bed was pouring water, which in turn was coursing into and under my tent. If I stayed, my entire shelter would be swamped. I had no choice but to tear down and keep going.

I ran down the trail in the gloaming, my sopping wet tent wadded in a ball in my frozen hands. It was a little more than seven miles to

Partnership Shelter, with a solar shower and a nearby visitor center. *Can I run that far like this without losing my fingers?*

I almost didn't see the campsite in the near darkness and my panicking state. Rain drenched me, borne by a ferocious wind that cut through my clothing, as the hypothermic quivering in my body grew worse. *I'm okay as long as I don't stop shivering.*

The site was a good one, and I took more time to set up than I had before, fighting my dysfunctional digits and my desperation to get inside. Finally, the tent was taut and I crawled in, dragging my pack into the vestibule and zipping it shut against the storm.

I sat there shell-shocked, trying desperately to think. *What needs to happen first?* Without feeling in my fingers, it would be nearly impossible to peel off my rain jacket and other soaked clothes, but I knew I had to do it.

Clumsily, I managed it. The frigid air blasting through the mesh of the tent shocked my bare skin while I fumbled for my sleeping pad. The windigo was raging tonight, its ravenous screams reminding me that here in the bleak mountain forest it was still winter.

Perched on a dry sleeping pad island in the middle of my wet tent, surrounded by islets of wet gear, I struggled into the dry clothes I carried for sleep. Then I wrestled my sleeping bag free from its stuff sack and wiggled into it. My body shuddered violently as I rocked back and forth, desperately trying to kindle my body's flame against the cold. I reached into the pile of unceremoniously deposited gear beside me and found a chocolate bar. I broke the frozen candy into pieces, stuffing them into my mouth until no more would fit. Slowly it melted while I sat there, the influx of calories fueling the production of heat.

Gradually I realized that the steady thrumming of rain pelting the tent had ceased. Yet, the howls of insatiable winter still shook the thin nylon walls. I unzipped the vestibule just enough to set up my Esbit stove, revealing that the rain had not stopped but transformed into heavy flakes of snow.

I cooked my noodles and pulled the steaming pot back inside, cradling it in Raynaud's-whitened hands. Slowly the uncomfortable heat bored its way through my wooden digits, mottling them with color and intense pain. I hoped the pot hadn't been hot enough to burn them. Eating quietly, I watched the steam rise—freezing in swirls across the ceiling of my tent—with tears sliding down my cheeks.

Belly full, exhausted from both miles and the ordeal, I clicked off my headlamp and sank back onto the pile of damp gear that was now my pillow. I slipped earplugs in to block out the shrieking storm.

By dawn my sleeping bag had absorbed the moisture of the tent, causing cold spots where the down had clumped together, losing its ability to insulate. I'd barely stayed warm enough. Despite sleep I was still exhausted from the difficult day, the brush with hypothermia, and the Raynaud's attack. Inside my bag my hands were warm, and for that I was grateful. I lay on my side and watched my breath curl away from me. Through the mesh door I could see that three inches of powder had fallen. Ultimately, the very thing that had threatened me the night before had also blanketed me, offering its own shelter. The windigo had departed, leaving the breathless silence of the forest after a heavy snowfall.

I made hot coffee and gulped it down quickly before it could cool. I would need a belly full of scalding liquid for what came next. With as much rapidity as my stiff joints could manage, I stuffed my gear into my pack and donned my wet clothes from the day before—thankful yet again for the wool shirt that kept me warmer when soaked than a synthetic would have. I emerged from the tent, stamping my cold feet into my frozen shoes, gritting my teeth against the pain. I was grateful that despite everything that had happened the night before, I'd remembered to maximally loosen the laces before falling asleep, so at least my shoes froze in an open shape I could get my feet into.

Walking down the trail, scuffling through pillowy flakes piled deeper than my feet, I felt my toes go numb. My hands were cold, but my fingers were still pink and functional. As long as I could get up to speed, I would reach the visitor center adjacent to Partnership Shelter within a couple hours. I mentally assessed my situation. My clothes would likely dry enough while walking. The tent was still wet and would transfer moisture to my dry things if I used it again without drying it. My sodden sleeping bag wouldn't keep me warm another night, and that was critical.

I'm going to have to hitch into Marion and use a dryer.

I sighed at the prospect of a lost day and pulled an energy bar from my coat pocket where it had been thawing. I munched on it mindlessly as I tramped through the snow. My shoes had finally thawed enough to flex, and with that my feet had regained some feeling. The bar gone, I crouched to snug up the laces of my now loose-fitting shoes as best I could. The upper was yielding, but the laces were still frozen. I yanked hard and retied them as snug as I could, settling into a faster gait toward warmth.

The visitor center was a welcome sight, and I headed directly to where a phone hung on the outside wall. There were notes in my guide about shuttle services in the area. However, a sign farther down the building caught my eye and I paused to read it closely: "Women's."

I bolted toward it. *A warm place to look at my guide and eat something.* I yanked the door open and a wave of warm air rolled over me. I stepped inside, crying with relief. To my disbelief and joy there was a hand dryer mounted on the wall. I set my pack down and threw my tent over the frame of one of the stalls, followed by my sleeping bag. Then I set to warming my hands and feet with the dryer, alternating the process with eating. I was surprised to see it was only 8:15. I doubted anyone would be in there anytime soon.

Every half hour I opened the door briefly to allow moisture-laden air to escape as my clothing and gear released trapped water into the warm air. After a few rounds with the dryer, my shoes were malleable and mostly dry. I started using it on my sleeping bag in short spurts.

By the time two women my age walked in at 11:30, I was almost completely ready to leave. They smiled and we chatted a bit as I moved my gear, packing away what was dry. After they left, I scrunched my sleeping bag in my hands a few times. It was slightly damp, but no more than it typically was from morning condensation. I ran it under the hand dryer a few more times, and at noon I finally headed back out into the snow.

The rolling farmland was lovely in its white cloak. However, the storm had contributed to treacherous conditions for crossing the multiplicity of fence lines in the bucolic scenery.

"Virginia is for lovers?" I muttered the state's motto while climbing yet another ice-covered wooden stile. *More like for monkeys.* I clambered down the other side, almost slipping on the last step.

Even in dry conditions, crossing the numerous fence lines of rural Virginia was exhausting business. *Three steps up, three steps down . . . over and over.* The fields were deeply drifted, the wind settling what seemed like the entire winter's worth of snow into thick piles along the edges, where the AT traveled. I relished the forested sections where the trees diffused the snow, leaving only an inch or two on the trail bed, even more than usual.

I missed Adam. He'd texted a handful of times in the past week and a half. It sounded like he was getting the long runs he needed, on trails without snow. I was slightly jealous. Despite his absence in the land of lovers, I was finding a deep contentment in the repetitiveness of backpacking. I seldom saw another person, and that added to my overall tranquility. I was alone with the sleeping trees and occasional deer.

Seeing footprints in the snow from time to time alerted me that there were other hikers ahead of me, but probably not many and probably not very far ahead. At my pace I would reach Katahdin in May—before the trail to the summit was even open. But my plan did not involve reaching the end of the AT before heading west. I wanted to go only as far as I reasonably could before the weather stopped me. I anticipated making it to the exposed White Mountains of New Hampshire before heading to the Continental Divide Trail in New Mexico . . . unless there wasn't time before my Pacific Crest Trail permit starting date of May 22. Although, with the frequency of winter storms still slamming into the Appalachians, I wondered if perhaps I should head to New Mexico now.

My head swam with logistics, but often it was the only topic I could occupy my mind with for hours while I made my way up and down the forested hills and across snowy fields. I wondered how much faster my socks and shoes would wear out with the repetitive nightly freezing and thawing, and how much longer my feet could withstand the abuse.

More like how long can my mind withstand it?

ANOTHER FRIGID MORNING called for a makeshift down coat. I wrapped my sleeping bag around my neck and shoulders, the ends tucked into my rain jacket. I knew it looked ridiculous, but this method had saved me many times. I checked my phone and was happy to see that I was nearly to the dirt road leading down to Brushy Mountain OutPost and the junction of US 52. Despite the delicious warmth afforded by my unorthodox use of the bag, I was certain to draw more attention to myself than necessary by walking in there with it still in place. The trail turned sharply up, and I arrived at the deserted gravel road more quickly than I thought I would. Reluctantly I put my sleeping bag away. Weak sunlight was filtering through the leafless trees, speckling the road as I sauntered downhill.

I set my backpack on the picnic table outside the small store and went inside. Half a dozen gray-haired men in flannel lounged around drinking their coffees and shooting the breeze. I scanned the shelves for something gluten free I could eat, and, seeing nothing, bought a large coffee. The woman behind the counter grabbed a Styrofoam cup and poured what was unlikely to be very good tasting black liquid in.

"You better get a place in town," one of the old men announced loudly, clearly addressing me.

"Yeah, a big storm is a'comin'," another added.

"Oh yeah?" I grasped the hot Styrofoam, grateful for the warmth against my hands. I had no doubt another storm was coming, but I'd walked through so many that I was nonplussed by the idea.

"Gonna get ten inches of snow!" the first man declared, almost jubilant. I wondered if it was because he enjoyed scaring hikers, or whether he loved snow.

"Well, I better get walking then." I smiled and left.

Outside I dumped a quarter cup of the powdered cream I carried in my food bag into the cup to mitigate the development of an ulcer and shouldered my pack. The wan sunshine had turned to brilliantly intense light, forcing me to put on my sunglasses. There was no sign in the sky of impending doom.

Nearly a foot? I doubt that.

Eighteen rolling miles ahead, Trent's Grocery was a short distance off trail and I had a box waiting for me there. I savored my coffee as I followed roads for a while before rejoining the trail. I'd need to hike steadily to make it there before they closed, but I didn't doubt I could make it. The sun was thawing both the forest and my body. As the stiffness melted from my muscles, I found myself striding along, faster than normal. Squirrels dashed around the forest floor for the first time since Georgia. I was grateful for more whispers of spring—even if there were also rumors of snowstorms.

At Trent's I sorted my box and packed up with just a couple hours left before dark. I stepped outside, where the sun was baking the front of the store, and smiled into the heat.

"Don't let the sun fool you. A foot of snow is coming tomorrow."

I turned slightly to take in the hefty man in overalls sitting on a bench in the sun, drinking either an energy drink or a beer. His meaty hand obscured enough of the can that I couldn't tell for sure.

"Really?" I looked up to the western sky and noted the thin horsetails swirled across the robin's egg sky. *Maybe they're right.*

"You heading to Wapiti tonight?"

"Um, yeah," I lied. I intended to camp somewhere in the woods before the shelter. There was nothing about him that seemed dangerous, but then again, I never disclosed my plans to strangers. Hikers had been murdered along the AT by people from towns—and Wapiti Shelter was one of those locations. I didn't intend to be on that list.

He nodded, "You'll have no problem getting to Woods Hole then tomorrow. It's a good place to wait it out and," he paused leaning forward to point, "you can head up the road here and take the Dismal Trail back to the AT. Easy to cross the crick. It'll save you walking back down the highway."

"Oh, thanks."

I pulled my phone out and looked at the map. I could see the route he was talking about. It would save me a mile of out and back. I pocketed the phone and gave him a small wave before heading up the road. To my surprise, the phone rang. *I thought I turned it off?* I pulled it out of my pocket to see Adam's name on the screen. My heart leapt with joy. I hadn't heard a peep from him in three days.

"Hello?!"

"Hey, where are you?"

"I'm leaving Trent's in Bland. Are you still in the Uwharrie?"

"No, I'm on my way to you."

"What? Why?"

"There's a massive winter storm heading your way. It's gonna hit the mountains around ten tomorrow. Do you think you can make it to Pearisburg by then?"

My heart sank.

"So, the old men weren't kidding, huh?"

"What?"

"The last two stops they've been warning me that a big storm is coming. It's the fish story—the snow depth just keeps getting deeper."

"You're looking at getting at least a foot, maybe more."

I could hear the concern in his voice, and I knew he could actually read weather maps. The crystalline cirrus over my head didn't lie either... there was *something* coming.

"I'll be in Pearisburg by ten."

"Okay, I'll find us a hotel and see you there. I miss you."

"I miss you too."

"Heather?"

"Yeah?"

"I'm not going back to the Uwharrie. I'm going to crew you the rest of the way."

"What?" I paused, uncertain what to say. "That would be great," I added.

"Love you. Bye."

"Love you too."

I switched the phone off and put it back in my pocket. Pearisburg was twenty-five miles away, and I would need to hike all the way to Wapiti Shelter tonight, leaving nineteen miles to cover in the morning. The math was nearly impossible without hiking well into the dark or waking up before dawn . . . maybe both. But Adam would be there, and he wasn't going to leave again.

I walked across the Dismal Falls parking lot and down to the water. The creek was deep, cold, and fast—and the falls were actually falls. It was far too deep to wade.

"Dammit!" *Why did I listen to that guy? I don't have time for this.*

It was true. To retrace my steps past Trent's to the AT and back to this spot just across the river would take me an hour at least. An hour that was even more precious now that I knew I was racing a storm. Memories of my hypothermic evening near Grayson Highlands sent me into a slight panic. I stomped around on the bank like a frustrated horse.

There was a thin log—a sapling really—six inches wide and twelve feet long spanning the water. It cleared the creek by only two or three inches and was coated with ice in the middle, where it likely submerged under load. I kicked it to determine its solidity. The log shuddered but didn't budge. I tested its pliability with one tentative weight-bearing step. It held without deforming.

"Dammit," I said again, puffing my breath out with a short sigh. If I fell in, I'd certainly go over the falls. I wouldn't drown or die—unless I hit my head—but hypothermia would be imminent and there would be no way of me making it to Pearisburg.

"You just can't fall," I told myself, stepping onto the narrow log, clutching my poles horizontally like a high-wire aerialist.

I shuffled across the river, my shoes barely clinging to the wet bark. Midway—where the river was at its deepest—the log sank beneath the surface, dipping my feet into the icy water. I felt a surge of adrenaline—inciting panic and fast movement—roaring from my abdomen to my legs and heart. I fought to keep my breath and my muscles in check, even as they quivered with the instinctual urge to flee.

"No," I whispered as my feet slipped on submerged ice.

My mind went to a place of such intense focus it was almost as though I blacked out. All I saw were my feet on the log underwater—and then I was lurching onto the ground on the other side. I fell, unable to keep my body from leaping away from danger any longer. I landed on the soft dirt and knelt there for a minute, uncertain if I was going to throw up. After a few deep breaths, I got up and stumbled along the blue-blazed trail back to the AT, unable to feel my benumbed feet.

I pulled out my phone to look at my map, hands shaking so violently it was hard to focus on the screen. Now that I was back on the trail, I realized that despite my attempted misdirection, I would likely end up camping at or near the shelter I'd told the man at Trent's—unless I took the old AT, now the Ribble Trail, four miles ahead. Taking this trail straight up the mountain would save me several miles and mean I could avoid camping anywhere near Wapiti. That shelter—or nearby it, depending on who you believe—was the site of a double homicide committed by a man from Pearisburg nearly forty years before.

I doubled down on my hiking speed. It was going to get dark before I even finished the alternate if I didn't hurry. My foot-shaped ice blocks were clumsy as I tried to walk fast.

I regretted sharing my destination, even unintentionally, with a stranger. I needed to ensure I camped well away from there for my own peace of mind now—and in order to get to Pearisburg before the storm did. The rhododendron-lined trail felt eerie in the dimming light. I glanced up through the trail-wide gap in branches. The sky was still mostly clear. Only a few trailing cirrus—harbingers of the storm—marred the perfect blueness of it. Such perfection juxtaposed with my crawling sense of irrational fear—the creeps—put me into an even more anxious mindset as I hurried along the trail.

"HO." MY DAD ALWAYS ANSWERED the phone with that monosyllabic statement rather than a traditional greeting. It was a comfort to dial my parents' number and hear that familiar sound. I wished I could call him now. Not that he'd intentionally quell my unease over a murder that happened nearly forty years ago nor a random encounter with a stranger trying to be helpful at a gas station. But his calmness as we discussed the weather or sports would dissipate my alarm through distraction.

"I'll be right over."

As a teenager, I'd heard him matter-of-factly responding to the person on the other end of the phone call that had awakened me at five thirty—an hour before my alarm. Head under the pillow, I'd gone back to sleep. I hadn't learned who the mystery caller was until my sister Louisa arrived for tea a week later.

Over strong English Breakfast, she'd relayed the phone call she'd received just before leaving for work—a call that was nothing more than heavy breathing on the other end. With her husband already on his way to work, she'd slammed the phone down and crept to the doors to make sure they were locked. Then she'd called Dad.

My mom's eyes were wide, and Louisa seemed surprised that Dad hadn't shared the early morning escapade. He'd listened to her recounting the story with a nonchalance that bespoke his firm belief that as a father he would always defend his daughters—with his life if necessary.

Now, with him gone, it was up to me to take care of myself.

I found the Ribble Trail and veered onto it as it climbed more steeply than the AT. The sun skimmed the horizon now. It wouldn't be long before I was in complete darkness on a trail that was neither as well marked nor as well traveled as the AT. If I didn't rejoin the white blazes before nightfall, getting lost could be a real issue.

Lost in the dark in a creepy forest with a winter storm bearing down on me. Great.

I imagined my dad pulling into Louisa's driveway that long-ago morning with his high beams on, illuminating any cranny where someone could hide and pouring light into the back of my sister's unlocked car. After he honked and revved the engine, my sister dashed from door to car, assessing its headlight-illuminated interior before jumping in. His pickup escorted her to the main road before he returned home as though nothing had happened.

After that episode, he'd arrived at her house every morning at 5:45 for the rest of the week.

TEARS WERE STREAKING DOWN my face as I struggled to breathe fast enough to keep climbing at a rapid pace—wishing my dad was there to guide me to safety now. Wishing I hadn't fled from home as soon as I could.

The trail turned to a jumble of rocks under a thick layer of leaves. I could barely see what I was tripping over, and I yanked my phone out to check the GPS. The red line of the AT was straight ahead. I blundered uphill directly without regard for the fact that I was crashing through brush—clearly not on any trail.

Cresting the rocky lip of the ridge, I stumbled onto a wide path next to a white-blazed tree and began to run in earnest. Up here crusty snow crunched underfoot as I plunged down into a small hollow and across a flattish area. It was fully dark, but I was too spooked to stop. The white paint on trees stood out ghostly pale in the lingering cosmic light as I dashed from blaze to blaze, haunted by phantoms in my mind.

The trail disappeared under compacted snow and I broke through, pitching forward onto my knees. I gasped in surprise and repeated the deep inhalation several more times in order to regain my composure. The forest was welcoming here; a cool breeze swept across the ground, caressing my tear-stained face. I wiped the snot off my nose with my sleeve and dug my headlamp out of my hip belt pocket.

You're running like a scared child, Heather. What on earth are you afraid of?

Back on my feet, I panned the light until I located the nearest blaze a few feet away. Walking over to it, I could see two more, and I headed toward them. The snow on the trail was only a couple inches deep and crunchy, but it was enough to obscure the tread in the flat light of a headlamp. I glanced at my phone to see where I was. It was only a little over a mile to Woods Hole—not that I wanted to barge into the hostel at eight p.m. If I woke up early, I could make it to Pearisburg by eleven at the latest. I settled into my night hiking rhythm until I spotted a place that seemed suitable as a campsite.

I used my feet to systematically scrape the seven inches of snow that was piled under the rhododendrons alongside the trail into a rectangular bulwark. The bare ground beneath was sodden and thick with rotting leaves, but it was a better base than the snow to camp on. I pitched my tent by rote. I had done what I needed to do to get to town before the storm and meet Adam.

The site was soft and guarded from the wind by my palisade of snow. I had two liters of water from Trent's in my water bladder, but I didn't want to cook dinner. Instead, I sat in my sleeping bag eating Swedish Fish one by one in the complete darkness.

Whenever I'd needed my dad, he'd been there. But now he wasn't. And I needed *him*. I needed him to tell me that he understood. That he was proud of me. That what I was doing with my life impressed him. To have him acknowledge that my wilderness savvy and my physical feats had at last removed his doubts about his uncoordinated daughter who was terrible at every sport she had tried. I'd always been grateful for his protection, but in the end that was never what I'd needed. I'd needed his approval.

Now, I needed to be brave enough to approve of my own choices.

I'm not even brave enough to hike calmly through a haunted forest.

I put the candy away and fell asleep.

The scent and taste of bacon faded as I opened my eyes inside a dark tent a few hours later.

"It's too early in the hike for food dreams," I muttered to myself as I rummaged in my food bag for something that wouldn't be too hard to eat while frozen.

I pulled a baggie of dark chocolate peanut butter cups into my down cocoon and ate them slowly. I'd barely had any town food indulgences on the hike so far, and I was certainly not carrying enough food with me. *Eating gummy candy for dinner doesn't help, either.* The ten pounds I had put on for this year of hiking was already gone, melted by the extra effort to stay warm and fight my way up and down mountains in the snow while averaging thirty miles or more a day.

Those pounds were supposed to last more than a quarter of one hike—and I still have seven thousand miles to go.

I finished chewing, listening to a winter wind raging through the trees yet again, not giving up without a fight. I sank back into sleep.

BY DAY, THE THICK RHODODENDRONS growing on either side of the trail were decidedly less creepy. These thickets had earned the AT the moniker of "the long green tunnel." But especially after nights like the one before, I knew it was more like an enchanted forest—full of dark secrets. As I left the evergreen bushes behind, the sweeping view from Angels Rest was made even more so by the lack of leaves on the surrounding trees, revealing a lavender-gray bank of clouds instead of sky. Brittle air rattled through gaps in the trees as I sucked the last of my water out of the reservoir hose, bemoaning the destruction of my water filter, which had frozen overnight.

I paused despite the cold burning my cheeks. *I don't want to stop early today. I want to hike.* I felt a familiar sense of frustration rising in my throat, tightening my jaw. I loved being immersed in nature, but I also hated being limited by it. I wanted to move forward toward my goal. Every day that I did fewer miles meant more days I'd have to hike farther in order to finish before winter reared her hoary head again across the mountains in October.

Fat snowflakes began to drift down from the dark clouds above me. I jogged as best as I could with a heavy pack on my back as the Appalachian Trail coiled into steep switchbacks down toward the New River. I knew I couldn't travel more than seven thousand miles on foot without facing winter, either now or later. I just had to choose.

"Now, then," I growled, picking up the pace.

Adam spotted me before I saw him. At his voice I lifted my eyes from my feet to peer through the opaque veil of snow rapidly enveloping the world around me.

"You made it!" The relief was obvious in his voice as he pulled me into his arms.

"Yeah, not particularly easy, but I did. Do you have any water?"

He pulled a bottle from his jacket pocket and handed it to me. I drained it and handed it back.

"I'm parked at the trailhead. The motel is at the end of this street across from the grocery store."

"But I wanted to get down to the highway," I protested.

"Heather, it's going to accumulate fast. I'm not sure I can even drive in it in a few minutes."

I noticed the slushy snow sticking to the road and acquiesced. "Okay, but I'm hiking out tomorrow."

"No, you aren't."

"Don't tell me what to do!" He'd been back for mere minutes, and it felt like he was already trying to alter my plans. I was hungry, cranky, and tired. I wanted support, not input.

At the truck I threw my pack in the back and climbed into the passenger seat, slamming the door. Without another word he started the engine, and we crept slowly down the hill.

By the time we'd unloaded things into the room and I'd showered, six inches of snow was piled on the ground and truck. We ran across the road to the grocery store, and I relished wandering the aisles, picking out a smorgasbord of food—notably, butter and bacon.

By the time the faint light of day had begun to recede behind the clouds, ten inches of snow had fallen and it was still coming down thickly. I stared at my phone, watching the weather radar. A massive purple blob covered my flashing blue dot . . . as well as most of the surrounding states. I sighed and peered out the window again. Mother nature was humbling me soundly.

"I guess I'm going to have to zero tomorrow." The words tasted bitter.

Adam nodded, and to his credit did not say "I told you so" in reference to our earlier squabble. Instead, he said, "I'll go to the office and make sure we can keep our room."

I went back to staring at the weather app, willing the blob to disintegrate.

"Okay, all set." He stomped snow off of his shoes. "Want to go get ice cream?"

I laughed at the ridiculousness of it. Then my stomach gurgled, weighing in that it very much wanted ice cream.

"Do you think they're still open?"

"Probably. There are still some cars in the parking lot."

"Okay!"

We dashed across the deserted road, plunging through the foot-deep powder in a direct line to the store, laughing. The mechanical doors slid open and we perused our options of frozen pizza and ice cream. At the checkout, seven employees loitered around the registers waiting for the word to leave.

I SLEPT UNTIL NEARLY TEN A.M., lulled by a sated belly and the quiet of a snowfall-hushed town. Even Adam slept late, then quietly browsed on his phone until I stirred. I rolled over to look at him, watching the minute movements of the muscles in his arm as he scrolled, and relished the feeling of being warm when I woke up instead of watching my breath, illuminated by headlamp, circulate in the freezing darkness.

"Coffee?" I asked hopefully.

He looked up and beamed at me.

"Good morning! Do you feel better? You slept hard."

"Yeah." I sat up as he began fussing with the in-room coffee machine.

"Did you know the Barkley started today?" he asked, handing me a steaming cup.

"What?! It's a week early." The infamously grueling ultramarathon across rugged terrain in eastern Tennessee was always April Fool's weekend.

He shrugged. "I guess it changed since we ran there."

"Poor bastards." The Barkley is almost impossible to complete and involves intense routefinding, with only fifteen individual finishers in the race's thirty-two-year history.

"Yup."

I scrolled the race updates on Twitter, at once thankful that I wasn't fighting the saw briars in this weather but also reminded, with a gut twinge, of my failure to get very far there despite four attempts. I needed to finish this hike in order to amend prior failures with a success.

"There's almost two feet of snow out there. I don't think the plows have even started yet. So today we eat and relax. You *need* to relax."

I nodded, sipping the coffee. This zero day was unplanned, but the visible toll on my body—not to mention bacon dreams—showed I was pushing myself far too hard on a hike that would last eight months, not two.

Marathon, not a sprint . . .

CHAPTER 6

VIRGINIA IS FOR LOVERS, PART 2

The mercurial swings of spring continued as I moved steadily north through Virginia, the state with the most trail miles of the entire AT. I waded through unbroken hip-deep snow after Pearisburg, then stripped to just my bra and shorts as I clambered through the rocky formation called Dragons Tooth on a hot, sunny afternoon. Every morning, I woke up cold in the back of the truck, unless Adam had willingly hiked his four-season tent out with me the final miles of the day. Those mornings were harder to get going. Leaving the warm comfort of the insulating tent and his presence was more of a challenge than fighting snow. I relished the increasingly sunny days and longer daylight hours, even as the threat of winter still glowered from the shadows.

We fell into a steady rhythm of support and incremental progress. He set up camp, broke it down, made me coffee and dinner. I hiked, each day becoming slightly more comfortable with leaving an item or two behind, whittling the eighteen-pound base weight of my pack steadily downward as I finally allowed my reliance on him to spiral increasingly upward.

We didn't talk much, each playing our roles, yet tiny seeds of resentment were still planted. Whenever I arrived at the truck or camp tired, he encouraged me to stop hiking, making it even harder for me to self-motivate. I was so happy to see him when he hiked toward me and share my day with him, but his response was usually flat and he was obviously bored. The Appalachian Trail was not direct, so sometimes my entire day was spent walking a distance that he drove in less than an hour. My excitement to see him waned in the presence of his resigned mood.

"What's going to happen with Umstead?' I asked, lying in the crook of his arm listening to the wind shaking the trees outside the tent on another bitter night.

"I still plan to run."

There was silence in the tent for several minutes as we each considered what we wanted from the other person. I wanted him to run the race he'd been training for, but I felt confused after his declaration that he was going to crew me the rest of the way when he'd returned to me in Pearisburg. His oscillation between being there and being gone gnawed at my heart. *What does he want me to do? What should I do?*

"I'll crew you." I uttered the words almost before I'd realized it.

"What?" In the darkness, I felt his head turn toward me in surprise.

"I'll crew you. Get me through the Shenandoah before the race and I'll crew you. By then I'll be through the highest country from here to Vermont, and the weather will be better after we get back. I can't pace you, of course, but I can crew you. It'll give me a few day's rest, which I probably need." I was surprised at how rational I sounded, having not previously thought about this plan.

"Okay," he agreed, with excitement in his voice I hadn't heard in months. "You're going to have to push pretty hard to get to Front Royal beforehand, though."

"I know. The Shenandoah is pretty flat and you can meet me literally every couple of miles. I can probably do forty miles a day."

"Thank you." He kissed my head and rolled over.

I listened to the wind, to his steady sleeping breaths, and to my heart asking me why I was relinquishing even more autonomy on this hike. I wondered if Adam was right.

Maybe I should quit. Maybe I just don't care enough about this anymore. It's nothing like I imagined it would be, anyway. I'm not on my own. I'm not enjoying the hiking like I usually do. Maybe I should just do it some other time—or not at all. He's sacrificed so much already. This is a small thing I can do to give him something to look forward to. Maybe spring will catch up to my pace with a few days off. Maybe . . .

I believe if you listen hard enough, the trees will share their wisdom. That night I listened intently but heard no answers—only the clash of seasons.

Pushing myself into the realm of thirty-eight to forty miles per day was harder than I thought it would be. Even with the added frequency of support and carrying nothing but a water bottle and a pocket snack, and despite the more than seven hundred miles I'd walked in the first few weeks, my body was not quite ready for it. The increased mileage also brought my neuroma pain back with a vengeance. Adam had to push me out of camp at first light, and at day's end we set up the tent by headlamp.

Even so, I reached Rockfish Gap at the southern end of Shenandoah National Park with just enough days left before Umstead to plow through the park. I hid my limp from him so that he wouldn't know what the push to help him was doing to me.

It will get better if I just keep using it, I lied to myself.

Back at elevations above four thousand feet, spring was showing no signs of arrival, but thankfully the park was snow free. Skyline Drive—the ribbon of road traversing the spine of the park alongside the AT—and the trails were deserted. It felt surreal to seemingly have an entire national park to ourselves. The leafless ridges revealed rippling hollows, valleys, and subridges cascading into the distance. *Virginia views are greater than Virginia blues.* I smiled at my rerendering of a well-worn hiking trope that the five hundred miles of Virginia seemed to drag on forever, demoralizing thru-hikers as progress never seemed to be made.

In the solitudinous trek through the park, I passed two milestones—the eight-hundred-mile mark and my first month on the trail—without much notice. Each day I found it more challenging to go fast enough without going either too fast or not fast enough—especially now trying to get through the park before Umstead. Across the highlands of northern Virginia, I reminded myself to rein in my drive when I began to feel swamped by the need to do more and more miles with the whispered reminder that six thousand more remained.

You're just going to do a few big days and then back to no more than thirty. You don't want to burn out or get more injured.

It was nearly headlamp time when I reached the turnoff for Gravel Springs Shelter on my final night in the park. "Mer!" I called out our signal into the gloomy hollow below.

Trees clacked together in response, driven by the ever-present wind pummeling the ridgeline. My teeth chattered in rhythm, and I felt a sinking feeling in my stomach when I heard no human response. This was my biggest fear when being dependent on a support crew. *What if he's not here? What if he can't get here? I only have a windbreaker. I'll get too cold waiting for him.* I rushed down the steps of the side trail, the hulk of the shelter looming in the gloaming.

I can get out of the wind in there at least, but that won't buy me a ton of time. I'm all sweaty. I'll get cold fast once I stop.

I rounded the front of the shelter to find our familiar neon green tent set up, but the campsite and shelter were completely deserted. I unzipped the fly and peered inside. "Adam?"

"Hey, you're here!" His voice came from behind me.

I caught my hair in the zipper backing up so fast.

"Dammit." I yanked my hair free. "Ouch! Yes, where were you? I was worried!"

He held up several bottles of water. "The spring is pretty slow."

"Oh. Thank you for getting water and setting up camp."

We settled into the tent, made dinner, and got ready for bed.

"You're only twenty miles from Front Royal. You did it."

"Not quite yet, but I should be able to get there by the end of the day tomorrow."

"You will. We can camp there and easily drive down to Umstead the next morning and get there in time for race check in."

I yawned and snuggled deeper into my sleeping bag. "I hope so."

Morning dawned cold, clear, and completely silent now that the wind had abated. I fumbled for my shoes in the vestibule.

"What the hell?"

"Huh?" Adam's groggy voice murmured from deep inside his quilt.

I started to laugh as I realized what had happened. I jostled him.

"Hey, look. You're gonna wanna see this."

He poked his head out of the warmth with a bleary-eyed look that said he doubted it. I lifted my shoes high in the air and then turned them upside down. Dozens of acorns poured out.

He lifted up on one elbow. "What? How did that happen?"

"Busy squirrel. Glad it didn't decide to chew into the tent." I stuffed my feet into the now-empty footwear. "I'll see you at the highway."

AS ADAM'S TRUCK HURTLED toward Raleigh at more than twenty times my walking speed, reversing my painstaking progress over the previous month, the overwhelming sense that something was terribly wrong gripped me. Hundreds of miles south, the air was warm and soft. The roadsides were green and abloom with flowers. The trees were in full leaf. It felt like time travel.

I felt displaced in the state park campground. The warm, slightly humid air was so unlike the dry, frigid weather I'd become accustomed to. The amenities—indoor plumbing and a level site in a real campground—were completely unlike the wild woods where I had spent most nights. Not to mention the hum of ultramarathon subculture with its brightly colored spandex and general noise infiltrating all corners of Umstead. It was all surreal after weeks of hiking through the woods mostly alone.

At predawn the next morning, Adam took off at the front of the pack and I settled in with the other crew people inside the race headquarters building. Despite all the time I'd spent around ultramarathons, very little of it had been in the position of crewperson. Usually I was the runner or, almost as equally, a volunteer. Here I had no job but to wait for him to run each 12.5-mile loop, dispense snacks, and give encouragement each time he appeared.

I made small talk with a few people but mostly just listened to the flurry of conversations around me as people talked about their runner's pace goals and the purported gravitas of various runners on course. I felt lost in a crowd of people who shared one of my hobbies. Ultrarunning was a niche and tight-knit subculture but also distinctly regional. In the

Pacific Northwest, Adam and I were universally known, but not here. I settled into a chair with my tote of supplies to wait.

Adam came and went through the station with the lead runners on pace for his goal time of finishing the hundred-mile race in under seventeen hours. I took soggy gloves he no longer needed and cheered as he vanished down the road again. I would be alone for another hour and a half. I paced the building for a while before sitting down in a corner by the fireplace where I could catch up on emails and social media. When Adam was due, I hovered by the door, waiting to see him appear. He was only a little slower than his first lap, just three minutes behind the leaders.

"What do you need? Are you warm enough? Here's some soup."

"I'm fine." He swallowed the soup and was gone again.

Two laps down, six to go. I struggled to stay warm without much to eat and without moving like I was used to. I made my way back to the fireside and tried to journal about the first month on the trail. *Has it really been only a month? It feels like four.*

Like clockwork, Adam came through the headquarters area two hours later. He grabbed the proffered water and snacks before taking off again. *He doesn't even need me here.* I went to the truck and put away the things he'd rejected for his race and organized some of the bins. I ate some of my resupply food—my body ravenous despite the fact that I hadn't walked in a day and a half. I made a mental note about what I'd need to replace.

What Adam can replace for me while I hike, I corrected myself.

Although we hadn't talked about it, I assumed he'd continue north with me after the race. *Then again*, I paused with my hand on the door handle, *what if this were it?* After the race he might just drop me off at Front Royal and go. *Go where?* I shook the thought away and firmly closed the door. *He said he was crewing me the rest of the way.* Then I made my way back across the tiny mud-slick parking lot to pace near the finish line like a caged tiger.

He was forty-five minutes late.

"It's over," he said, handing me his bottle to refill.

I gaped at him. "What? You're still on pace! You just ran fifty miles in eight and a half hours. You've got plenty of time."

Don't quit. Please don't quit. If you quit, I can't handle thinking it's because of my bike.

He shook his head.

"Are you quitting?" I asked, barely audible.

He looked at me like I'd spoken French.

"Of course not. I'll finish it, but I'm not going to get the time I wanted."

"Oh."

You're not going to succeed, and it's my fault. Even though I'm here. Even though I'm trying to make this work.

He took the refilled bottle from my hands and trotted away again. I stared after him, unable to understand his math. From where I stood, he seemed to be right on time, but he'd been a competitive ultrarunner for many years and if he said it wasn't possible, he was probably right.

I resumed pacing the race HQ. At the front of the room a small table was set with random race paraphernalia and a copy of *Trail Runner* magazine open to a face I recognized. I paused to read the caption. *You've got to be kidding me. Why that issue?*

I picked it up and glanced through the article about Scott Jurek's Appalachian Trail supported FKT, set just a month before I started out on my self-supported AT record in 2015. I wasn't mentioned in the article. *Why would you be? This is a running magazine and he's a runner. Your record was a hiking record.* I felt even less at home than I had earlier.

I flipped through the magazine, looking for something else to read. Many pages later I saw a small sidebar and my face. Petulantly I laid the magazine back down with that page open and smoothed it down to stay that way. I drifted back to the fire, wildly hungry but aware that I really couldn't eat my fill of the food in the kitchen for the runners, pacers, and crew.

It began pouring icy rain and I moved to the doorway. *Runners will start struggling and dropping like flies in these conditions.* Adam appeared, wordlessly grabbed his rain jacket, and took off again. I glanced at my phone. He'd taken two and a half hours for that lap.

Darkness came again and with it more cold rain. Adam stayed consistent with another three-hour lap. Soon after he headed out for the seventh time, a deluge of beleaguered runners in various stages of hypothermia began to pour into the building. Their crews shepherded soggy charges into the room and arranged them close to the fireplace, displacing me. I started shivering too. I could feel resentment curdling my empty stomach.

They can all go home or to a hotel tonight. They'll shower and be warm. I have to sleep in a tent and go back to sleeping in a tent indefinitely, hiking in worse weather than this for God knows how long.

I shook my head at myself, trying to get my mind back on what was important: Adam.

I'd been awake for almost twenty hours, and I knew it was affecting my mood. I needed to feel like there was a purpose in me being here, away from the AT. I went outside, dashing from the door to the pacer tent, getting drenched in the process.

"My runner needs a pacer for his last lap," I said loudly so that the woman behind the table could hear me over the thumping music blaring from the finish line speakers.

"Which runner?"

"Adam Lint. He should be here in an hour-ish."

"Oh, wow, he's quick. Grant? I've got a runner for you."

A short man about Adam's age with a jovial face darted over to me, his effusive energy nearly tripping him.

"Hi, I'm Grant." He shook my hand rapidly.

"Hi. Uh, I'm Heather. My runner is Adam. He should be here in about an hour. He's had a bit of a hard day, but he's doing really well so I just want to make sure he finishes strong. He probably just wants some company."

"No problem! I can do that! I'll just run to my car quickly and get a couple things, and I'll be right here waiting."

"Okay. Thank you, Grant."

I lurked by the door, so cold I couldn't feel my fingers. It was hard to see runners coming off the course aside from shadows as they approached. Once they entered the well-lit lap area, they quickly disappeared into a sea of neon polyester and spandex. The winner crossed the line followed by the next three finishers. Adam still had a lap left. I congratulated the winners as they were ushered by, cringing inwardly. *Adam should be here right now. This was his goal time.*

I stared blankly into the dark, becoming shockingly aware of how much I needed to sleep. Adam was standing in front of me before my eyes focused and I realized he was there.

"You okay?" he asked.

"Yes, yes. I just didn't see you. What do you need?"

"Layers."

For the first time all race, he came to my staked-out corner of the HQ and sat down. I peeled his soaking-wet shirt off and gave him another to put on. He applied glide and I refilled his water bottle. He stuffed some food into his pockets and grabbed his remaining dry jacket.

"I'll probably just be walking this lap so don't expect me in under four."

"Wait!" I grabbed at his elbow as he moved rapidly toward the door.

"What? I gotta get going before my muscles seize up."

"I, I got you a pacer. His name is Grant." I looked up and locked eyes with Grant, who had been eagerly bouncing from foot to foot under the pacing tent. He beamed when he saw me with a runner in tow and ran toward us.

"What? But I don't need . . . "

"Hi! I'm Grant. You must be Adam!" Grant enthusiastically fist bumped Adam. "You all ready? You need anything? I can grab you some water or snacks?"

"Um, yeah. I'm ready." Adam shot me a look over his shoulder as he followed Grant's enthusiasm into the night.

I was relieved to see the two of them cross the finish line a few hours later. I was more than ready to be back at camp.

I'D NEVER HELPED BATHE an adult before—and I was worried I might need to.

Back in the campground, less than twenty-four hours after we'd left, I followed Adam as he hobbled to the bathhouse. *If I ran a hundred miles in twenty-one hours, he'd have to carry me.*

Luckily, all I had to carry were his clean clothes and a towel. I reluctantly followed him into the men's room and helped him strip, thankful that he insisted on bathing himself. I self-consciously stood outside the stall watching through the space below the door as mud ran off his legs and swirled around the tiled floor before slipping down the drain. I was relieved that no one came in.

We slept until eleven a.m.

"So, back to the AT?" I asked as he settled stiffly into the passenger seat.

"Yeah." He leaned his head back and I started driving. Piloting a vehicle felt frightening, and I gripped the steering wheel with white knuckles.

"Do you want to stop to get some food?" I asked after several hours of complete silence.

"I don't know."

I glanced over at him. He'd been dozing and wincing in equal measure as we barreled north again.

"It's been three hours and you didn't really eat anything this morning," I coaxed. "Look, there's a McDonald's at this exit."

"No."

"Well, I'm hungry. And I need to pee." I took the exit and pulled into the restaurant. "Are you coming in?"

"No."

I sighed and went in by myself. He was limping loops around the truck when I got back.

"What do you need?"

"I just need to sleep, dammit, Heather. Leave me alone."

I bit my cheek and got a bag of chips from the back of the truck. I crawled into the driver's seat and started eating them while scrolling through Google maps for a motel that we could afford.

"What are you doing?"

"I'm taking you somewhere to sleep."

"We can't afford a hotel."

"We can afford this one. Get in."

He didn't protest any more. The dumpy motel was less than ideal, but it didn't cost much more than the campground we'd stayed at in the park. He crawled into the bed and immediately passed out. I did our laundry, relieved not to have to interact with him in his sleep-deprived, moody state.

"Par for the course," I muttered to myself as I finally got into the shower after all the chores were done. Sleep deprivation was just part of being an endurance athlete, and I was certain I'd been moody and grumpy with him over the previous weeks as well.

The next evening, we turned onto the 522 heading toward the AT crossing where I'd left the trail four days prior. Adam, now fully rested, reached across the seat and took my hand.

"Thank you for coming with me and taking care of me."

"You're welcome."

"What's wrong?"

You were an ass to me yesterday, I thought, and asked the burning question that hadn't been addressed. "What happens now? Are you done?"

"No, of course not. I'm here. I'm going to keep crewing you."

I let out the breath I'd been holding for what felt like a week. "That's great. I'm really glad." *He's committed to this now. It will be different.*

"Of course. You thought I was just going to leave you in Virginia and take off somewhere? I told you I was going to be here for you." He squeezed my hand tightly. "I love you."

"I love you too."

CHAPTER 7

THE MID-ATLANTIC

Returning to the trail after a handful of days off felt comforting. My life was once again orderly, focused, and straightforward. The frequent road crossings where I met Adam meant I carried only a small amount of food and water in my pack. My foot seemed recovered after the rest and with less weight. The brief absence had even allowed spring finally to catch up to me, and I felt its warm breath on my neck as I made my way along the C&O canal outside Harper's Ferry, West Virginia. Though the trees were still gray and leafless, a close inspection of branches revealed swollen buds on the verge of bursting.

The skies were mostly overcast as I crossed the dozen or so roads intersecting the trail at regular intervals throughout Maryland. In contrast, the forest ground was soft and smelled of fresh dirt. Sprigs of green and a few specks of color—short-lived early flowers springing to life—poked through the uniform brown of last year's leaf litter. I squatted beside a splotch of yellow trout lilies and admired their fragile beauty, from mottled leaf to nodding trumpet head atop a slender stem. So delicate and yet strong enough to bloom in the near wake of winter, when nights still dropped into the thirties and the wan sun was frequently hidden.

"Thank you," I whispered to them, trusting their reassurance that winter was finally over.

By the time I reached the Mason-Dixon Line, I was hiking in short sleeves. South Mountain, and the end of the Blue Ridge I'd followed since Springer, was not far ahead. From there the mountainous ridgelines gave way to a broad break in the Appalachian Range—the Cumberland Valley. My pale arms pinked in the sunlight as I reached the Appalachian Trail Conservancy office in Boiling Springs—the heart of the valley—at noon a few days later. I sat outside the shuttered office next to Adam sipping Cokes with two other thru-hikers I'd been just behind for more than eleven hundred miles.

"We're going to head to the restaurant for lunch, wanna come?" the woman asked us.

"I don't think so. Thank you." I watched as the two of them headed off in the direction of town.

"Uh oh," Adam mumbled, staring at his phone.

"What?"

He looked up. "You're not going to like this."

My heart sank. Perhaps the trout lilies had lied.

"There's a cold front coming in. Five inches of rain tomorrow. And two to three more the next day."

I stared at him blankly. The sun was forcing the thermometer on the side of the building upward as we spoke, with a promise of reaching eighty by midafternoon. "Eight inches of rain?"

"At least it's not snow."

"Do you think we can go to your sister's house tonight instead of tomorrow?"

"Um, I can ask her, but I thought you wanted to make it to Duncannon before we went there."

"If I run the rest of the day, I can make it to Duncannon by dark."

Adam paused, obviously checking my math in his head. "You can probably do that. It's another twenty-five miles and you've got about seven hours before dark."

I was already on my feet and tightening my shoelaces. "I need you every five miles at least. I'll need water, electrolytes, and a snack ready."

I pulled my shirt off in anticipation of the summer-like heat and in just my sports bra took off down the street toward the edge of town, not bothering to wait for my new plan to be confirmed.

Hours later I reached the edge of the flatlands and began ascending Darlington Ridge. My hamstrings clenched taut from the sudden shift in elevation after being forced to run all afternoon. I chugged water from a spring surrounded by golden daffodils, remnants of the homestead that had once been there. I powered up the switchbacks, swinging my arms hard to make up for the reduction in pace. The trees opened as I neared the top, and I paused briefly to look back across the giant valley I'd just crossed to the prow of the Blue Ridge as it faded away into the distance.

Descending the north side of the ridge, I ran through forest and fields with the hulk of Cove Mountain looming directly ahead, separating me from the town of Duncannon, which sprawled across the confluence of the Susquehanna and Juniata Rivers. "And miles to go before I sleep," I whispered to myself. Adam was parked at the bottom of the hill.

"You're doing great," he said, handing me my water, snack, and electrolyte drink requests as he had all afternoon.

"Thanks. I hope I can make it before dark. It's a long climb up there. And rocky." I pulled my shirt back on. The sun had dipped low enough now that I could finally wear it again.

"I'll drive around and hike toward you with your headlamp just in case. Amber said it's no problem if we get there late."

"Okay."

A mile later, I stepped across a clear stream after finally leaving fields for thick forest. The trail curved sharply and began to ascend in earnest. The twenty-eight miles I'd already covered that day reverberated through my legs as I resolutely climbed, gaining five hundred feet in half a mile. *Only seven more miles. You can do this.* I cheered myself along silently, wishing we hadn't slept in that morning.

I reached the gas line clearing at the top of the ascent as the bottom of the sun kissed the horizon. The trail on the other side of the clearing deteriorated into the sea of rocks that Pennsylvania was infamous for.

C'mon. I coaxed my feet to move faster, to lift higher, to clear the impediments.

Now on the ridgeline, it was a fairly level walk to the shelter turnoff and from there a steep descent to the river. I willed my exhausted legs to run again and to my surprise they did, quivering in response as I danced across rocky terrain. Despite my focus, I still stubbed my toes repeatedly.

The hot day softened around me, and for the first time since Georgia I heard birds chirping their evening farewells from the trees.

Adam was at the shelter junction when I arrived.

"You don't have to run anymore. You've got plenty of time."

"Thank God." I slowed to a walk, grateful to return to a pace that my body was attuned to, and followed the AT downward in the dimming light.

Not far from the shelter was a hammock hung in a tree and a man who appeared to be thru-hiking reclined beneath it, strumming a mini guitar. A warm breeze spiraled up from the Susquehanna and dried the sweaty hair clinging to my neck. I felt intoxicated with endorphins, the sunset light, the music, and the summer air in the middle of April. We made our way down steeply to where half a dozen parties lounged on Hawk Rock for the first warm sunset of spring, likely feeling the same headiness as me. We reached the top of the first series of rock steps and descended rapidly.

I SAT IN A FUNK, staring out the window of Adam's sister's house watching the deluge pummeling the yard. I certainly didn't want to be walking in the rain, but I also wished I was making forward progress instead of sitting in a guest room with an aching foot. Yesterday's run or the rocks, or maybe the combination, had triggered my neuroma. I absentmindedly massaged my swollen, tender forefoot, and was surprised when my phone beeped. I halfheartedly picked it up to read the text from Apple Pie.

"Hey! I've got free time. I was thinking I could meet you in the Delaware Water Gap and crew you north from there. If you want help, that is . . . "

"Are you kidding?! I would love that!"

I excitedly began to calculate how long it would take me to get there and began hashing out plans. *Maybe Adam and I will even be able to backpack together, with her there to shuttle.*

Adam came in from his run, dripping wet.

"Guess what?"

"What?" He stripped the wet clothes off and wrung them out in the bathroom sink adjacent to our room.

"Apple Pie is going to come crew me north from the Water Gap! You could finally join me hiking!"

He paused and looked up at me with excitement and relief on his face. "That's great! I need some time to myself. I can go to my parents' house for a few weeks. I'll meet you in San Diego."

He hopped into the shower, oblivious to my crestfallen expression. I stood gripping the sink for a moment before returning to our room to resume watching it rain—and to cry.

FOR THE REST OF MY TIME THERE, Pennsylvania disavowed the magical taste of summer it had offered me in the Cumberland Valley. It rained every day after I reached Duncannon, rendering the rocky trail slippery and slow. Adam struggled to dry things out while I walked. Over and over, after miles of slogging, I would climb into the truck, water streaming off my jacket and rain paints, puddling on the floorboards.

Yet again, I sat in a puddle of rainwater on the vinyl truck seat, my white, cold fingers grasping the steaming cup of tea he'd made for me, trying to hold it still despite my shaking. After six nights of setting up in the rain, our tent and bedding were hopelessly sodden, along with our moods. The conversation we'd had at his sister's had been a frequent topic over the last week. We'd just rehashed it another time and quickly descended into an argument, with me again asking him to join me on the trail—so we could repair our month of accumulated resentments and tiffs—and him staunchly refusing. The weather seemed like the only safe topic.

"Does the forecast look any better?" I asked hesitantly as I sipped hot tea.

"It looks drier, at least. But not very warm. Around forty."

I was already dreading going back outside into the wet. But it was only four p.m.

"Have you heard from Apple Pie?"

"Yeah, she's still planning to meet us in the Delaware Water Gap." I said the words slowly, as they still touched a tender spot in my heart after our fight that morning.

"Good."

"Yeah."

Once the tea was gone, I took a deep breath, got out of the truck, and headed up the hill away from the trailhead. It was raining less, mostly mist, and I pushed the hood of my rain jacket back to alleviate the annoyance of constant rustling over the top of my ears. I'd be at the Water Gap the next night. And then Adam was leaving again. I felt frustrated with his back and forth. I wasn't sure I could trust him to stay gone, but I also wasn't certain I wanted him to come back and crew since the roles of crew and supported were so uncomfortable for both of us.

I wished yet again that he'd just get out of the truck and hike with me instead of crewing. He wished I'd quit hiking and go to a tropical beach with him. There seemed to be no middle ground.

I want to stop feeling like my pursuing my passion is ruining his life. He's the one who decided he wanted to crew—I never asked him. Then why can't he follow through on what he promised to do?

I wanted to feel supported in spirit, not like his crewing was a frustrating task he was halfheartedly committed to. Daily texts sent from across the country where he was happily doing something else would have felt better than having him here with an impatient attitude.

On the plus side, the rain brought hundreds of little efts out into the open. The tiny salamanders blended in among old leaves despite their vibrant orange coloring. I found their presence a welcome distraction from the thoughts circling in my mind as I hopped around frantically to avoid squishing any of them.

"I hope things will be better between Adam and me when we're united in a common goal—thru-hiking the Pacific Crest Trail together," I said to the juvenile newts adorning the rocky trail.

They made no comment.

BEING HANDED OFF to another caretaker was strange. As I listened to them discussing my schedule and my preferences, I felt like a child being dropped off with the sitter. We moved boxes from the pickup into Apple Pie's SUV, and I tried not to chime in, *It's not like that! I'm not needy.*

Instead, I bit my tongue, grateful I would be free to keep hiking with a daypack for the immediate future. *This conserves my energy, and I need to just roll with it. When I move on to the PCT and CDT, it's going to get very hard very quickly.*

On every long-distance hike, I'd found my body at its peak by the time I'd walked a thousand miles up and over mountains. By now, having done thru-hikes of two-thousand-plus miles six different times over the years, I knew there was a certain inevitability to it. I already felt that sense creeping into my body, but it was hindered by something. *Perhaps the cold? Or the crewing?* I wasn't sure, but I knew that soon I'd feel invincible—until I wasn't. The decline was just as predictable as the peak. Somewhere around two thousand miles, the boundless strength and power would begin to ebb, and I would coast to the terminus exhausted.

But on this quest the termini were fluid. One thru-hike would end, but then I'd go to another, and a third. Much more flow would be required before I could ebb.

Will I decline after two thousand miles all the way to the end, four thousand miles later? Or will I be unable to continue after I finish one thru-hike . . . or two?

Adam closed the now nearly empty truck bed, the last of my items having been transferred into the next vehicle. Being crewed for most of the Appalachian Trail could only help extend my indefatigable miles. *And once those are exhausted, will another level of strength and invincibility come?* I followed them into the house where we were staying that night.

There's only one way to find out.

Nature rewarded my surrender to yet another chapter of spontaneity with dazzling sunshine as I climbed Kittatinny Ridge the next day and began my trek across New Jersey. With Apple Pie meeting me instead of Adam, the pall of resentment that had hung heavy over my hike faded away. We read gossip magazines in the back of the SUV and took side trips to the high point of New Jersey and yummy restaurants. We hiked together, camping in the woods in our matching green tents. I missed Adam, but I didn't miss the aura of sadness that clung to him. I wasn't great at being supported, and he wasn't good at supporting me. The combination had been dreadful, maybe even detrimental. I expected to get a message any day that he was headed to Costa Rica, finally going to the tropics without me. Instead, he messaged me a week after he left to tell me he was thru-hiking Pennsylvania's Mid State Trail.

"Have fun," I replied, even though I wanted to say, "Why not hike with me?" Then I turned my phone off altogether.

Over the last week I'd already navigated the slabby ridges of New Jersey that bled into southern New York and scrambled through the iconic Lemon Squeezer in Harriman State Park. Soon I'd traverse Bear Mountain to cross the Hudson River. For the first time since I reached Virginia, I felt like I was making progress. To celebrate, Apple Pie and I scarfed down pizza in the sun.

"See you soon, sweetie!" Apple Pie called after me as I headed into the woods. I smiled and waved, her encouragement and love bolstering me in ways Adam hadn't.

Back on trail, the forest and I both relished the warmth pouring down on us. All around, the shrubs and trees of southern New York were quickly waking up, bursting with bright new leaves. I threaded my way past cars to the pedestrian lane on the Bear Mountain Bridge, already sensing the pulse of the earth flowing through the Hudson just ahead. Among the most powerful and amazing aspects of the Appalachian Trail were the rivers. These arteries of the continent—Susquehanna, Hudson, Delaware, and more—were massive, deep, and wide. Only crossing the Columbia compared on the western trails. Each time I reached one, I found myself bowled over by the sheer power of them, uncontrollably emotional at their simple existence.

The cars roaring past me faded into the periphery of my attention as I crossed the carotid of the Northeast. Tears began to pour down my cheeks at the vast might of the Hudson far below me, and I stopped halfway across the bridge. There I tilted my head back and howled at the top of my lungs, my own vitality released to flow with it. Whether my own energy could sustain me through this endeavor or not, Earth had plenty to share if only I could learn to draw upon it.

"Thank you," I whispered to the river.

CHAPTER 8

VERMONT

"Shit," I said for the thousandth time as my feet disappeared into the snow, followed by my legs all the way to my crotch.

I glanced at my phone again to ensure I was still on the AT, or at least close to it. My blue dot blinked near the red line. *Close enough.* I veered left onto packed snowmobile tracks leading steeply upward. For the first time in hours, I wasn't sinking in.

"No doubt the snowmobilers went up Glastenbury too," I muttered. I glanced at the phone again. I was about fifty yards from where the line of the AT went up the mountain. *Still going the right way.*

After the bare trail, budding trees, and spring rains of New York, Connecticut, and Massachusetts, entering Vermont's Green Mountains heralded a sharp regression back to winter—which I thought I'd left in Virginia. *Too fast for my own good.*

After another thirty minutes of slogging up the snowmobile trail, I glimpsed the abandoned lookout tower, its metal footings blending in with the black tree trunks spiking out of the dazzling white snow. I blinked a few times. *It's like staring at a barcode.* My eyes were tired of trying to make sense of the binary world surrounding me. Exhausted, I leaned against the metal leg nearest me and took a selfie. *Might as well document the moment.*

I unwrapped a snack bar and chewed it ravenously with my eyes closed. It had taken me hours to get up Glastenbury. I thought about the day before with its thirty-eight-degree temperature and pouring rain as I'd hiked through slush up Harmon Hill and nearly wiped out repeatedly on the icy rocks descending to the road. Today had been sunny, and despite the snow I was stripped down to base layers and sweaty from the effort of the snowy ascent. Opening my eyes from their much-needed break, I pulled out my phone again.

"Moving slow. Just got to Glastenbury. Been breaking trail in deep consolidated snow. Might be after dark getting to the road."

Apple Pie responded surprisingly quickly. "No worries. I'm heading in right now with snacks and headlamps."

"Well, I'm not going anywhere standing still," I said, putting the empty wrapper in my pocket and orienting myself with my phone. I plunged into the hip-deep snow again. No snowmobiles had gone past the tower. After two months of fighting the weather, I was grateful to be heading to New Mexico soon, despite the red flag warnings and drought conditions there. Extreme dry heat sounded rather delightful at the moment.

After a few minutes of plodding, I was surprised to find a set of deeply postholed tracks leading through the snowy forest. *Someone has been up here on foot recently.* Double-checking religiously for a bit, I confirmed that they were doing an accurate job of following the AT down. So I relaxed my phone-checking vigil, relieved to not have to think so hard for the first time all day. The summit of Glastenbury was just below four thousand feet. I hoped that by the time I dropped a thousand to Kid Gore Shelter I'd be in less snow.

Stepping in the other person's tracks was easier than making my own, but it still wasn't easy. Their stride was much longer than mine, forcing me to make awkwardly lurching steps. Every five minutes I checked my phone to verify my position, especially since I couldn't easily pick out white blazes on tree trunks plastered with snow. The harsh shadows of the forest threw off my balance when I tried to wear my sunglasses, and without them the sun reflecting off of the snow sent red speckles dancing across my barcode vision. The world I walked through was a bewildering combination of black and white, lurch and progression.

Ever so gradually, the depth of the snow relented. The icy crust grazed my midthigh, then my kneecaps. As the postholes shallowed to midcalf, I noticed shades of green in the forest around me. I paused, taking a deep drink of water with my eyes closed, uncertain if the color was a retinal response to UV or whether there were in fact bushes emerging from their winter cloaks. I swallowed and opened my eyes. Among the many straight lines of black were the oblate profiles of leaves, emerald jewels against their neutral setting. *Spring is here somewhere.*

Kid Gore Shelter appeared out of nowhere, empty and cold. The snow had diminished to slush and mud as I passed by, and I finally felt like my tired legs could move naturally. The air rising off the snow was surprisingly warm even though the sun was low in the sky. I slipped my sunglasses on now that the shadows weren't impeding my steps and hurried forward. The window of late afternoon warmth wouldn't last much longer, and sunset would follow quickly.

"Whoop!"

I looked up at Apple Pie's voice. "Whoop!" I called back, waving.

"You aren't even going to need the headlamp!"

"Thank God! There was so much snow all the way up to the last shelter." I fell into step behind her as she turned around and headed back north. I was grateful to just follow her dark blonde ponytail and not think for a while.

"Yeah, I figured. I took a nice break at Story Spring and read the shelter log. There's a couple of women ahead of you trying to do the Calendar Year Triple Crown too."

"Really?!" I was shocked. I hadn't heard of them, but then again, I wasn't reading shelter logs.

"Yeah, sisters. But it sounds like they're planning to quit."

"I don't blame them."

I was regretting my decision, made in Massachusetts, to hike to the New Hampshire border before flying to New Mexico to complete part of the CDT. *Maybe I should have flown to Durango and hiked all of New Mexico instead of trying to get through Vermont.* I shook my head slightly to erase the thought. For the thousandth time since Springer, I reminded myself that there was no right choice, no one method, no one way. And even if there were, I would never know.

I have only one chance, one choice. There aren't any redos in life.

I'D NEVER STOOD IN SNOW fog before, and I was mesmerized.

It swirled around my ankles and drifted upward, oddly warm and cool at the same time, planting clammy kisses on my bare face. Stratton Pond was just visible through the mist, the black water covered by patchy ice and snow. It was mystical, haunting—a hallowed moment in the midst of my morning push deeper into the Green Mountains. The hairs on my neck prickled with sensation. No one else was around to witness the silent beauty, and yet I was confident I was not alone.

As day burgeoned, the sun burned through the mist, turning the top layers of snow to slush and the bare plots of dirt to mud. I was grateful I wouldn't be there when mud season truly started. It was sloppy and difficult enough now.

By the time I reached the massive parking lot south of Bromley Mountain, it felt like summer. The sky was clear blue, and I was warm enough to take off my tights and hike in shorts. I threw my layers into the back of Apple Pie's SUV and drank the Gatorade she'd bought me in town.

"I think I can meet you on the other side of the mountain at Mad Tom Notch," she said, pointing at the icon on the app.

"Oh yeah? That's a dirt road—it might be snowy."

"Yeah, I asked a few people in town. Sounds like it's open to just past the trail crossing."

"Well, that's great. That won't take me long at all. I won't even need to carry anything."

"That's what I thought."

A short time later I postholed past the hut at the top of Bromley, thankful I'd been able to skirt the snow lingering on the ski slope as I'd ascended. I reached the woods line, looking forward to a fast descent to waiting food. Within a few feet my foot broke through an icy crust into flowing water. I took another step with the same result, only this time my shoe slipped on the hidden rocks and I pitched forward, twisting my knee hard as I fell.

My hands crashed through the fragile crème brûlée surface, smacking rocks and slipping in mud. Frigid water streamed through my fingers, turning them to ice instantly. I fought my way up, too shocked to even swear, although that didn't last long. I grabbed a tree branch to steady myself and looked down. I was covered in blood where the icy crust had cut my shins and forearms. The palms of my hands were scraped and oozing too.

"Dammit!"

I looked up at the sun, suddenly resentful of the sixty-five-degree warmth hitting the backs of my bare legs. *I shouldn't have worn shorts and left my gaiters in the car.*

I took another tentative step, wincing as the snow cracked and sharp edges raked along my already scraped shin. I looked down the mountain. The trail was completely covered by thin snow, the sound of gurgling meltwater nearly deafening as it roared along unseen. *This is going to suck.*

I sighed deeply and plunged forward.

At the bottom of the torturous descent, I staggered out onto the road, bloody legs burning. Apple Pie honked and waved cheerily, but then her smile faded when she saw my condition. She jumped out of the car, her blue eyes full of worry.

"Are you okay?"

"Icy crust on the snow," I managed before bursting into tears.

She embraced me and led me to the car. "C'mon, get in."

"But it's only four o'clock. I need to keep hiking," I sobbed.

"Nope, you need to eat, drink tea, and read a gossip magazine," she said, loading me into the passenger seat. She drove us down the road to a sun-drenched cul-de-sac.

I stared blankly out the windshield as she got out the stove and made us both tea. I sipped it mechanically, feeling a desperate mixture of guilt and exhaustion rising in my throat. I hadn't had a day of under thirty miles since Duncannon, nearly a month prior. I couldn't break the streak now.

She's right, you know. You're worn out and underfed. You need to rest more than you need seven more miles. She's helping you recover to keep going, not trying to derail your hike into becoming a tropical vacation like Adam was.

I'd been on trail less than two months and had managed to hike almost eighteen hundred miles across eleven states. *It's a marathon, not a sprint.* My left foot throbbed, reminding me of the near-constant pain I'd been hiking with. I finished the tea, feeling my anxiety lessen slightly.

"You're right," I said, handing her the cup and grabbing my water bladder. "I'm going to go wash up."

I came back from my ablutions free of blood and mud, and flopped in the back of the SUV next to her, where I applied triple antibiotic ointment and gauze to my scrapes. She handed me a gossip magazine and a chocolate bar.

"Better?" she asked.

"Much," I said, biting into the treat and enjoying the warmth of the sun on my bandaged legs. It was easier to rest around someone who was happy.

"Look what I got in town!" She held up a pair of hiking boots.

"Ooo, pretty! But are they functional?" We both hiked in sneakers.

"I don't know, but they were on sale and cute. So . . . " We both giggled.

A FEW DAYS LATER I stood outside the vehicle, gripping a steaming cup of coffee and grinning as Apple Pie took a picture of me.

"I'll see you at Gifford Woods. Call me from the top if anything goes wrong!"

"Thank you!" I waved as she drove away, heading toward real civilization to take care of work while I faced the highest point on the Vermont AT—Killington Peak.

I walked through the chilly forest on a bare trail, happily sipping the coffee. A scuffling noise caught my attention, and I looked over to see a porcupine lumbering out of sight into the underbrush. The sun was up, but the light was gray and dull, enticing crepuscular animals to stay out past their bedtimes. It was not quite spring here, but it certainly wasn't winter either. I paused to note a small sign on a tree that read "Katahdin 500."

"Oh, that's not very far!" I exclaimed, and immediately laughed at myself. *Only a thru-hiker thinks like that.*

I finished my coffee and tucked the cup into my backpack just as I began stepping on snow. From there the AT climbed steadily toward the lofty summit shelter at just below four thousand feet. If Glastenbury, many miles to the south, was any indication, I was in for a very long slog. I glanced down at my torn tights layered under knee-high gaiters. My shins were still bruised and marred by the wretched descent into Mad Tom Notch. Even though it was colder today and the snow was likely to be much firmer, I was not willing to risk slicing and dicing myself again.

My breath came out in little huffs as I struggled to simultaneously climb the mountain and punch tracks into ever-deepening snow. Now that the entire slope was a swath of untracked white, I focused on locating blazes on the trees and walking from one to the next. Without a visible trail, my route was undefined, merely point to point. As I climbed, the air temperature dropped, firming the snow, and I sank in less. I was grateful for that slight reprieve as I worked incredibly hard to plow my way upward.

I floundered around in a surprisingly soft area of snow, searching for the next blaze. Tree branches smacked me in the face, and I felt for a moment as though I were drowning in them—disoriented. *Something is wrong!* I felt panic rising. *Where is the next blaze? Am I lost?* Then one leg plunged even deeper into the snow, leaving my other leg suspended and twisted sideways. I flailed my arms; my buried foot was not touching dirt. *Calm down!*

I took a deep breath to quell the fear enlivening my limbs. *Stop fighting and distribute!* I flopped backward, like a drunken snow angel, and gripped the snow with my outstretched hands. I wiggled my hips until I managed to straighten my surface leg enough to push, resurrecting my buried leg from its snow grave. Free of the hip-deep postholes I lay still, starfished across the surface of the snow in the midst of a silent forest. The sun broke free from its cloudy prison and dazzled my surroundings. On a tree ten feet from my face—at snow level—was what looked like half of a white blaze. *Is that really a blaze? It has to be. It's too rectangular to be natural.*

Holy shit. The snow is six feet deep here. No wonder branches are smacking me in the face.

I pulled my sunglasses out of my pocket and slid them on before army crawling forward a few feet. Carefully I got up and stood still. The snow held my weight. *Thank God.* I pulled out my phone and looked at it. *Another thousand vertical. And the sun is going to soften this snow fast.*

I took a few tentative steps and pitched forward as my left foot broke through, although only half as far as before. I repeated my extrication maneuvers and panted for a few moments on hands and knees.

I'm going to have to crawl up this damn mountain, aren't I?

It was almost easier to ascend straight up through the snow on hands and knees than it had been to try and walk where the trail wove through the forest. Every ten minutes I would try to walk again, inevitably post-holing into snow that lay deeper than I was tall. The solar radiation reflecting off of it simultaneously softened the surface and warmed me so that I had no fear of getting too cold. *As long as I'm off this mountain by dark.*

Only a couple hundred feet below the summit, a cool fog rolled up and blocked out the sun, a by-product of the rapid evaporation happening below. I attempted to stand and took a few steps, my face clenched tight, expecting to crash through once again. But I didn't. The air was suddenly chilly and clammy. I put my jacket on, relieved to be walking upright again, even if I had to dodge tree branches that would normally be out of reach above my head.

Just below the summit, a flash of orange caught my eye, standing out brightly against the white background. I perked up, thinking there was someone else crazy enough to be hiking up here.

"Hello!"

There was no response and I hurried forward. More orange revealed itself in the form of plastic tape stretched across the trail.

You might be an early NoBo if the ski resort hasn't yet removed the out-of-bounds markings, I thought wryly. (NoBo is trail lingo for northbound.)

I was relieved to see that the snow was almost nonexistent in the forest beyond Cooper Lodge, a very old stone shelter. Slushy, but only ankle deep—an almost unimaginable contrast with the side of the mountain I'd just ascended. *I'll take it.* I stopped to eat a snack and text Apple Pie an ETA.

Then I sent my sister an update: "Hey! I'm almost through Vermont, ready to head west on Monday!"

I chewed, thinking about how much of a shift it was to be texting my sister from a mountainside when for most of my life she'd been absent, separated by the generational age gap as well as geography. The domino effect of my losses that began when our father died had—surprisingly—brought me to her doorstep in Florida.

The phone chimed.

"Good luck! Are you doing the Cascades first or the Rockies? Take care."

"A little bit of New Mexico and then the PCT!"

It was in the previous months, living right next door to her in our deceased grandmother's vacant home that Marie now owned, that I'd begun to really know my sister. I was amazed to discover we were shockingly alike, from habits to mannerisms. One afternoon as I sat on her couch using the internet while she bustled around the kitchen staying busy doing nothing that I could see, just like I often did, I had an abrupt realization.

I wasn't the black sheep. I just didn't know the other one in the flock.

My sister had left home at eighteen and married a Navy man a year later, when I was six weeks old. They lived all over the world and raised two children. I had always admired her beauty and auburn hair, both much lauded by the rest of the family. Shy and keenly uncomfortable in my own body, I had wanted nothing more than to be like her.

And now I'd discovered that I was, just not in the ways I'd wanted. Instead, we shared a sense of adventure, prized our private space, and even had similar little quirks of speech and facial expressions.

"Go girl!"

I smiled, so grateful for her encouragement. No one else in my family had ever championed my hiking. However, in these last months of preparation, Marie had asked a thousand questions, more eager to understand than judge. She'd beamed over articles about me and my book contract. "I'm so proud of you!" she'd gushed as I said goodbye.

Her exuberant pride in me was unlike anything I had experienced from anyone else in my typically reserved family. I finally felt like there was someone in my family I could connect with, who cared about what

I had dedicated my life to. I looked forward to growing our relationship even more once I was done with this hike.

I finished my food and then hurried down the trail, pleased that while the descent was intermittently snowy, it was easily manageable. *Everyone always said Marie was the most like my dad. Maybe if she's proud of me . . .*

Spring was prevalent along the AT north of Killington. Slushy patches of snow dotted the trail here and there, but mostly it was clear trail and greening forest. The narrow path of dirt, rocks, and roots marked by swaths of white painted on the trees had been my home for two months and two days now—almost all of it in harsh weather. *In fact, it's been my home for nearly an entire year of my life in total between this, my FKT, and my first thru-hike that I started fifteen years ago next week.* No wonder stepping onto the Appalachian Trail always felt like coming home.

I relished the sun pouring through the trees as I walked, lost in thought about the next stage of the hike, which was rapidly approaching. *Meet Pie and Greenleaf at VT 12. Hike with Greenleaf this afternoon and tomorrow morning. Get to Hanover tomorrow and go home with them. Zero and swap out all my gear for the desert. Leave winter gear here for when I come back in the fall to finish up the AT. Fly to Albuquerque and take a Greyhound to Grants. Hike to Mexico. Take the Greyhound to Tucson and stay with Sirena until my flight to San Diego. Meet Adam and stay with Scout and Frodo. Start the PCT on May 22, our permit date.*

I stopped as I realized that I was on the edge of a cliff. I turned around and looked into the sunny forest behind me. It looked like trail. *What the . . . ?*

I retraced my steps, keeping my mind in the present rather than weeks ahead. A hundred yards back was a white blaze. I turned around. The trail most definitely went to the cliff edge. I walked back over and cautiously peered down. A ladder was bolted to the rock.

"Oh good, still on trail," I muttered, turning around and swinging down the ladder. *I'm almost to the Whites, after all.*

The trail ahead in New Hampshire was known for its rocky brutality and the need for hands-on scrambling. In fact, most of the hike to the end of the trail from here, including the iconic ascent of the Hunt Spur to the terminus on Mount Katahdin, necessitated three points or more of contact. While hardy New Englanders trekked through the White Mountains even in winter, there were deaths every year. The AT up there would be coated in deep snow and rime right now, with arctic winds that could cut through every layer of clothing I owned. The huts, normally staffed, would still be boarded up, removing any safety net from the exposed landscape. I could do it, but it would be an extreme risk for me to continue on—one that I was not willing to take.

I'd rejected high altitude mountaineering when the reality of my limitations with Raynaud's had set in several years prior. The Whites in winter were an alpinist's training ground. I knew I had no business up there at this time of year. I walked along the mostly level trail, basking in the sunshine. *Besides, New Mexico sounds amazing right now.*

I couldn't wait to leave the rocky trail for the mostly level road and desert of southern New Mexico. Perhaps there my foot could finally recover from the neuroma pain that had plagued me since right before I entered the Smokies. Most days I didn't think about it too much; compartmentalizing pain was something I had learned to excel at. But the rocks of Pennsylvania had been excruciating. Day after day, while it snowed and rained, all I could do was try to find my rock Zen and keep going. To let go of every expectation, including the idea of getting through a Calendar Year Triple Crown without a physical toll.

Trading Adam for Apple Pie, and extra cushioned shoes for the worn-out pair I'd been wearing, had enabled me to keep climbing, fording, and singing to myself even in the worst of it. Snow, oddly, had been the best respite for my feet. Its softness acted as extra cushioning against the uneven terrain. Even though nature smiled gently on me now, I knew that—truly—it had no compassion, no qualms about being difficult or making things practically impossible. Sometimes I had even felt as though it relished my suffering.

Now I ducked under long lines of tubing crisscrossing the forest, running from tree to tree. I followed one, confused as to its purpose until I saw it hooked into a tap in one of the drowsy trees. *Maple syrup lines!* I laughed at the realization and rested my hand against the maple that was just waking. *Perhaps this tree will sweeten my breakfast in the future.*

I continued downhill toward the ribbon of road visible in the distance, where I would meet Apple Pie and Greenleaf. The Appalachian Trail was not a gentle thing. She was more like a mischievous wood elf throwing rocks, roots, fords, and inclement weather at you, laughing so hard that springs burst from her bouldered face. I'd learned to accept her impediments and to laugh along with her at the absurdity of it all. Despite my aching feet, I broke into a run, airplaning my arms and grinning—embracing the sheer joy of being alive in nature.

PART II

WESTWARD

CHAPTER 9

SOUTHERN NEW MEXICO

I felt displaced in the air.

It was odd to cross the Connecticut River by foot on a balmy late April evening, then get into a car and drive away, choosing to trade thick forest for desert. Now I had committed myself to returning later for unfinished business among the spruces, rocky rivers, and wide-open ridgelines of New England. Business that would have to wait for me to trek the length of the Pacific Crest Trail—twenty-six hundred miles—and however much of the Continental Divide Trail I could before October, when winter threatened to close access to Mount Katahdin.

I wondered if I should have stayed the course, albeit much more slowly, in order to finish the entire AT first. I felt the pull of those last two states tugging on me even as my plane soared over the Midwest. I hoped the pull to complete what I had started would be strong enough to get me through the moments ahead when I wouldn't want to walk anymore. The Appalachian Trail had always felt like home, and I had adapted this journey's itinerary to accommodate hiking the PCT with Adam in the belief that I would miss that home enough to push me through.

I hope I'm right. I have to be right. It will. It will.

After a long twenty-four hours of travel and half a night of sleep in a motel, I stepped outside into the desert sunshine, blinding after two months in the gray-spring Appalachians. I walked across an overpass to reach the Continental Divide Trail where it followed old Route 66 through Grants, New Mexico. In a small triangle of green where the overpass road diverged from the renowned highway of kicks, a solitary tree spread its welcoming branches. I walked over to it as though it had beckoned me by name.

I paused beside it, laying my hand lightly on the furrowed bark. Most likely I would finish the entire Calendar Year Triple Crown right here, at this tree. After I finished the PCT and the AT, I would end with the CDT, hiking back to this tree from the north.

If I finish. My pack was heavy with water, and the day would only grow hotter. My first one hundred miles southbound from Grants would be mostly along roads until I reached my resupply box in Pie Town. Though I'd longed for warmth for what seemed like forever, I knew the heat radiating off of the blacktop would become unbearable by late afternoon. I gazed up into the cool canopy.

"I'll be back," I whispered, promising both the tree and myself.

I strode along the once-famous road, my legs feeling strong and light without snow and mud hindering them. My new, highly cushioned running shoes ameliorated the pain that had been my constant companion for more than fifteen hundred miles. I glanced up at the Route 66 sign and felt a sharp constriction in my chest. *My dad was here.*

A car sped past me and I pictured what this must have been like in 1955, when my father came flying through on his pedal-to-the-metal journey from Saint Louis, Michigan, to Navy boot camp in Oxnard, California.

"There's nothing out there," he'd declared whenever I spoke of my hikes in—and love for—the desert.

Back then, there probably wasn't much. Nothing except open terrain, cacti, canyons, lizards, coyotes—and all of the other things I loved about this landscape. He'd made the drive in three days, and in his retelling it was often unclear whether he'd slept at all or only for a few minutes when he could no longer keep the car pointed straight on the lonesome road.

I reached the end of the old highway, where it merged with the modern interstate. I crossed another overpass and descended into the quiet, open land to the south. In the harsh light of morning, the world beyond the city limits looked barren and uninviting. *He would have careened through here at the same time of day, bound for an alien encounter late that night outside Yuma.*

I was glad to leave Route 66 and the city behind. Despite walking on roads, I experienced a peace in the desert seldom found elsewhere.

The day passed in the metronymic manner I had missed in the early season struggles of the AT. I stopped once, at a closed ranger station along the highway, and filled my water bottles to the brim from an outside faucet. From beneath my hat, I marked the wide arc of the sun as it blazed a path across the sky, throwing my body into a confused state of profuse sweating as the ambient temperature rose above eighty—and much hotter on the radiant road. As the sun eventually began to sink, I followed the contour beneath ruddy cliffs, grateful for the relief of the nascent shade. *Was it only three days ago that I was striding through the just-awakening forests of Vermont investigating maple syrup taps?*

Though the AT felt like home and the memory of white-blazed bark floated in my mind and heart, I was surprised to find a new sense of homecoming here in the desert, a manifestation of the surge of love that had filled me on arrival.

I nestled into the sand beneath my sleeping pad that night, relishing the way it cradled my tired body. Darkness came quickly, and with it a surprising dip in temperatures. I dozed off immediately, exhausted from flying, riding, and hiking thousands of miles in forty-eight hours.

I WAS IN THE OLD BUICK with my dad, hurtling through the desert night, the radio long since plunged into static and silence as we stared ahead, our future unseen. A bright light flooded the car as it oscillated across the no-man's-land all around us. My dad muttered, "Aliens," as he nudged the speedometer over a hundred even as I yelled.

"No! Dad, it's a train!"

I felt more than heard the *ba-bump* he had so often described as his car tires ricocheted across the metal rails, waking him from his trance in time to barely regain control of the vehicle as the orb of the train's light passed seconds behind him.

I sat bolt upright, my heart pounding, bright moonlight shining in my face. I clutched my chest, willing my heart to slow down by taking deep lungfuls of the dry air. As the adrenaline ebbed, I pushed back my sleeping bag and crawled out of my tent, blinking at the full moon's brightness. I stood there silently in the desert, listening to the far-off yip of coyotes and the soft susurrations of something unknown in the brush nearby. *Full speed ahead almost cost you, and me, our lives.*

A solitary coyote sang out, so close that goosebumps sprang up along my arms. *But maybe it's really what saved you. Maybe it's what will save me too.*

I crawled back into my tent and fell dreamlessly asleep.

ROADS HAVE ONE DISTINCT BENEFIT over trails: they are fast. My feet flew along the graded, level surfaces without pain. Thirty-four miles into my day, at four p.m., I reached a ranch that offered free water and camping to hikers. I greedily drank bottle after bottle of water, chatting with the few other hikers who were there, all heading north in opposition to my southward trajectory.

Against the flow yet again. Always different.

My dehydrated body slowly rejuvenated after two long days in the brutal sun. It was another sixteen miles to Pie Town, where my resupply would be waiting. *Just enough time to make it by dark.* I took my phone off of airplane mode and read the text from Apple Pie that came through, my brow furrowing with dismay.

"Checked the tracking number on your box. It won't be there until tomorrow."

I turned the phone back on airplane mode and put it in my pack. She had mailed the box for me several days before I'd headed west, with a guaranteed delivery before I arrived. Suddenly the relentless push through the hottest hours of the day on the road seemed meaningless. Even if I made it to Pie Town tonight, there wouldn't be a box there for me. *What if it doesn't show up tomorrow either?*

I filled all of my water containers and wandered away from the other hikers. Near the edge of the property, I found a cozy spot under the sprawling arms of a juniper to pitch my tent. The sun wouldn't set for several more hours, but in the sparse shade I could rest, which I knew I needed.

I ate and drank as much as I could hold, and then I lay back on my mat, letting the sage-scented breeze and growing shadows cast by the tree dance across my naked body. I woke up with the moon in my face again, shivering from the cold. I rolled over, grabbing my sleeping bag and snuggling inside it. *I'm so tired, even though I stopped early. Why am I so tired?*

My body's response was to sink into unconsciousness.

DAWN WAS BARELY TINTING the sky orange when my body had slept its fill and woke me. I sat up and quietly went about my morning ritual: coffee, breakfast, dressing, packing. I crept over to the spigot and refilled my water again before following the driveway past a smattering of tents back to the dirt road. I brushed my teeth as light bloomed across the sky. The crunching of gravel under my feet sounded loud in the quiet dawn.

I walked into the dusty restaurant parking lot ten seconds after the UPS truck pulled in. I hurried forward as the driver walked inside with a familiar-looking box. *That's my box!* I wanted to call after him, but I recognized the futility. I was just relieved to know it was there.

After I'd collected it and sat for a couple hours eating, talking to more northbound thru-hikers, and repacking, I set out on yet another road. This one was paved and would weave past ranches and homes across the pine and sage desert for twenty-two miles before finally entering the national forest. The pressure to reach my box alleviated, and with the assurance from NoBo hikers of several water sources along the road ahead, I allowed my thoughts to wander until they naturally ceased and I was simply there, walking through warm pinyon desert alone.

I reached the head of Govina Canyon just before dusk the next day, grateful to be high up on the ponderosa-covered slopes of Wagontongue Mountain. I staked out my tent as the cool evening air began to settle, chilling my sweaty body. *I wonder if it will be below freezing tonight?* The thought seemed laughable after having just spent four days hiking in the direct sun where temperatures kissed triple digits. However, the desert is variable in ways the uninitiated can't understand. Some of my coldest times on trail have been sleeping among cactus and sand.

As the last rays of sun filtered through the trees and gilded my tent, I surveyed my campsite. "Home for the night," I announced to no one and the universe. *I'm not sure there's anything more wonderful than waking up beneath ponderosas.*

Inside my tent I quickly changed into my warm night clothes and draped my damp shorts and shirt on the tent's clothesline to dry. I filtered water into my dried beans and gulped them down with tortilla chips and chunks of avocado before they were completely rehydrated, not caring about the weird half-crunchy texture after another nearly forty-mile day. I tucked the water filter into the foot of my sleeping bag—just in case it would dip below thirty-two—and snuggled deep into the down.

The moon was sliding upward into the lapis sky. Nearby an owl hooted, and I heard the muffled sound of feathers pass overhead. I began to drift off to sleep, brought back momentarily by the excited yipping of a pack of coyotes in the near distance. I smiled even as my consciousness was dwindling. *Nothing better than waking up beneath these trees, except perhaps falling asleep beneath them to owl call and coyote howl.*

THE CDT THROUGH the Gila National Forest was mostly on dirt roads. The springs I expected to have water did, but everything else was bone dry. The other hikers I met told me about the extreme drought conditions they'd been hiking in, although it was already evident to me by the brown grass and powdery dust that rose in little puffs as I walked, infiltrating the weave of my socks.

I stopped only twice in thirty miles, once for water and once to eat. Two months of struggling through snow, mud, and rugged terrain had conditioned my legs for constant motion. On the flat, clear terrain they propelled me forward at a brisk clip. However, the mercury was again above ninety, and the punishing sun took a toll on my as yet unacclimated body. My nose bled and I staunched it with a piece of cloth torn from my shirt. By late afternoon my water supply was precariously low, despite having set out from the last spring with a gallon and a half.

I hope there's water in T-Bar Canyon. I hope there's water in T-Bar Canyon. Over and over the phrase echoed through my overheated mind.

Like a mirage, two hikers appeared on the savannah-like horizon.

"Is there water in T-Bar Canyon?" I asked hopefully.

"Uh, I don't know where that is," one of the guys responded.

I pointed vaguely behind them.

"The canyon you just came up. Before you climbed up here onto the plateau."

"Oh, yeah, there was some water at mile 82.7, if that's what you mean," the other guy chimed in.

"Okay, thanks."

We carried on in our opposite directions. I had no idea what mile point anything was at. When I first trekked this trail in 2005 there were no apps for it, and I carried a guidebook that named features and gave geophysical descriptions. Thus I knew this landscape by names on the map, not by waypoints logged as digits counting up or down to a final number.

Now I pulled out my phone and looked at the app for the first time since I'd left the network of roads after Pie Town. The mileages were not the same for me as they were for a northbounder. I sighed and put it away. My feet scuffed along, my dehydrated and tired legs unwilling to lift them any higher.

I know there's water down there somewhere, even if it's the reservoir.

As I reached the loose, rocky descent toward the blue reservoir, I drank my last sip. Looks were deceiving. As clean as it looked from here, I knew it was murky cow water. *I hope there's water in T-Bar Canyon.*

Thankfully, there was. The water that coursed through the narrow canyon was crystal clear, the muck having been skimmed out by the reeds and long grasses, acacia, and willow that lined the banks. I filled a bladder and filtered into my mouth as I walked, keeping an eye on the stream. For now, it babbled playfully along, mirthful and mischievous, but at any minute it could dive underground. After a couple of miles, I waded in to my ankles and filled all of my water containers, despite having drunk my fill while I walked. Then I climbed up and away from the stream, glancing back a few minutes later to see that the water no longer flowed aboveground.

Exiting T-Bar Canyon onto jeep roads, I was relieved to find myself walking in long shadows. It was already eight p.m. and finally cool enough to be comfortable. A short while later I found a campsite under a large tree and stopped for the night, with nearly forty miles on my feet for the day yet again.

By morning I'd drank half of my water, and I committed to rationing over the hot, dusty road miles and steep ridgeline separating me from the Gila River. "There's no water until the Gila and you've got to go up and over Aeroplane Mesa," I admonished myself as I set off in the cool morning air, longing for coffee.

The sun crested the mesas not many minutes into my day, drenching me in sunshine. *I will never complain about being too hot*, I told myself, thinking of the frigid Appalachians and the many hours I'd longed for unbridled sunlight like this.

I reached the dirt road junction that led up to the Gila River High Route and turned eastward, the sun now positioned for a full-frontal assault. I pulled my visor as low as I could and watched my feet as I climbed. The wind picked up as the day warmed. Unlike the cold breath of the windigo, this felt like walking into a hair dryer.

By the time I reached the Aeroplane Mesa Campground, where I would go over the ridgetop and descend to the Gila River, my water was gone. I stood under a pine tree and ate a packet of Trail Butter, the only palatable thing I could ingest without getting extremely thirsty. It was still five miles to the river. I resumed trudging uphill.

The climb was easy compared to the agonizingly slow descent. Loose rocks threatened to turn my ankles and sharp cacti overhung the tread in several places. I skidded on the steeper bits, recognizing that my hyper-cushioned road running shoes were massively out of place here. Even when I finally glimpsed the brown ribbon of river gliding through the forest below, it took half an hour to reach its banks.

I stopped as soon as I reached it, removed my shoes, and waded into the water. Its coolness stripped away the heat of the last several hours.

I scooped a gallon of water into the gravity filter bag, hung it on a pine tree, and plopped down against the trunk. Putting the filter hose in my mouth, I closed my eyes and let the water trickle in like a jerry-rigged IV.

After a liter had passed through my dry throat, I transferred the hose to one of my water bottles and sat up straighter, suddenly very hungry. I devoured my lunch as well as some of the snacks I hadn't eaten because of thirst. I dropped an electrolyte tablet into the now full bottle and switched the hose to another one. I pulled my soaking wet socks off and rinsed my feet in the river, thankfully washing away the grit that had been rubbing them raw for the last few days. I poured a quarter cup of sand out of each of my shoes, shaking my head at the amount.

"Ridiculous," I muttered.

Hydrated, fed, and sand-free, I waded across the river. While many hikers opt to traverse the Gila itself for many miles, I'd already done the "100 Gila Fords on the Wall" hike in 2006. In 2017 I'd hiked the Gila High Route; while devoid of water, it was a pleasant trek overland through pine forest to the road accessing Gila Cliff Dwellings National Monument on the other side of the ridgeline that formed the southern boundary of the Gila Gorge.

"Up we go," I said, climbing up and away from the river on faint tread.

I meandered through minor dry drainages and relished the modicum of shade the pines of the High Route cast on me. Beyond their boughs I could sense the heat blooming. The air in shafts of sunlight danced with the energy of the sun. Once more I was amazed at how little I needed to refer to my map. Having hiked through this area less than eight months prior, I still had a clear memory of it. Once again, I marveled at my mind's ability to create maps of the places I had walked. Locations where I'd camped more than ten years earlier leapt out at me as I traversed the Triple Crown trails for the third time.

There is something innately human about walking long distances like this, roaming across landscapes looking for water and safe places to spend the night. Being out here unlocks a primal part of my memory. Places I have slept are indelibly stamped in my mind. Necessary to humans who traveled the same routes in pursuit of game for millennia, the ability to recreate the way to them is a latent survival skill unused by most. When the trail changes and takes me somewhere new but there is water on the old route, I remember the way to go. The places I've slept badly are just as memorable. Where I've encountered bears or high wind, my brain reminds me not to stop there.

I feel more human walking through the wild than anywhere else.

I crested the ridge as the sun dropped behind the next one, still blazing hot. The wind rose with the shifting angle of light and roared in my ears, scouring my face with its arid breath and airborne sand. I followed the trail through many ups and downs, avoiding the first descending trail option because my memory reminded me of the terrifying encounter there a year before with an olive-colored northern black-tailed rattlesnake—even though I knew it was unlikely to be there this time through.

Instead, I powered through the undulations along the ridge, growing thirstier and thirstier as I went. *Will this ever end? I'm not going to make it to Doc Campbell's tonight at this rate.* The only place to buy supplies on the dead-end road several thousand feet below closed at four p.m. I pulled out my phone and looked at the time. Five. *I should have known.* I slowed my pace and resigned myself to not reaching my resupply until the morning.

The first cooling shadows of the evening were puddling beneath the trees when I reached the Little Bear Canyon Trail. Far below me to the left, I glimpsed the Gila River. To my right, the canyon of the West Fork of the Gila sprawled out of sight in lengthening shadow. I stopped and marveled at the multiplicity of hues staining the sky and land around me. Deep indigo shadows poured over mauve and buff rock. Splotches of emerald vegetation illustrated life carving its way in every nook and cranny possible; bent shapes of wind-gnarled trees gave the landscape a look of frozen movement. The western sky blazed coral and gold, tinged rose and lavender where the approaching night kissed retiring day. My shoes were full of sand again, my face was burned from the sun, and my ears rang with the wind's assault. Yet, as I swallowed the last sip of the Gila River I carried, I couldn't help but feel deep, abiding joy at the beauty surrounding me.

My God, New Mexico, I love you.

I WOKE AT THE FIRST fluttering breeze after a still night. Soft gray light pervaded my tent. My mouth was cottony. I sat up and drank the water I'd gotten from a nearby spigot before bed, then began to pack up. I moved slowly, my joints and muscles inflexible from another forty-mile day coupled with mild dehydration.

I stumbled down the loose embankment to the trailhead and refilled my water, chugging a liter without pausing for breath. It was only three miles to Doc Campbell's, which wouldn't open for several more hours. But the day was young and cool, so now was the time to walk. I started down the road, wrapped in a meditative blankness of mind.

I reached the outpost just as the sun was beginning to warm the day. Plopping down on the cement pad under the awning in the back, I plugged my phone and battery pack in to the outlet to charge. Meanwhile, I logged on to the Wi-Fi and began catching up with online tasks that had been forgotten for days as I walked.

"Hey! Mind if I use the other plug?"

I glanced up to see a young man and woman in front of me.

"Oh, sure. Go ahead." I scooted over a bit so they could plug their devices in next to mine.

The woman flopped onto the picnic table bench across from me with an air of exhaustion that was surprising for eight a.m.

"You thru-hiking?" the man asked, sitting down next to her much less dramatically.

"Yeah, kind of. I just started in Grants and I'm going to flip-flop," I responded, keeping my explanation as simple as possible.

They both nodded.

"Get the hot out of the way and miss the snow in the south San Juans both. Good strategy." The man dug around in his pack and pulled out a box of mini cinnamon rolls.

The woman took one and shoved it into her mouth, whole.

"You guys are northbound?" I ventured.

"Yeah, mmmph," the woman spoke around the pastry. "But not the way you think."

I lifted my eyebrows a little.

"We did the Columbus route," the man filled in, taking a small bite of his roll. This meant they'd started at one of the alternate termini of the CDT. This original route ended farther east, at the border crossing into Puerto Palomas, Mexico, just south of Columbus, New Mexico.

"It was awful!" the woman exclaimed, having swallowed the roll. She waved her hand at him for another one. "It was so hot and there was no water."

"None?" I asked. "I was planning to go that way."

"There was water," he amended, casting the woman a sidelong glance. "Just not a lot. I wouldn't be surprised if some of the sources are dry by the time you get there."

I thought about all the warnings of no water I'd received from other NoBos already. Even so, all the permanent sources were full. *If you've done this trail twice, you understand the difference between maybe water and sure thing water*, I reassured myself.

I opened my app and scrolled ahead. *No point in asking them the names of the sources.*

"So, what about this water source?" I handed my phone over to him. "This is where I'm heading tomorrow."

He glanced at it and then at me. "You'll have a hard time getting there by tomorrow. That section is a hellacious bushwhack. But regardless, that spring is literally dripping. It took us three hours to get a gallon of water."

"We camped there three days ago. We had to because we'd run out of time to hike by the time we finished filling our water," the woman added.

"Hmm, thanks." I set my phone down. I'd spent two hours the night before studying the Columbus route. It had been twelve years since I'd hiked it, but the route in the app didn't match my memory at all. Then again, at one point we'd walked up a dirt road described in our guidebook only to find ourselves on someone's ranch. Thankfully, they'd allowed us to pass through, regaining the national forest a mile beyond their house. It was unlikely that passage was still allowed. *Probably many other situations like that have changed the route.*

The sound of someone unlocking the shop door sent all three of us springing to our feet. Inside, the couple browsed the shelves while I went straight to the desk and asked for my resupply box. Back outside, I opened it and began throwing things into my pack. I looked up in my app the number of a trail angel couple in Mimbres and sent them a message asking if I could stay with them that night.

It would be more than forty more miles on roads for the day, but I'd bypass the bushwhack, pass by sure water at a campground, and avoid relying on the dripping—possibly dry—spring that was the only water source in that entire section. *Besides, at this point you've been hiking forties almost every day anyway. So what if this ends up being about fifty total?* With my water bottles fully restocked and snacks stashed in easy-to-reach places, I took off up the road into the already harsh sun.

The yellow orb was still bearing down on me nine hours later. I texted the trail angels.

"I'm sorry, I'll be later than I thought. Probably eight p.m. Is that okay?"

I hadn't stopped except to get water at the camp many miles and hours ago. My whole body felt wired into mechanical movement at a singular speed—forward at just under four miles per hour. Despite the cushioned shoes, my feet and shins were aching. The soles had softened in the heat, growing sticky on the hot blacktop. Now that they were resolidifying in the marginally cooling temperatures, I gained back some additional momentum with every step. My water was gone and I was still a little more than five miles away.

My God, it's so hot here. I can't even swallow without it hurting.

It was not the hottest I'd ever been, but it was the hottest I'd been for many years. With three miles to go I felt myself weaving, struggling to stay the course. All I wanted to do was sit down and pour cold water into my mouth—and over my head. I stared hard at the white line and tried to put my feet on it, both to keep me walking straight and also to step on the coolest part of the road. The stance required to do so was too narrow, and I tripped myself. My next tactic was to focus on planting my feet on each side of the line, the inside of each sole touching it. This method worked.

I reached the turnoff to their house as dusk graced the sky. After pushing relentlessly all day I stood on their front step, uncertain of what to do or how to act. These people were complete strangers who made themselves available to help thru-hikers. I would need to provide at least a modicum of sociability, yet every molecule of my being was screaming for my most basic need: water. Finally, I gathered myself enough to ring the doorbell.

A woman who looked to be nearly seventy answered the door.

"You must be Heather! I'm Helen," she said, holding the door for me. "Welcome."

"Thank you." My words cracked like the desiccated mud around dry springs, my throat barely capable of making intelligible croaks.

"This is John," she said, introducing me to her husband as we walked into the kitchen.

"Hi Heather, we were just preparing dinner. Is salad and chicken okay with you?" he asked.

I nodded.

"Here, you must be thirsty." Helen handed me a glass to fill with water.

My vision had already begun darkening at the edges. I was aware they were talking, and yet I heard only a rushing sound. I fumbled with the faucet. *Just get water.* I held the glass under the stream of cold water, watching as my hand wobbled, struggling to keep water entering the glass. To my surprise, my hand, the glass, and the water all disappeared and I heard a thump in the far-off distance.

"Heather! Are you okay?' Helen's voice was nearly drowned out by a deafening ringing in my ears that had replaced the rushing sound.

I winced as I rejoined my body, now supine on their kitchen floor. My head was throbbing where I'd hit it, and my legs felt stiff, hard, bloated. I was still very thirsty. I struggled to push myself part way up and tried to focus on their faces with my swimming vision.

"I'm okay." The words were labored. "I just need some water. And to put my feet up."

Helen put the glass of water in my hand and I drained it. John helped me to my feet and I staggered into the dining room, barely able to walk without passing out again. Once we reached the dining table, I sank gratefully onto the cool wood floor and propped my feet up on a chair. I closed my eyes until the spinning stopped, aware of just how ridiculous the whole situation was. A dirty, unknown woman had entered this generous couple's home, passed out in their kitchen, and was now lying flat on her back with her feet up on their dining room chair.

"I'm so sorry for that! I walked here from Doc Campbell's today without stopping. The blood is all pooled in my legs. I just need to invert them until my body realizes I'm not walking anymore and reestablishes normal venous return," I explained, grateful that my brain was working again after a glass of cold water. My legs and feet began to tingle. "I'm so sorry. It should only take like five minutes."

"You do whatever you have to do to take care of yourself," Helen said from the kitchen doorway, seemingly nonplussed by the whole thing.

I relaxed, letting my body restore equilibrium, listening to the clank of dishes and the sound of cupboard doors in the next room.

It's okay to let others take care of you, Heather. Just let them. And let yourself take care of you too.

"Doc Campbell's is pretty far away," John said, setting a bowl of crisp salad on the table above me.

"Yeah, I took the roads though." I hauled myself up into a chair and they sat down as well. "I hiked this route once before, a long time ago. It seems like it's changed?"

"Yes, they even took down our Continental Divide sign on the highway," Helen sighed, passing me the platter of baked chicken.

"I thought so! I got to the pass and it looked so familiar, but I remember there being a sign that it was the divide." I served myself heaping portions of chicken and salad.

"It's dry out there this year. We've had only two or three other hikers—not many do this route anymore. But they've all reported that even the cattle tanks are just mud puddles," John said, taking the platter of chicken I passed him.

"It's definitely hot," I concurred. My skin was still radiating heat, despite my copious application of SPF 50 throughout the day.

"They'll close the forests soon." Helen shook her head. "If they don't, people can't celebrate Memorial Day without someone starting a fire."

I nodded. I was grateful to be heading south and away from the ensuing chaos for hikers when the forests did close. I knew it was inevitable, having seen it happen several years in a row when extreme spring droughts turned the forests to tinder. As we ate, we chatted quietly about their experiences as trail angels over the years and their life in the Mimbres Valley. I helped clear the table and do the dishes until Helen shooed me toward the bathroom.

"You've helped enough. Now get in there and take as long of a shower as you want. I'll wash your clothes when you get out."

It felt surreal to stand in a black stone tiled shower with limitless water coursing over my skin. Days' worth of dust swirled in snaky streaks down my legs, coiled around my ankles, and slithered down the drain. *I'm not nearly as tan as I thought.* I laughed, watching my skin turn three shades lighter as the suds slid off.

Afterward, I joined Helen and John on the couch in the living room wearing my sleeping clothes while the rest tumbled in the washer. John handed me a thick journal, the log signed by everyone who had stayed with them over the years. I flipped to the beginning—2006, the same year I'd hiked the CDT for the first time—and smiled to see familiar names from so long ago. I made my way through the many pages, enjoying the pictures some had sent them from the completion of their hikes, until I found my eyes on a blank page. I took a pen from the coffee table and scrawled my own thank you.

It was ten thirty and I was barely able to keep my eyes open as Helen handed me my fresh laundry. "Are bacon and eggs okay for breakfast?"

"Um, I mean, yes, but I want to get going really early. I need to make it to the hot springs tomorrow. You don't have to get up to make me anything. You've done so much already."

"Nonsense, we're normally up at six. Is that okay?" John asked as they followed me to the door.

"Six is great," I said, stepping outside into the cool night air.

"See you then!" They bade me goodnight and gently closed the door.

As wonderful as their company had been, standing in their yard in the dark enveloped by the chirping of crickets was better. They had offered me a room in their house or the use of their guest RV, but I had declined, knowing I would sleep best on the ground inside my tent as I had done for so many weeks now.

I made my way to a patch of lawn fifty yards from the house and set up my tent by moonlight. Their place was near the river, and the addition of just a slight bit of humidity to the air made it feel clammy after the utter dryness of the past week. Surprised at the rapid cooling, I collapsed into my sleeping bag.

I WAS GRATEFUL FOR THE two convenience stores I passed during the forty miles of blazing hot road walking the next day. The scenery around me was the barren kind, remote and seemingly lifeless, the kind my dad would have hated. *To thrive here you must not move during the day like ignorant humans. Only by night.* Despite knowing this, I doggedly moved forward without taking breaks, simply because it was easier than stopping and then having to start again. Hours and miles passed on the remote roadways, with cars going by only infrequently. *I wish I had the option to move at night like the lions and coyotes.*

By three p.m. the sun had crested its zenith and the temperature spiked. I was certain the radiating heat from the pavement, combined with the unbridled direct light, was sending the real feel temperature soaring far into the hundred and tens. My legs quivered from the relentless miles, chronic mild dehydration, and loss of electrolytes through sweat that evaporated so quickly I missed its presence altogether. I knew my body was struggling with the extreme change in climate. I pulled out my phone from where it was stashed in an interior pocket to protect it from the furnace in the sky. Faywood Hot Springs was another four miles.

I'd hoped I was closer, and the truth was crushing. My head ached and I drank most of the rest of my water, reserving a few sips for that point in the next hour and a half when I knew I'd be out of my mind with thirst. I slipped the nearly empty bottle back into the side pocket of my backpack and leaned forward, placing my hands on my knees, bowing my head before the sun—god of the desert. The road trended westward here, directly into the brutality of the afternoon. I gasped raggedly, needing air and yet nearly vomiting from the arid, sweltering inhalation.

How long? I held my palms to the sky, using them as crude sundials, counting how long until the moment that occupied my thoughts for hours of every day in the heat: the moment the shadows would begin to grow and I would finally feel like I could breathe again.

Too long. You've got to keep going. I stared at my feet, leaning heavily on my knees again, struggling to take another step. *Will I die right here? Mummified in a submissive stance?*

Something beside my left foot twitched, or perhaps my eyes finally discerned the pattern. An enormous horned lizard, the full length and breadth of my hand, rested on the gravelly shoulder. It was by far the largest one I'd ever seen. His black eyes disappeared and slowly reappeared as he blinked at me.

I've walked more than twenty-one hundred miles already. The full scope of what I was trying to do began to feel real to me for the first time. *Five thousand plus to go.*

"Oh, Great Guardian, I accept your good omen of longevity and self-reliance as I continue forward on this quest." I whispered my gratitude to the tranquil reptile, then pushed off my knees with several lurching steps, face forward into the sun.

Just before five p.m. I hobbled into the cool lobby of the hot springs office and sank into a chair, my lesson learned from the night before. I conversed with the woman behind the desk, explaining my hike and why I didn't want to stand immediately, as pulsing, stabbing pain shot through my calves. The more intense the waves of pain grew, the more broadly I smiled, asking questions about the history and chemical makeup of the water to keep myself from screaming. As the pressure began to ebb, I dared rise and hand her the clipboard registration I'd filled out.

"Your campsite is here," she said, circling a number on the map. "This is the closest hot spring, which is clothing optional and has an attached bathhouse. There is a potable water tap here, right beside your site. I'll be here until ten tonight if you need anything."

I thanked her and went back outside into the crushing heat, thankful that my site was under several acacias. Their filigree leaves cast feathery shadows onto the ground. I set up my tent and ate dinner at the picnic table while drinking bottle after bottle of water. There was hardly anyone else in the quiet campground, which suited me just fine. I refilled my bottle for the fourth time as the first earnest shadows cloaked the edges of my tent site.

Cooler now, I strolled over to the bathhouse and showered gratefully in cold water. I sudsed my clothing as well, rinsing away the salt crust that had developed during the day's miles. Then I opened the door to the hot spring pools to see one man reclining in the closest spring.

"Hello!" he greeted me.

"Hi." I paused, looking at the three pools.

"I'm in the hottest one. That one over there is the coolest, and the one in the middle is, well, the middle," he chuckled.

"Thanks." I strode to the coolest one. The thought of getting into hot water was revolting, bordering on nausea inducing. Yet, I knew the therapeutic water with dissolved minerals was precisely what my legs and feet needed.

I sat on the edge of the pool and eased my lower extremities into the water. My skin prickled, resenting the heat. *Out of the saucepan and into the fire.* I grimaced and forced my legs farther in.

"It takes some getting used to," the man chimed in, clambering out of the hot pool and strutting to the middle pool.

"Mmmhmm," I murmured. He was talking rapidly and I struggled to follow along.

My mind was melting just as rapidly as the tense muscles in my legs. *I'm exhausted.*

I'd given myself fourteen days to hike from Grants to Puerto Palomas. This was day seven. I'd reach the border in two days if I maintained this pace. *I don't have any other choice.* Deming was thirty miles away and the border another thirty-five, without options to camp in between. *Unless I veer into the Floridas.* I grimaced thinking of the rugged, trailless mountain range some hikers added to break up the final sixty-five-mile road walk on the Columbus route.

"I love it here. I stay every time I get sent out here to the mining reclamation." The man's voice penetrated my wandering mind.

"Ah, yeah. What type of mine?" I asked absently.

"Asbestos." He got out of the middle pool and made his way into the cooler one opposite where I was perched on the edge.

The sun was now lower than the top of the high wall surrounding the pool area, and for the first time since I woke up in the cool backyard in Mimbres, my skin dimpled with goosebumps as a gentle breeze flowed across it. After the last two days of pounding out forty-plus miles in the heat, thirty seemed so much more doable. And Walter, a trail angel who was hosting me the next night, was already expecting me. I was silently grateful for the network of trail angels arranged by one of my followers in Columbus.

I glanced up to see the man looking at me expectantly. I was vaguely aware that the rhythm of his voice had changed from going on about himself to asking a question that I'd missed.

"Uh, I'm sorry. What?"

"I said, what brings you here?" he repeated, sounding slightly annoyed.

"Oh, I'm walking across the country," I simplified.

"Wow! That's pretty amazing. Where'd you start?"

"That's, uh, complicated. I hiked the Appalachian Trail this spring, now I'm on my way to San Diego," I trailed off. There was no easy way to explain what I was doing, especially to someone who didn't hike.

He nodded emphatically. "I have a buddy who walked that trail."

His voice settled into a rhythm of self-centered storytelling again, and I let my mind go blissfully blank, nodding occasionally. After another five minutes he paused, and I extricated my legs from the water and stood up.

"Nice chatting." I headed toward the exit.

"Yeah! I'm in cabin 4 if you want to stop in for a beer later."

"Thanks, but I have to get up really early." I dodged the invitation and darted for the door.

"Good luck!" he called out, returning to the hot pool.

The sky was indigo overhead and lavender at the western edge, the violet gradient between the two revealing a smattering of stars. The sunset wind was stronger outside the enclosure, swirling dust into small tornados by my bare feet as I walked back to my tent on rejuvenated legs. I paused at the pump and chugged water again. At my site I ate a snack and crawled into my sleeping bag, where I dreamed of the lush beauty of the Gila and Mimbres valleys.

The next morning, walking along the deserted highway, I was firmly reminded that I was now traversing the Upper Chihuahuan Desert, far from rivers and forests. My next water was at a store in Deming. At three mph I would get there in ten hours. I willed my hot springs–treated legs to pivot faster than that. *Let's do it in eight and a half.*

I could see the gas station plaza for more than an hour before I finally reached the commotion of civilization coursing through the parking lot and store. I wandered inside, lost in the four aisles of brightly colored packaging. I finally bought a Coke, a liter of cold water, and a bag of potato chips before going outside to hunch down in the scrap of shade thrown by the Reddy Ice cooler.

I downed the soda in two big gulps but ate the chips slowly. I felt dazed from the sun. The thermometer on the roadside sign said eighty-five, but it felt like a hundred. I opened the messages on my phone and reread the directions from Walter. I input his address into Google Maps and was relieved to see his home was only two miles away and not far off of the route I'd take out of town in the morning. I forced myself slowly to my feet and threw the empty chip bag and soda bottle into the trash. I took a slug of water—a full third of the bottle—and threaded my way through cars and pedestrians back to the road.

Outside Walter's small bungalow I followed the texted instructions down a tiled path, through a shady pollinator garden to a casita in the back of the property. I found the key under the mat and unlocked a brilliant blue door. I stepped inside, grateful to be out of the sun. The well-insulated building was stuffy but noticeably cooler. I heard a crunch and looked down to see that I'd smashed a cockroach under my shoe. *I hope there aren't too many of those.*

Turning on the fans, I set my pack on the kitchen table and stripped down before showering in cold water. I refused to get out until I'd begun to shiver.

Afterward, wearing my shower-washed hiking clothes, I wandered the tiny space, taking in the southwestern art on the walls. It was cozy, and I was thankful I had a free place to sleep indoors. I pulled the rest of my clothes out of my pack and washed them in the sink, then hung them to dry in the closet. I dumped everything else on the bed and headed back into the heat wearing my now empty backpack.

It was a half hour walk to Walmart, but without the weight of my gear it felt easy. After I had cooled down in the shower, the heat felt manageable, and the air-conditioned store felt downright luxurious. I wandered around buying food for the next two days as well as a new hiking dress—actually a beach coverup—to wear on the Pacific Crest Trail. Briefly I thought of Adam. *I'll see him in a week.*

I hadn't heard much from him since I'd been in the desert, and there were times I forgot about my off-trail life altogether. I was gripped with a sudden anxiety. *What if he doesn't show up?* I'd chosen a disjointed approach to my CYTC in order to accommodate thru-hiking the entire PCT with him. Oddly, I felt like I would be more upset that my plans had been so distorted for no reason than by his absence if he didn't show. I shook my head to clear those thoughts and texted him a picture of the dress.

"New hiking dress to wear on the PCT with you!"

Then I texted Walter. "Hi Walter. I found the casita, thank you! I'm at Walmart now, getting a few things. I'll be walking back soon."

I threw the dress into my basket and headed to the checkout. As I scanned the items, my phone dinged and my heart leapt. I pulled it out expecting to see Adam's response, but it was Walter.

"I'm on my way home from work now. I will come pick you up in twenty minutes. No need to walk any extra!"

The excitement that had turned to disappointment was quickly replaced by gratitude that my walking was done for the day. I responded and finished checking out. Then I settled on a bench outside the door in the shade, sipping kombucha. After fifteen minutes a car matching Walter's description pulled up and the driver's window rolled down, revealing a man in his early seventies.

"Heather?"

"Yes! Hi, Walter." I ran around the car and hopped into the passenger seat. "Thank you so much!"

"You're very welcome," he said.

At ten I finally excused myself from Walter's living room and made my way to the now cool casita. I sprawled on the bed, thankful for the belly full of homemade food. The recent widower was an avid hiker, and we'd spent hours talking about our respective adventures. But now it was well past my bedtime, and I was planning another first-light start to beat the heat. I sank deeply into the pillow and was enveloped by a blanket of silence.

The chiming of my phone alarm jarred me out of heavy sleep. I stumbled into the kitchenette where the phone was plugged in and shut it off, swearing under my breath. *I hate mornings.* It was dark in the casita, but outside the windows the silhouette of the garden was faintly visible, etched in shades of charcoal. I'd fallen asleep in my hiking clothes, so all I needed to do was put on my shoes and backpack, and step outside into the cool predawn.

I made my way through the still-sleeping city of Deming. Sporadic gusts of warm air heralding the return of the as-yet-unseen sun swirled around my ankles and swept across my bare arms. At the southern edge of town, I reached a gas station that had just opened. Cars were beginning to merge onto the streets, dogs barked from fenced yards, and I veered into the bustling convenience store. I bought a calorie-laden iced coffee drink, just like everyone else in line, feeling more American than I had in a long time.

The sense of compatriotism faded in the parking lot, where I chugged the drink so I could toss the glass bottle into the trash before walking thirty-five miles due south rather than jumping into a car and driving to work.

Seven hours later I crested a small hill, blasted afresh by hot air barreling northward out of Chihuahua. My water was gone, but at least the town of Columbus was in view a few miles ahead—and just three miles beyond that, Mexico. Cars were sparse on this road and I was surprised to see a cyclist coming uphill toward me. As the rider drew closer, I saw that it was a woman with long blond hair streaming from under her helmet. She swerved across the highway and pulled up alongside me. Before she spoke, I knew who she had to be.

"Liza!" I exclaimed, not asking.

"You're almost there!" Still pedaling, she reached into the handlebar pannier and pulled out two water bottles. "I'll see you in Columbus!"

I took them, thrilled to discover that they'd been packed in ice and were almost painfully cold in my overheated hands. I emptied one in a single gulp and then half of the other because I knew it would be better now than in ten minutes when it was warm. I strode down the gentle descent with renewed vigor and purpose.

Liza had followed me online for a long time, and she'd orchestrated my stay with Walter the night before, as well as a ride back to Deming to catch the bus. She'd even offered me the opportunity to camp at her home in the Columbus commune.

"The trail provides." I whispered the mantra of thru-hikers everywhere.

As I approached the border, Liza emerged from the day parking lot and fell into stride with me. I followed her through the gates where the Mexican border patrol agent smiled and waved. He asked Liza a question and she nodded, "Si, si."

I looked questioningly at her.

"He asked if you are the hiker. I've told everyone about you."

I smiled at him as we walked into Palomas.

An unorganized throng of people lined the streets and started cheering as Liza led me toward the city center. Bewildered, I followed her to where even more people were clustered around the statue of Pancho Villa. They parted as we arrived, and a band of guitar and accordion players began to play. Everyone was clapping and singing. I stood there, dazed.

"They are so excited for you! It's a celebration in your honor," Liza smiled.

"Gracias. Gracias. Gracias." I repeated it over and over as people shook my hand and said congratulatory things that I could understand even without speaking their language. Despite my dehydration, tears puddled in my eyes and overflowed.

After fifteen minutes, I began to feel myself swaying. My hours of walking combined with thirst, hunger, and sheer relief at being done with my march across the desert were taking their toll. The scene had begun a rolling celebration around the town, with people dancing and tourists taking pictures. I wasn't sure how long I needed to stay, but I knew if I didn't want a repeat of the incident in Mimbres I had to sit down. Luckily, Liza noticed and supplied me with yet another bottle of water, and she gently began to peel us away, translating my gratitude and explaining my fatigue. The audience effusively bid us farewell and continued the party in our wake as we made our way back through the border to Liza's car.

"I can't believe you organized a mariachi celebration for me," I said, sinking into the passenger seat.

Liza laughed, "They love any chance to celebrate and they love hikers. So does Columbus. Which is why you have a room at the motel for two nights if you want it. The whole community went in to pay for it."

My mouth gaped. I felt like my heart would burst from the swell of gratitude cascading through me. I didn't know how to express it, so I simply said, "Thank you so much."

Liza pulled up at the motel and made sure I was settled.

"All right, I know you're exhausted. Just relax now. I'll be going to the café," she pointed across the street, "at six for dinner, and you're welcome to join me if you want. But take care of yourself however you need to."

"Thank you," I said again, unable to formulate any better words in my tired, hot, overwhelmed brain.

Liza waved and drove away.

I stepped into my room. Someone had preemptively turned on the AC and I mentally blessed them. I showered, drank as much water as I could hold, ate most of the food in my backpack, and collapsed on the bed.

For the second time that day, my alarm pulled me from the deepest depths of unconsciousness. This time I didn't swear at it. *I only have to walk across the street.*

I rolled out of the bed, stomach growling loudly. I'd slept four hours but felt like it was a drop in the bucket compared to what I truly needed.

Stepping outside was a rude reminder of the environment I'd temporarily left behind. Although the sun was steadily descending, it was still sweltering. *Air conditioning is the most magical invention on earth.*

I crossed the empty road and opened the screen door to the café. Liza was already there with three others. She waved me over.

"I'm so glad you made it!"

"Me too," I smiled, sitting down.

TWO NIGHTS LATER, I LEANED my head against the window of the Greyhound speeding westward across the desert. It was well past hiker midnight—nine p.m.—in the middle of May, and my eyelids drooped with sleepiness. But I was pensive, anxious, with a stomach churning for a reason I couldn't put my finger on. A pale sliver of moon was slung low in the starless sky.

Why are the stars gone? Ah yes, the glow of city lights, Pilot stations, and the Golden Arches—I'm back in the world of humanoids. Like any animal, I was uneasy there. My landmarks—the stars, the soft sounds of nighttime, the feel of the ground beneath my body—were obscured by unnatural light and rapid transportation.

I'd now walked more than twenty-one hundred miles in two and a half months, yet I was feeling as though it had simply been a warm-up for the main event. For all the challenges of constant locomotion, there was an abiding comfort there. The trail was the only place I felt completely whole, completely natural, complete. I'd become so at ease in that world that a couple thousand miles of continuous ambulation didn't seem like anything out of the ordinary.

The freeway passed out of the city and into the sparsely settled land straddling the border between New Mexico and Arizona. I felt calmer now that I could see stars freckling the sky. Though I hadn't always been comfortable in the darkness, now I craved its embrace. Ever since I had conquered the Night inside of me by walking through the dark, my fear of the earthly night's denizens had transformed into connection with them. The night that I roared into the face of a mountain lion on the slopes of Mount Hood, I became indivisible from it. *A lion can inhabit LA's Griffith Park, and a lioness can ride a Greyhound.*

The lion once symbolized my great fear of darkness. Now it showed me the way. Both the lion and I could move among the people surrounding them, each of us longing to be wild and free. I peeled my face away from the window and leaned back, closing my eyes. I had only a few more days to lap up the soft indulgences of "real life" before my feet touched sand again. *Before I return to* my *real life out there.*

CHAPTER 10

SOUTHERN CALIFORNIA

Adam and I moved through the desert in silence, following the winding tread of the Pacific Crest Trail. After hiking thirty-eight miles our first day, and more than thirty miles so far on the second day, we'd each fallen silent for our own reasons.

Despite the week of rest before we began, I was still physically exhausted. Adam was frustrated by the serpentine path rising and falling at a gradient suitable for horses. At every switchback, he cursed and made remarks about wanting to cut between them to reach the top faster. His desire for the directness of Appalachian hiking was misaligned with the personality of the gentle PCT.

All you did was talk about not wanting to hike the AT when we were there, and now you want this trail to be like that one. I resisted the urge to point out the irony.

We hiked without speaking for most of the afternoon as the intense sun beat down on us. I could tell he was uncomfortable in the complete open of the San Felipe Hills. After the previous week on the CDT, I was unaffected by the soaring temperature as we moved ever closer to summer in the West. The buff ground radiated much less heat than pavement, so it felt cooler to me even though the ambient temperature was higher than it had been in New Mexico. Now, with the sun blocked by the hills in the west, he was noticeably perkier.

"We're almost to the campsite," I said, after glancing at the app on my phone.

"Great!"

We rounded another rolling curve and heard voices. To my dismay, two tents were already crammed into the small site. My heart sank. There were no more sites listed for several miles.

"What are we going to do?" I whined, my fatigue getting the better of me.

"Well, we can go squeeze in there with them or keep walking," Adam responded, irritably, his momentary cheerfulness gone.

I sighed deeply. There wasn't room for us, but it was almost dark. With a little huff of frustration, I started down the trail again. Adam followed close behind. We were gradually winding down toward Barrel Springs, located at a trailhead still many miles away. Dusk in Southern California was like being cast into the midst of an impressionist painting. Blue, hazy valleys were layered beneath a fiery red-and-orange-streaked horizon line, which in turn faded from lemon to lavender upward into the inkiness of space. Sunset winds picked up with surprising ferocity, casting fine sand into my eyes.

"Here." I stopped and pointed to a generally flat area right alongside the trail marred by myriad small holes.

"What are these?" Adam asked, poking at the holes with his trekking pole.

I shrugged. Nothing was emerging at his disturbance, and I stomped around a few times. Still nothing.

"It's a pretty shitty site, but I'm tired." I threw my backpack down and yanked my headlamp out. He shrugged and followed suit.

I woke up several hours later feeling like I'd only barely fallen asleep. *I shouldn't have drunk all that water with dinner.* Unzipping the tent door, I slipped my feet into my flip-flops, waddling a few steps outside. The wind had died down and the air was deliciously cool as I gazed up at the star-studded blackness above me.

"Ow," I said, sitting back into the tent and looking at my right foot, expecting to see a cactus prick.

Instead, I choked, unable to breathe or speak. I gasped raggedly, attempting to get words out.

"Adam!" finally one came.

He stirred at the sound of my hoarse shriek.

"What?" he mumbled, not sitting up. I smacked him several times, unable to get any more words out.

"What?!" He sat up, irritated.

I pointed frantically at my foot. "Scorpion," I managed, my need for air finally overriding the panic.

He stared dumbfounded for a moment, then reached for his own flip-flop and in one quick movement swatted the arachnid off of my foot, through the open tent door, and into the dark desert. Then he flopped back down on his sleeping pad and closed his eyes. Almost immediately, he began snoring lightly.

I zipped the tent door shut as quickly as I could with trembling fingers, still struggling to breathe, my inhalations coming in harsh gasps. My skin crawled and I clawed at my clothes and sleeping bag, terrified that other scorpions were inside the tent. I moved my pack and my other gear. I lifted my sleeping pad and shined my headlamp into my sleeping bag. I stripped and redressed. Then I sat there shaking, aware that my right foot was tingling. I clicked my headlamp back on and studied my foot carefully. I couldn't see any marks. *Am I seriously imagining this?* I checked my entire space again, bumping Adam several times in the process. He responded with several unconscious grunts.

Stop being OCD, Heather. There aren't any scorpions in here. I sank back onto my mat, my exhaustion beginning to seep through the adrenaline.

How long does it take to have an allergic reaction? Did I even get stung? For all the thousands of miles I'd walked in desert terrain, I'd never so much as seen a scorpion before. *Go figure—my first time and it would be on my foot.*

I pulled out my phone and connected to the faint available network. I searched Google for insight as the weird tingling throbbed through my toe. *Scorpions can inflict dry—venomless—stings.* I clicked the phone off, having established that if I were going to have a severe reaction I would have done so by now. My breathing had regulated. I'd never before been so afraid that I was rendered unable to breathe or speak—even on this trail when I ran into mountain lions alone. I closed my eyes and prayed for sleep to find me again.

It didn't.

I lay on my side, watching the western sky turn violet and then transition through lavender to gray, knowing that the hidden horizon on the other side of the hills was flaming. I rolled back over to stroke Adam's thick black hair. He smiled and peered out of mostly closed eyes.

"Good morning," he mumbled.

I smiled back weakly. "It's morning, all right."

DESPITE HIS FRUSTRATION with the character of the trail and my overall fatigue, Adam and I fell into our well-established, easy rhythm of hiking from dawn until dusk, averaging thirty-five miles per day. I reminisced often, at what was likely an annoying level, but he didn't seem to mind. Reestablishing our hiking partnership, cemented on our CDT thru-hike the year before, felt good. *This is why I wanted him to hike with me, not crew me. We're so much happier when we're both hiking.* Through our steady big-mile days, I reached three months and more than twenty-four hundred miles into my Calendar Year Triple Crown attempt and began to wonder if I would ever again feel anything but tired.

Every morning it took immense effort to pry my crusty eyelids open and begin the daylong process of trying to force as much fluid into my body as possible while walking as far as I could. We started hiking just past dawn in the cool air after eight hours of sleep, and every day I anticipated bouncing along, rejuvenated by the rest. Instead, I dragged, my mind foggy and my legs leaden. I'd been dreaming of the PCT since the first winter storm hit me in March on the AT, yet now that I was on it I was decidedly not having fun.

Am I going to be this tired the rest of the way? I was well past the end of the invincible mileage point, and my worst fears about my endurance had crept into my every waking thought. *Maybe this is just too much for me. Maybe I can't do this, not happily or healthily anyway.*

Additionally, the trail was far more crowded than I'd ever experienced before, although I was well aware that the numbers were nothing like those found on the AT during prime season. I had known deep solitude in the pristine emptiness of the PCT twice before, so walking through a desert full of toilet paper blooms and newly created campsites hacked from the scrub—not to mention crossing paths with insular trail groups who barely interacted—left me feeling old and grumpy. Fortunately, now that we were hiking together with the same goal, Adam's morose mood was fading into memory, and that was enough to buoy me despite my disappointment about those other aspects of the experience.

Contrary to how it sounds, the PCT is not a trail along one continuous ridgeline. In fact, in the desert one feels as though the trail is wending its way from sleeping giant to sleeping giant, following the crest of each of these massifs before descending to the low desert floor in between them. Again and again, we tiptoed beneath their rocky edifices, through pines that whispered to us, and fell asleep under the stars before descending to trudge across the lower terrain separating us from the next mountain.

A week into the hike, we spiraled down from the heights of Mount San Jacinto as light faded behind the hulking mountain that pierced the sky nearly ten thousand feet above us. Adam began singing something ridiculous, rhyming *Jacinto* with made-up syllables, and I laughed. We were beginning to find ourselves in harmony again.

"This descent takes forever," I interrupted him.

He sang louder, switching to a Beastie Boys riff, "No sleep 'til fau-cet!"

I giggled. The reliable Snow Creek faucet was down there somewhere in the dark canyon to our right. No longer able to discern whether I was putting my feet on rocks or rattlesnakes, I clicked on my headlamp and so did he. The night wind swirled upward and around us, mixing hot and cold air into tantalizing eddies that alternately warmed and chilled us. Our pace increased as we were rejuvenated by the reprieve from the sun and by increased oxygen as we dropped in elevation. With one final series of switchbacks, the trail finally dumped us into a wide flat with a water fountain incongruently situated right in the middle.

Adam chugged the last of his warm water.

"First we should make sure it's on!" I admonished, trying the faucet.

He shrugged and pointed at the ground, which was was clearly wet. Just then cold water, piped directly from snowmelt and springs pouring off of San Jacinto, spurted out. He filled his bottle and chugged it, and I rolled my eyes. *One of these days he's going to get giardia.*

Slightly jealous, longing to gulp the cold water, I filled my bladders to filter in camp. We found a spot to pitch our tent a short distance away from the smattering of other tents we could see scattered in the scrubby bushes.

Sleeping in was not an option on the east-facing flat. Hot sun pummeled our tent at 5:30 the next morning. Despite drinking my fill the night before, I awoke cotton mouthed. We refilled our water and trudged into the windy, sandy plain that stretched between us and the I-10 underpass visible four miles away. This broad pass between the massifs of San Jacinto and San Gorgonio was subject to intense wind and blowing sand. It housed massive wind farms that bedecked the low hills and slopes in every direction. While the otherworldly barrenness was engaging, it was also terrible to walk across.

"Finally!" we said in unison as we reached the cool shade and wind protection of the freeway underpass.

"Jinx!" I added, heading toward the coolers that were stationed near the gap between eastbound and westbound lanes.

"Gatorade?" I asked Adam, and he nodded. I threw him one of the free drinks and took another for myself.

"The one benefit to more hikers is that there is way more trail magic these days," I said, drinking half the beverage in one gulp. It was eight a.m. and I already felt dehydrated.

"Yeah," he agreed, putting his bottle into the provided trash can. "You want to go to the wind farm?"

"Definitely. That climb up and over to the Whitewater is brutally hot. I don't have enough water to make it."

We left the shade of the freeway and plunged into the heat. It was shocking even after just a few minutes' reprieve. *The last time I was here, it was eighty degrees at five a.m. I wonder what it is now?* We made our way along the outskirts of a subdivision before reaching a short diversion to the Mesa Wind Farm complex. Inside the blessedly air-conditioned office, we sank into chairs and split a pint of ice cream that they had on hand for hikers to purchase.

Forty-five minutes later, we finally pried ourselves from the chairs and filled our water bottles for the long seven-mile climb and descent into the Whitewater River drainage. As we left, I paused to look at the indoor/

outdoor thermometer by the door. *It's a hundred degrees and it's not even the hottest part of the day yet!*

Despite each of us carrying three liters of water from the wind farm, we were both out by the time we reached the loping switchbacks leading down to the river. From the heights, it wasn't obvious if the rambling, wide, gravelly bed even had water in it. *You know it does*, I reassured myself as I felt anxiety clutching at my heat-nauseated stomach. The Whitewater was the largest river crossing on the PCT in all of Southern California. Flowing from the Sand to Snow National Monument and ultimately the slopes of the twelve-thousand-foot San Gorgonio massif to the northwest, it was a perennial water source.

At last, we reached the sandy embankment and could see the rush of cold, clear water racing across the otherwise arid desert. I was struck by its dissonance. While it was the rainbow that was supposed to symbolize the promise of God, the gushing Whitewater—a river flowing through the desert—seemed like a far more tangible promise than ephemeral prisms in the sky. I dropped my backpack, walked into the ankle-deep water, and lay down with nothing but my face above the surface. The cooling rush of snow-birthed water enveloping me as sand and smooth stones pressed into my back was divine. This was a promise that I could feel—one that coursed over my body and assured me that I would not die of heat or thirst on this day. *That's the kind of promise I trust.*

ON JUNE 4 WE WOKE UP under a massive ponderosa pine, scenting our tent site vanilla. The sweet smell combined with the sharp resin emanating from the thick layer of shed needles that cushioned us was inextricably linked with so many of my PCT memories. I rolled over and slipped a small wrapped gift onto Adam's sleeping pad when he went outside to pee.

"What's this?" he asked, crawling back in and picking it up.

"Happy birthday!" I said.

He tore it open to find a small sock doll that matched the one hanging on my backpack, both made by Apple Pie while she followed me through New England.

"I can't believe you've been carrying this for almost four hundred miles!"

"It's not that heavy. Besides," I grinned mischievously, "you get to carry it the next twenty-two hundred!"

The Angeles National Forest was hot and quiet. We passed several groups of hikers but otherwise felt as though we were alone—odd for a locale so close to LA. It was the height of afternoon when we finally topped out on a long ascent a mile or so from the remote North Fork Ranger Station. We paused to take in the view of the rolling terrain northward. I pointed toward the valley where the Acton KOA was tucked alongside the Santa Clara River and the brown hills we'd make our way through after that.

"And that's where Agua Dulce is." I waved my hand toward the barely discernible break on the other side of the hills. "Holy shit!"

"What is that?" Adam asked, seeing the same pale gray cloud bulging upward from where I was pointing.

"It's a fire cloud!"

We stood in shock as the desert view of unbroken shades of brown and green undulating into the distance was marred by a massive column of smoke rising rapidly, mushrooming over the hilltops in the distance.

"Did we just see a wildfire start?" Adam finally said.

"Yes, and we're screwed. That's on the trail."

"Are you sure?" He gazed at the growing bulbous cloud.

"Positive."

I'd hiked through this section three times before. The meandering path between where we stood and the Agua Dulce home of the Saufleys, trail angels and personal friends, was firmly etched into my memory. *I hope Donna and Jeff are okay.* Slowly I turned away from the gut-wrenching sight, and we made our way down to the ranger station where a dozen hikers and a volunteer were spread out at picnic tables.

"Did you see the fire?" one of the hikers asked as we walked in, pointing northward emphatically.

"Yes," I said, irritably. I walked to the water jugs on the table and began to fill my bottle.

"I wonder if it's on the trail," a woman mused, leaning against her backpack in the shade of a tree.

"It is."

I could feel all the eyes settling on me at my assured statement. Just then the cell phone sitting on the table by the water jugs rang and the volunteer answered. He made a few noncommittal sounds, glanced at me, and hung up.

"The fire is on the PCT about a mile north of Agua Dulce. The trail is closed. No reroute has been put into place yet."

A pall fell over the group. I glanced at Adam and he nodded. We began the barren, rolling descent to the Santa Clara River nestled deep inside Soledad Canyon. The fire would only get bigger the longer we waited, possibly evacuating Agua Dulce.

That night we slept uneasily amid the brown hills, the harsh smell of smoke drifting into our tent from time to time. The next morning, tired and anxious, we marched silently to the Antelope Highway underpass and through the alien features of Vasquez Rocks State Park. Their forms would ordinarily inspire wonder and conversation, but instead we were laser focused on reaching the resupply point and the trail angels to get some real answers—ideally before any evacuations started. I was hoping the frequent wildfires that happened each summer along the PCT wouldn't derail our hike.

The next hours were chaotic as we tried to buy supplies and decide on a course of action. Several fire agencies were battling the blaze, containing it in the canyon where it had begun under unknown circumstances. Wild speculation spread as rapidly as flames throughout the community and the hikers. Adam and I sat in our room at the Saufleys', sorting our food. I was grateful to have a shower and get our laundry washed. I desperately wanted the rest day we'd intended here, yet my gut was telling me to get out now. *But how?*

"Hmm?" Adam asked, and I realized I'd spoken my thought aloud.

"Just wondering what to do," I replied. "They may get it put out and we can hike on tomorrow, or they may keep it closed and we'll have to walk the narrow canyon roads all the way around."

Adam nodded, then shrugged. Donna had already warned us not to walk the winding roads with their nonexistent shoulders and high-speed traffic. Despite my desire to connect my steps, I was inclined to agree.

Needless risk. But it *was* important to me to walk every step. Three hikers had left the day before, heading through an off-road-vehicle recreation area to avoid the roads and the fire, but no one had heard from them. We theorized they were lost in the vast maze of unmarked trails.

"The section of trail that's closed is only five miles," Adam said. "If there were just a way to get to Martindale Ridge, we'd be fine."

By six p.m. the gray cloud no longer loomed over the town, and the word filtering in was that the fire was out. Donna's tall form came hustling toward us.

"I have an idea," she said. "There are some old roads west of the trail that you can take up to Martindale Ridge."

Adam and I looked at each other.

She pulled out a map and pointed. "See, you take the road out of Agua Dulce past the PCT turnoff, then go down this road here. Behind this ranch you can just go straight up and cut across the open here. There's no trail, but it's easy. I ride my horses this way all the time. After this little arroyo you'll hit the old fire road and go up. You'll be close to the fire closure there, but I've checked with several folks that you'll be outside of it. Then it just takes you away as you climb, and you rejoin the PCT at the top."

Adam pulled out his phone and studied his GPS app as she talked, nodding. "Yeah, I see it."

"I think they're going to keep this section of trail closed indefinitely, and the PCTA isn't going to recommend hikers walk the roads. So if this works, I can send people this way. But I don't trust just anyone to be my guinea pigs," she laughed.

"We'll do it," I said, not hesitating. My gut agreed with Donna, even if I was a little scared to go tromping off into the desert hills near an active burn area. If her connections had told her the fire was out, I trusted that.

We ran back to the trailer and packed rapidly. We weren't sure how long the alternate route was, but once we reached the PCT we'd need to walk at least four more miles to water and camping—and only about four hours of light remained. Armed with Donna's verbal directions, fresh supplies, and plenty of water, we took off into the unknown.

Once above the canyon on the old fire roads, we could clearly see that the fire was indeed completely out. Fire crews were loading their equipment and driving away. I felt a sense of relief wash over me. *It's not going to blow up while we're passing through here, and we'll be well beyond it tonight.* I hurried forward to catch up with Adam.

"Huuuuhhh," I gasped sharply. He turned around, his face registering the fear I felt as a searing sensation tore through the sole of my left foot—the one that had been the source of so much pain on the AT.

"What happened?" he asked, coming back to where I stood, unable to move.

"I . . . I don't know. It's just . . . pain." I lifted my knee, my foot dangling from my ankle. "It's unbearable." I could barely breathe.

"Did it feel hot?"

I nodded, gingerly setting my foot back down and easing a small amount of weight onto it. My foot throbbed intensely. "It felt like a hot knife slicing across the sole of my foot."

"I've seen runners tear their fascia. They made exactly that face—pain and surprise."

"What now?" I asked in a whisper. We were standing in a no-man's land between a wildfire closure, the PCT, and a cross-country swath of rugged land.

Adam glanced up the remaining thousand vertical feet to Martindale Ridge, then back at me. He didn't say anything.

What can he say? I'm dead in the water.

I leaned forward and tried to walk. Pain radiated up my leg, my knee buckled, and I stumbled. He caught me.

"I can go back to town and get help."

"No, no . . ." I forced myself to stand normally, clenching my eyes shut against the blinding pain. "What can be done for it? If I tore my plantar fascia?"

He shook his head. "Not much, I don't think. I mean, I think they can do surgery, but usually just rest until it heals. Can you flex your ankle?"

I lifted my knee again and pointed my toes, then flexed my foot up. The latter was excruciating, but possible. I looked up at him, searching his caramel eyes for an answer.

"Well, that's good. It's not a total rupture or you wouldn't be able to do that. Maybe you just did a partial tear or tore a bunch of scar tissue."

"Let's get going. It's a long way to water."

"Are you sure?"

I nodded. He waited a moment and then turned around to resume climbing. I followed him—grinding my teeth—and focused all of my energy on walking without falling, despite the jolts of pain shooting through my foot and leg.

We didn't reach the water cache at Bouquet Canyon Road until after dark. We fumbled around under the trees locating the water jugs and refilling our bottles. I texted Donna, letting her know the route would go.

"Thanks, but PCTA has officially closed the trail all the way to Bouquet Canyon. Hikers will have to take Ubers. Good thing you went when you did."

THREE DAYS LATER, I LAY in the tent as gray morning light seeped in, too hot to sleep, thinking about my first year as a long-distance runner, a decade prior. I flopped my legs out of the tangled sleeping bag and stared at my feet. They were flat. Bunions that had been there since I took my first duck-footed steps now bulged on four toes. But my feet had never seemed to know that they couldn't run or hike. Until now.

"You shouldn't run."

The podiatrist had said these words as he entered the room with a manila file in his hands. He hadn't even looked at my feet—only seen their shadow on film.

I looked at the basis of my ambulation that had already carried me across the country three times, up many mountains, and to the finish line of several ultramarathons. He might have been right.

I'd left his office with a prescription for orthotics I never wore and had continued to hike and run, covering at least twenty thousand miles since then. My big toes definitely pointed inward more, my biomechanical shortcomings compounding my congenital deformity with every single step.

How much more damage will come in the remaining five thousand miles of this hike?

In the days since I'd torn my fascia, my foot had gone from excruciating to swollen and stiff. My feet had never known they weren't supposed to function properly at all. Not run. Not scramble up mountains. Not hike thousands of miles faster than anyone else. They had just carried me onward without complaint. *Until now.*

In Tehachapi I'd bought cheap plantar fasciitis support inserts for my shoes. I hoped they would alleviate the symptoms, not only of the injury but also the chronic ones—the ones that had taken me to the doctor in the first place so many years ago. I was accustomed to the fact that my knees hurt sometimes and that pain worked its way up into my hips and back, creeping upward from feet that did not believe anyone else's assessment of their abilities.

I massaged them gently, stretching and flexing them as gray light gave way to gold. *Thank you for carrying me so far.*

Beside me Adam stirred. I nuzzled into him, grateful that I hadn't known I couldn't do the things I'd done until after I'd done them. I hoped that continuing to place blind faith in my body to overcome limitations was the right decision.

CHAPTER 11

SIERRA NEVADA

While the Pacific Crest Trail is known for the tremendous beauty of a seemingly endless viewshed, it's often overlooked that the southernmost seven hundred miles wend their way through desert landscapes. Although there are ascents to the high peaks of Southern California, like San Jacinto, the majority of the first part of the trail is unremarkably barren. This monotony causes many aspiring thru-hikers to falter in their quest, either going home or getting into a car to move ahead to more awe-inspiring portions. However, like the roads of New Mexico, the miles through scrubby, cactus-laden hill country were a boon to my body. I had neither the energy nor the desire to climb excessively—or think too hard. Losing myself in the rhythm of walking on the packed sandy ground for fourteen hours a day was meditative and, in an odd way, rejuvenating.

The inserts in my shoes seemed to be helping. The pain had gradually subsided, and then the swelling as well. I stared down at my feet as we shuffled through the sage toward Kennedy Meadows. KM, as it's called by hikers, marks the end of the desert and the point of entry to the mountains of the High Sierra. My left foot was still tender, but since the tear outside Agua Dulce it had continued to answer my demands to carry me another three hundred miles.

I sent gratitude toward my foot and to my body as a whole. Despite injury and fire, we were on pace to complete a nine-hundred-mile month. *Thank you.*

We reached the KM General Store, where at least a hundred thru-hikers sprawled in the yard, on the porch and steps, and anywhere they could sit rather than walk. They clapped and cheered our arrival, as was tradition for anyone who made it there. I half smiled as I hobbled up the steps behind Adam. I wanted only one thing: ice cream.

Though gradual with the occasional undulation, the next sixty or so miles were essentially all uphill. Leaving Kennedy Meadows felt like a milestone ending to the arid desert, but it was really more of a gateway. Stepping through that portal, we entered not desert but not mountain either. Instead, the next day or two of hiking was through a transitory zone of sage until we ascended into dry pine forest. Finally, after leaving the sagebrush completely behind and wending through conifers, the massive emerald meadows—replete with the snow-powered rivers the region was known for—would begin to appear. The PCT then meandered through idyllic beauty until at last it deposited us in the shadow of the highest summit in the contiguous United States, Mount Whitney.

After the steep haul up and over a ridge separating our previous camp in the Rock Creek drainage from Crabtree Meadows, the gigantic parkland below the high point, we dropped our packs for a second breakfast.

"So you're going to wait here?" Adam asked for the eighth time.

"Yes, I've climbed it twice. And I don't need to do it again, especially in the middle of the CYTC."

"Okay, if you're sure, I'll leave all my stuff here and run." Adam began divesting himself of his backpack, walking sticks, and waist pack.

"Yeah, in fact, I think I'm going to set up the tent." I started rummaging through his pack and pulled out our tent, packed away only a few hours before.

He filled his twenty-ounce water bottle and tied his fleece around his waist as I deftly staked out the shelter and threw everything inside to keep it corralled. He kissed me on the cheek.

"I'll be back in five hours, but don't worry for seven," he said.

"That's why I have the tent set up. Have fun!"

I watched as he loped across the meadow, his many years as an elite ultramarathoner evident in the fluidity of his stride now that he was free of the cumbersome backpack. I crawled into the tent and organized his things in a couple of neat piles, loading the food into our bear can. Then against my better judgment, knowing how much farther we had to go to our next resupply at the Red's Meadow General Store and that I wasn't going to be making progress toward it for the next five or more hours, I ate.

"Oh my God," I mumbled a few minutes later, surveying the empty wrappers and snacked-on items surrounding me. *I'm going to run out of food.* I stuffed the remains back into the canister, shocked at how much I'd eaten in an insensate daze.

I secured the can outside and then sprawled out in the amazing spaciousness of having a two-person tent all to myself. Sun dappled the silnylon through the pine boughs above me, and my gaze softened, lulled by the interplay of light and shadow. *I'm so exhausted. I don't know how I'm going to keep going.*

"Mer?"

I roused a bit at the sound of our special call. "Adam?" I sat up, momentarily confused as to where I was.

He leaned into the vestibule, grinning. "Did you get a good nap?"

"What time is it?" I asked, befuddled. "Did you get to Mount Whitney?"

"It's four and yes. I ran all out. It felt great."

"Oh my God. I slept for almost five hours."

"Do you want to just stay here tonight?"

"Uhhh . . ." I thought guiltily of the food I'd eaten, including some of his chips. "Not unless you do. I mean, you just ran sixteen miles to fourteen thousand feet."

"I feel great! I've got lots of adrenaline going."

"Okay, let's get to Tyndall Creek then, so we're set up for Forester Pass in the morning."

"Sounds good." Adam began breaking camp while snacking on his chips. "Man, I guess I ate more of these than I thought. I'm getting low on food."

"Um, you had some help," I admitted guiltily, stuffing my sleeping bag into my pack. "I'm so sorry! I don't know what happened to me. It's like I had a food blackout."

"Hmm, well, I think it will be okay. I brought a little extra for this shorter day. But maybe ask me next time?"

"I will. I'm sorry." My eyes welled up. For the first time since starting the PCT I wasn't tired or hungry, but I regretted pilfering his chips. Food was gold to a thru-hiker, and we were in the longest stretch without a resupply on the entire trail—almost two hundred miles.

"It's okay. You needed it," he said, drawing me close and holding me. I sniffled and nodded.

WE LEFT OUR CAMP the next morning bathed in the shadow of the massive rock wall that Forester Pass was notched out of. No matter how many times I climbed this pass, I was always in awe of the vast Sierra views unfolding as the PCT spiraled upward on trail tread blasted from vertical cliff walls. We reached the top—the highest point on the entire trail—and gazed into the living heart of the Range of Light. Below us, a snowy basin cradled turquoise tarns that flashed in the sunlight, gemstones in a granite crown. In turn, these fed the roaring waters of Bubbs Creek that bounded down into the deep valley in front of us, a valley we would follow until turning right and ascending again to Glen Pass twelve miles away.

We ate quietly and quickly, each noting our low food stores without much comment. *The only solution is to walk more each day.* Then we slipped and slid down the snow-covered trail to the tree line. From there it was an enjoyable gradual downhill walk as we followed the creek. After a while I thought I heard voices.

"Do you hear that?"

"Yeah, sounds like a big group."

Just then we saw a small sign stuck in the ground: "Trail Magic .1."

"Trail magic?! Out here?" I exclaimed hopefully at the thought that someone had brought free food for hikers to the middle of nowhere.

We quickened our pace and in a few minutes entered a large camping area where at least twenty thru-hikers were gathered and hot dogs were cooking on a small grill. A table was set up with condiments, and coolers full of soda were stationed at either end.

"Welcome to the trail magic!" a man holding tongs whooped. "Got two dogs coming right up!"

We ate—and ate more when encouraged. Our fears of not having enough food melted away in the midst of the extreme generosity. After an hour we looked at one another and nodded. It would be easy to stay here, like most of the other hikers were planning to do. But we had miles to go before we could sleep, especially if we wanted to meet my goal of completing the trail in eighty days. So we bid our angels farewell with deep gratitude and hiked onward.

The Sierra passes were snowy, but not as snowy as I'd seen them before. Deep trenches, sometimes hip deep, were carved into the snow by thousands of feet trudging through before us. Slowly but surely, we were gaining on the bubble of hikers as we doggedly made our way northward thirty-plus miles at a time without regard for heat—or now snow and altitude. The Sierra, like all of Southern California, passed in a haze of beauty and walking. My body was robotic in its mission to move, no longer struggling to adapt as it had on the AT. Now it was my mind that had to shift, embracing the aspect of work that finishing this gargantuan endeavor would require.

"What do you think about while you're hiking so far every day?" is a common question from those who've never thru-hiked. The truth is that there is no single answer. Left to its own devices, my mind ran rampant. I mainly thought about food: macaroni and cheese, hot coffee, ice cream, milkshakes, hamburgers—pretty much anything that wasn't in my backpack.

But I also thought about how bad I smelled, especially when the long ascents in warm sunshine amplified the sweat, and how much I looked forward to the next time I got to do laundry and take a shower. I would mentally count the days, even though the ablutions were rather pointless since I'd stink again within twenty-four hours.

My mind wandered the landscape, thinking about the way the sun created shadows that played on the water, the ground, and the trees. I contemplated the birds of prey that swooped overhead, and the chipmunks and squirrels scampering in avoidance. I wondered what made the tracks and the scat along the trail. My attention also focused on the sound my feet made as they rhythmically struck the ground, inevitably making me think about how far I had to go and how far I'd already gone.

I often thought about the people I missed—my family and friends. I thought about how wonderful it would be to sleep in a comfortable bed with no alarm clock. But also, I thought about how absolutely beautiful it was to be out here and how very lucky I was to be hiking.

Sometimes I contemplated what I wanted to do with my life when I grew up. This reminded me that I was already grown up and still hadn't figured out what I wanted to do with my life. But then I'd think about the fact that I was doing exactly what I wanted to do with my life.

Other thoughts were more logistical. I'd think about where the next water was and whether I should stop to eat at the bottom or at the top of the climb. How far it was until I could sleep.

And sometimes—blissfully—I thought about absolutely nothing.

As we dropped thousands of vertical feet down from Donohue Pass into Tuolumne Meadows at the northern end of the longest roadless stretch in the Triple Crown, I pondered what a wonder it was to follow a single drop of water born from alpine snow to verdant meadow and beyond, over cascades frothing white, plunging down a canyon before sprawling sapphire across vibrant green meadows until at last we parted ways. The water taking its path to the sea and me again going upward, back to northern Yosemite's mountains and sky. Both journeys equally inevitable, equally powerful.

However, before we climbed into the remote sector of the park, we veered off trail to the Tuolumne Meadows Store for immediate sustenance and much needed resupply, days after our meager options at Red's Meadow Resort.

"Forty percent behind you," Adam said as we sat on the picnic tables outside the store, where I spooned coffee ice cream into my mouth at an alarming rate.

I paused. "Really?" In my desire for food, I'd forgotten the milestone.

He smiled and gave me a hug.

"Almost halfway," I smiled. "But it's still a long way to Canada."

"In a very good way," he added. "We're together."

I teared up. "Yeah."

Our togetherness was enhancing the experience on the PCT rather than detracting as it had on the AT. *I just have to keep hanging on to the knowledge that every hike has its ups and downs. I hope it's mostly ups from here.*

As much as the High Sierra section is renowned for its difficulty, the northern part of Yosemite and out to Sonora Pass was not a cake walk. Rocky, tough climbs and deep river fords continued to challenge us. But I knew that these paths with their hardships were what had formed me—were forming us. By foot and mile, they transformed our thoughts, priorities, and bodies.

We left the park and traversed the open rolling hills and passes as we headed toward Sonora Pass and the resupply point in the second, northern, Kennedy Meadows. This landscape was distinct in a sea of sameness, the hulking bald hillsides breaching from the forested valleys like whalebacks cresting the ocean's surface. Snow glistened, melting rapidly in the face of the savage sun. Our feet were soaked from slush and splashing through runoff.

It was in choosing to push through the hardships—heat, rain, snow, mosquitos, dehydration, daylight, and darkness—not just on this hike but through all the miles that had come before that I'd grown to be who I was. I knew that braving whatever lay ahead would help me find a metal core able to withstand whatever came my way in the years ahead. Despite how weak I often felt—perhaps because of it—I could still sense an inner strength, which grew daily.

You chose your path, Heather; now walk it. Every damn step through every damn hard and fearful moment.

I looked up. Adam was far above me on the loping trail, forging through what I assumed was his own set of challenges. We were both growing through this experience. I hoped we'd find ourselves bound closer together on the other side.

We reached the top of a ridge marked by a weathered sign pointing toward Emigrant Pass. My mind wandered to thoughts of those who had traveled through this convoluted landscape in wagons, seeking something better than what they'd left behind. Now, thousands of other seekers pass through here every year on very different journeys. *Perhaps in a thousand centuries, these rugged giants will be nothing more than rolling hills where cows graze what were once lofty summits.*

I wondered if those future people would know about us—the women and men who'd once ascended to these heights on rock and snow, our feet carrying us here for recreation. Would they wonder about us and our motivations just as I mused about those who'd come through with oxen and wagons? *When these heights have been laid low by wind and water, will the memory of us—the ones who stood atop the world and were kissed by the sky as we walked more than two thousand miles—persist in legend?*

Will I find what I'm seeking and will it be better than what I've left behind?

At last, the ribbon of highway coiling through Sonora Pass became visible far below. We made our way downhill, carefully negotiating the icy snow still clinging to the northern aspects of the large bowl the PCT descended. It was getting late in the day, but we hoped to get a ride to the Kennedy Meadows campground and store to resupply ourselves. We reached the deserted road and stood there in the growing shadows, our hope diminishing by the minute.

"Bottom of the food bag dinner tonight and no breakfast," I said dejectedly after half an hour of anxious waiting.

The sound of a sputtering engine laboring up the pass sent a jolt of hope through me, and we jutted our thumbs out. The beater slowed to a stop and we hopped in for the ten-mile ride down the steep, winding road.

"Where to?" the driver asked with a thick German accent.

"Kennedy Meadows. It's about ten miles down the road," Adam answered from the front passenger seat.

"Oh, yes, I think I know the place."

I dug through the miscellaneous climbing gear in the back seat to find the seat belt clip while the car shifted jerkily and sped down the 108. The driver took the first turn at a relatively safe speed but careened around the next two dangerously fast. I wondered briefly if he was intoxicated.

"So, what are you doing?" the driver asked.

"We're, uh, hiking the Pacific Crest Trail," I answered, clenching my hands on the seat edge as we swung wide around another curve. "What about you?"

"Oh, yes. I have hiked on that trail. I come up from San Francisco every weekend. I'm mostly climbing though. Do you know the Sierra Club Peaks List?"

"Yeah," I nodded, bracing myself as we approached a signed hairpin.

"Can you use the parking brake if your brakes don't work?" the driver calmly asked Adam.

I felt my stomach somersault. *This is how I'm going to die. Not a bear or a mountain lion or a rockslide. In a car accident, flying off the side of the highway.*

"Uh," Adam said, staring at the brake pedal that the man had pushed to the floor. We were slowing slightly, but nowhere near enough to navigate the sharp turn that was rapidly approaching.

"Yes, you can!" I called urgently from the backseat. *Engage the damn thing now!*

The driver pulled up on the emergency brake lever as we entered the curve and the car screeched and shuddered around it. We passed the pull off for a viewpoint and he engaged the brake again as we screamed around another hairpin. He was mumbling something in German—either a prayer or cursing. *Maybe both.* All small talk ended as we each set our mental affairs in order until at last the road leveled out alongside the Middle Fork of the Stanislaus River.

"You can just drop us off there at the turnoff." Adam pointed at the brown national forest sign a quarter mile ahead.

"Are you sure? I think it's a mile or two down the road."

"That's fine!" Adam and I both replied with enthusiasm—not for walking an extra couple of miles, but for getting out of the car alive.

He swerved onto the shoulder, employing his unorthodox braking technique, and the car fishtailed wildly in the gravel before stopping just past the turnoff. We hopped out, thanked him profusely, and turned down the road toward the pack station.

"I thought we were going to die," I said quietly, holding out my hand, which was still visibly shaking.

"Me too. I wonder if he's going to get back to San Francisco like that?"

I shook my head. "The e-brake will burn out way before that. I hope he just pulls over in the next town and gets it fixed."

We walked down the paved access road toward the campground and store. Adrenaline still flowed through my body, moving me faster than normal. I was no stranger to terrifying moments on a hitch, but after this one I found myself more inclined than ever to simply walk.

MY DAD WAS NOT CAPABLE of driving anything resembling the speed limit. Rocketing down the road at twenty over was normal with him. Yet, he'd never been in a collision—although he'd been close. The panic I'd felt in the brakeless car had been akin to the time my dad picked me up after school and speeding down M-57 in the rain hadn't seen the stopped semi waiting to make the left. Not until I urgently said, "Dad?!"

I was still a year shy of driver's training, but I would never forget what I learned in the next few moments. There was oncoming traffic and wet roads. My dad braked gradually, calmly steering the car onto the right shoulder. The tires hit gravel and grass as we passed within inches of the semi. He deftly regained his lane and carried onward.

I felt my skin crawl with fear, as though I was trying to escape my own body. He glanced over at me.

"That was a close one."

I desperately wanted to be able to find the tranquility in the midst of terror that he possessed.

AFTER A MUCH SAFER HITCH back to the trail in the morning, we followed the PCT north as it undulated through deep forest and open ridgelines, passing from the El Dorado into the Tahoe National Forest. My body and mood ebbed and flowed with it, lagging on the climbs and relishing the ease of the ridgetops. Day after day passed in a hazy realm of wake, walk, eat, walk, eat, sleep, repeat. Sometimes I told Adam rambling stories of my other times through the area just to keep myself awake. We passed dozens of people every day and even more tents in the crepuscular hours. We had clearly caught the so-called bubble, where the majority of northbound thru-hikers were clustered within a hundred miles or so of one another.

From time to time, I would revive with a sudden onslaught of energy that came from an unknown source. My pace would quicken, and my attention would suddenly be laser focused on the sound of wind rising and falling through the pines swaying over our heads or the sunlight patterns they cast on the brown trail tread. As we climbed up to the high plateau south of Anderson Peak, I felt this surge of energy coursing through my legs and lungs. I pounded uphill, taking the lead from Adam as we emerged above the tree line into bright morning light. Crisp wind swirled and cut, but I was pushing so hard that it was a bracing relief from the sweat pouring off of my body.

Ahead of us a red-headed hiker was also making his way upward, his long, curly hair flying in the breeze. For a moment I was drawn into a flashback of gaining on my ex-husband in this same spot thirteen years earlier. In present time I caught the hiker as we crested the ridge below Tinker Knob, the thin brown line of the PCT winding visibly across the soft green slopes of mule's ear for more than a mile ahead of us. The wind roared, making conversation impossible. Sensing me, he glanced back, his face registering surprise as he stepped aside. I smiled my thanks as I passed by him. Despite the hair color, he bore no resemblance to the man in my memory, and I turned my focus northward toward the diminutive tip of Anderson Peak.

Beyond it—within the gaps of blue-cast mountains—lay Donner Pass and I-80. Several figures dotted the panorama, spread out along the brown ribbon demarcating our shared destiny. I heard Adam jogging up behind me as he often did when I hit four mph. *I'm hiking too fast. I need to conserve.* But when the power of the land was in me—funneling upward from the earth—I walked faster. Who was I to deny it?

I'm strong enough. I just need to rest and eat more later. I remembered the vending machines at the interstate rest area just off trail and decided to maintain momentum. *Ice cream in twelve miles. Zero day in thirty-eight.*

Despite my overall fatigue, I managed to reach the rest area in three hours. I barely paused, hurrying inside with my wallet in hand.

"No!" I cried out loud, not caring that it drew the stares of the automobile-transported visitors milling around me. "The vending machines are out of order! All of them!" I started to cry as Adam arrived.

He punched some buttons on each machine in vain hope that the signs were wrong. Nothing happened and he turned back to me.

"I'm sorry, hon."

Tears poured down my face and I felt my legs rubberize. In my mad frenzy to reach ice cream, candy, and soda dispensers, I'd eaten next to nothing. My knees buckled and I swayed. Flashbacks to Mimbres hit me and I reached my arm out for Adam. He caught me and half carried me outside to the picnic tables at the far end of the rest area. I lay down on the grass with my feet propped up, sobbing uncontrollably.

"All I wanted was some ice cream," I sniffled. "Why do they have to be broken now?"

"It's okay. You just have low blood sugar and need to eat." Adam pulled a chocolate bar out of his backpack and broke off a piece, sticking it in my mouth in between my laments.

I closed my eyes as the sweetness melted and rapidly entered my bloodstream, countering the exhaustion. The eighteen miles we'd covered in five hours was a blistering pace compared to our norm when we were shuffling up hills. Adam sat next to me, feeding me more chocolate.

"I'm worried about you, Heather. You've lost a lot of weight. You have to either slow down or eat more. You're almost four thousand miles into this hike, but you've got at least three thousand more to go. You can't push yourself like that."

"But I wanted ice cream," I reiterated pitifully, propping myself up on my elbows.

"I know. But we're taking the day off at Scott and Michelle's. I'm sure we can have ice cream there." Adam patted my hand. "Lots of ice cream."

I sniffed again and got up, clambering onto the picnic table bench and dumping out my food bag. A half day ahead of schedule with only twenty-six miles to hike to our pick-up spot, I now had a surplus of food—just not what I craved. Despite the unappealing nature of the same old bars, cookies, candy, and chips, I started eating and kept it up while Adam filled our water bottles from the drinking fountain.

He's right. I'm burning through stores much faster than I should be at this point. And I have a really long way to go. Slow and steady. Slow and steady.

Once again, I came to after a blackout food binge, startled at how much I'd eaten—all the surplus and then some.

My resolve to take it slow lasted only until the next morning, when we awoke to twelve gradually downhill miles from our rendezvous location with Scott. I took off at a four-mile-per-hour pace again with Adam intermittently jogging behind me. We reached the road crossing just as our friend Scott leveraged his lanky frame out of his truck, planning to hike toward us for an hour. I felt bad ruining his outing.

"I'm sorry, we're early," I apologized, looking longingly at the vehicle.

"Not a problem! You guys hungry?" he asked, pulling two coolers out of his truck. One was full of drinks, the other contained fresh food. He also presented a grocery bag full of nonperishable snacks.

"Oh my God! Thank you!" I was overwhelmed yet again. Scott had brought me a similar spread as trail magic on my fastest known time PCT hike in 2013. "You didn't have to do this."

"I've gotten so much trail magic over the years, I love a chance to pay it forward," he said with a wave of his hand. "This sandwich is gluten free," he said, handing me a bulging turkey wrap from the cooler.

We lolled in the shade at the trailhead eating and visiting for what seemed like forever, although it was only an hour. A few hikers went by, returning from the nearby town and walking past us to begin the relentless climb of the Sierra Buttes. They cast longing glances—some more furtive than others—at our feast.

Once my hunger and thirst were sated, I began to feel anxiety. *I should be hiking on tonight. I can't afford to take a day off if I want to finish this.* I took several deep breaths and listened to Scott and Adam talking without registering their words. After another deep breath I reframed my fear. *I can't afford* not *to rest and eat if I want to finish this.*

That night as I fell asleep, clean and with a belly full of steak and veggies, I contemplated with gratitude how the man whose record I'd broken on the PCT and his wife had become such close and enduring friends. They'd spoiled us with food, and we would stay through the Fourth of July holiday before getting back on trail on July 5. *Tomorrow will be my first zero day since May 21.* The unbroken chain of thirty-plus-mile days for more than a month had severely depleted me. But now, thanks to my friends, I was going to rehabilitate somewhat.

"Thank you for Scott and Michelle," I whispered softly to the universe and drifted into a deep sleep.

After forty-eight hours of eating and sleeping, Adam and I hit the trail ready to make our way through the transitional landscape of Northern California. Over the next few days, we crossed the halfway point of the PCT—as well as of my entire CYTC.

"Happy birthday!" said the text message. "Bought a card then realized I had no place to send it! Hope you have a great day and stay safe."

I smiled at my phone. Marie's messages were always bedecked with emojis and positive energy.

"Thank you! I'll get it from you when we get home. We're almost to Oregon!"

"Yah, did you go south to north on this one?"

"North. I've got a thousand miles left on this trail and about twenty-five hundred miles left on the CDT/AT. I'm just over halfway!"

I slipped the phone into my pack pocket and heaved myself back to my feet. Some of those thirty-five hundred miles still needed to be walked that day, and soon we would leave the Sierra for the Cascades by circling the southernmost stratovolcanoes on the route—Lassen Peak and Mount Shasta.

I LAY UNDER A PINE TREE eating cheese with my legs propped up in the air against the trunk. My bare feet were pale, with dirt streaks between the toes where the fine-grained dust of the PCT had infiltrated my shoes and socks. My legs were perhaps tan, but it was hard to tell since the layer of dust stuck to dried sweat was so thick. I realized too late that my ponytail was now also getting coated in the powder-fine dirt while I lay on the ground. *Oh well.* I had never cared much for appearances. I thought back to scenes from my first marriage, to Remy.

"But I don't want to go to a fancy salon. I like going to the beauty school," I protested as Remy pulled up out front.

"I'm sure you'll like it. The women I work with all recommended it!" he encouraged me, waiting for me to get out of the car.

Reluctantly I went to the appointment he'd made—I hated the haircut.

Back under the tree, I plunked the last bite of cheese into my mouth and picked up a chocolate bar. It was melty in the heat, getting all over my face and fingers and mixing with the omnipresent dirt. *God, I stink*, I thought.

On a dreary Christmas morning, I gingerly held a fifty-dollar bottle of perfume and sniffed it carefully.

"Um, thank you?"

"Do you like it?" Remy asked, evidently proud of his gift selection.

"I guess so. But it's a lot of money for perfume. I don't really even wear perfume."

"Well, maybe you should."

Remy had always been booking me spa days and buying expensive perfume for gifts. He never understood that I preferred dreadlocks and dirt. *Was it any wonder it didn't work out?*

We'd thru-hiked together, yet he couldn't understand that I was the same person off trail as on—simple, frugal, and rather dirty. That before making any purchase I weighed the cost in terms of how much hike I could buy with that money instead, which led me to make almost no purchases aside from food.

I poured water on my chocolate-covered fingers, which only made chocolate mud. *Dammit.* I sat up, wiping the dirt and chocolate from my face and hands onto my skirt and furiously shaking pine needles out of my hair as the text from an ex-boyfriend danced through my head. *"I know when you've spent the night, even though you're gone when I wake up, because I find little bits of leaves and pine needles on the pillow. Calling cards from a wild woman."*

My wild otherness was titillating. I realized now that the steady flow of men who'd come into my life had done so because of my otherness—and my wholehearted commitment to not bend to convention in order to attract them. Wedded to nature above all else.

I looked over at Adam, who was just finishing his lunch. I noticed chocolate stains on his shirt as well and smiled. We exchanged the "I guess we should go" glance and began packing. I wondered if he, too, would get tired of me running to the mountains. I thought of our struggles on the AT. *I guess in a way he already has.*

The problem with inviting a wildling into your life is their inherent unpredictability. *Feral is one way of putting it.*

I picked up my backpack. As exhilarating as the unknown may be, over time the draw would cease to outweigh my partner's need for conformity and stability. In the face of expectation, I was likely to flee into the mountains.

And I had every time. *Will it ever be possible for me to not go?*

"I forbid you to thru-hike again," the pine needle ex-boyfriend said when I returned from a three-week trip. He erroneously thought an ultimatum could force me to stay.

I packed my bags and moved into my car, then in with a friend. Six months later I was walking across the country again.

And again. And again. Here I was thru-hiking again. This time for so much longer than ever before. But Adam was with me, the first time since Remy that I'd hiked with a partner. Remy and I couldn't sustain a relationship off the trail. I wondered if this time it would be different.

"Move home and marry a farmer," my dad had entreated me when our divorce papers were final.

"No, Dad."

Would a farmer understand my passion for the mountains? Unlikely.

Farmers were stable, irrevocably connected to the ultimate stabilizing force—the earth. No doubt my dad felt as though he would no longer need to worry about me if I were attached to fields that never moved. Farmers, like the land they worked, provided. My father's father was a farmer and his father before that. All tied to the black, loamy soil of mid-Michigan—soil they themselves were now part of.

I watched Adam's athletic build power uphill in front of me. A former member of the US World 100k Team, he was faster and stronger than I could ever hope to be. He'd also been raised on a farm in central Pennsylvania.

Would a farmer follow me to the mountains? This one could, and had.

Perhaps my dad was right about what I needed for once.

AS WE AMBLED THROUGH THE HOT, thick forests of Northern California, I felt stronger than I had since New Mexico. *Maybe the second wind comes after thirty-five hundred miles?* I mused. It was fortunate we were moving faster now because even as we steadily plowed north, wildfires were springing up behind us as well as to the east and west.

Smoke infiltrated our daily life; the air we breathed was always scented with a campfire smell. My heart grew heavy as the smoke thickened, even while sunsets became sublime from the particulates in the atmosphere. So much of the wild forests that I loved had burned—were burning. I grieved their loss even while the fear of the trail closing prodded us to take even fewer breaks and forgo any additional rest days. California had become a tinder box, and we didn't want to be caught in the flames.

Oregon was not far now, and beyond it lay the familiar home trails of Washington.

CHAPTER 12

OREGON

"Do you hear that?" I asked as we made our way through the smoky air near South Brown Mountain Shelter.

"Kinda," Adam answered.

Instead of escaping wildfire complications, we had seen a dramatic increase in the intensity of the smoke in the air ever since we'd reached Oregon. Every time we gained a vista, we scoured the horizon to see if any fires were visible. Unlike the obvious column outside Agua Dulce, however, the entire sky was cloaked—foggy, but not from water vapor. Coughing fits woke us up at night. So did my dreams of being trapped in a burning building, recurring almost nightly. *What is this doing to my lungs? I don't want to die of COPD like my dad when I've never smoked. Should we get masks? It can't burn like this forever, can it?*

The engine noise roared again louder, unmistakably close now.

"I don't think that's an ATV," I said. "It sounds like it's coming from overhead."

We emerged from the forest onto a red lava rock trail, indicative of the geology of the Cascade Range, which we would traverse the rest of the way to Canada. We wound around the base of Brown Mountain and the roaring came again, louder than ever.

"Holy shit!" I yelled over the noise, looking upward. A helicopter was only a few hundred feet above us with a bucket swinging below.

"Is that a water bucket?!" Adam yelled back, as the chopper disappeared over Brown Mountain.

"Yeah! It's probably getting water from Fish Lake," I said, waving in the direction of the large unseen lake just to the west. "But that means there's a fire nearby."

Without further discussion we surged forward, our hearts pounding and terror rising in our chests. Our greatest fear was finding ourselves trapped in a fire with our only option to go through, something I'd experienced before when hiking in Washington. I remembered how the moments inside the conflagration had passed with a surreal slowness.

Even though I was trying to flee that blaze, I could not help but gaze at the inferno surrounding me, mesmerized by the flames licking upward along trees and sweeping across the ground, turning everything orange and then black. Charred, flaming tree limbs broke free and fell to the ground on all sides—torches setting new blazes. I was dimly aware that my body was moving quickly, plunging downhill in a small stream to keep my shoes from melting to the hot ground. But my mind was still, fixated on each detail of the terrible beauty of a fire-engulfed forest.

I'd slipped and tripped over debris in the runnel, holding my shirt over my mouth, hoping that my rapid assessment of the map had been right about this drainage taking me back to the trail a mile farther down. Though I knew I was practically running, my mind registered nothing quickly, instead keenly cataloging what might be my final sights.

At last, I'd stumbled onto the trail again, luckily right at the boundary of the fire. I'd emerged from the flames calmly, pausing to have a brief, coherent conversation with the shocked firefighter in full Nomex who had witnessed my appearance from the creek bed, but as I made my way downhill from him at a sprint my body shook incessantly. I'd survived, but I had no desire to repeat the experience.

The helicopter buzzed overhead again and again, back and forth from Fish Lake to the unseen fire. Finally, an hour after its first pass, we reached the highway crossing. There were no signs posted, no personnel stationed. The helicopter was more distant now, heading south of us.

"What do you think?" Adam asked.

"Well, the fire is definitely south of us and they're actively fighting it. I know the next section of trail has a lot of lakes and wetlands. So I guess we keep hiking?" I shrugged.

"Yeah, it would be signed if it was closed. And," he pointed at the three cars parked in the small trailhead, "there are obviously other people out here."

We pushed hard through the hot, windless forest, partially to put distance between ourselves and the fire but also because the mosquitoes were unfathomably horrendous. Without a breeze, we had to move fast to keep them from landing, but even that method failed as we hiked through dense clouds hovering above the trail. The wetlands of the Sky Lakes Wilderness that were our savior from the flames spawned myriad relentless, bloodsucking demons that couldn't be stopped.

"Ugh," I cried, trying to move my head net aside enough to cram a cookie into my mouth. Twenty mosquitos flooded in.

"This is unreal!" Adam called back as he clambered over yet another fallen log.

"The amount of deadfall or the mosquitoes?" I asked, giving up on the snack and smashing the head net against my face with both hands to kill the bugs.

"Both!"

After several hours of racing along, clambering over dozens of fallen trees, I began feeling dizzy. Unable to eat or drink without exposing my face, I'd opted to do neither. Now that decision was catching up with me. Making matters worse, thick smoke had begun to fill the air again, alerting us to yet another fire in the vicinity. *But where?* I climbed over a log that was nearly chest high and got stuck astride it, neither of my legs reaching the ground. Marooned, I let myself flop face down onto the wide log in exhaustion. *It feels so good to stop.* Thousands of mosquitoes descended on me. I felt them landing on my legs and arms and, for the first time, I didn't care. I was too exhausted to combat them.

"Go on and save yourself," I called, melodramatically.

Adam turned around and came back.

"What are you doing?" he asked, swiping mosquitoes off my body.

"I can't do it. I'm exhausted. Just leave me here." I closed my eyes.

"Oh, come on, Heather. Here." He grabbed my arm and pulled me over the log. "Now drink something."

I obeyed, and he swatted away the insects that tried to infiltrate my head net while I gulped down a liter of water.

"Okay, now let's go. There has to be a campsite soon."

Rejuvenated by the water and brief rest, I hurried after him.

In camp, securely away from the insects and fed, we laughed until we cried at my antics.

SMOKE FILLED OUR TENT ALL NIGHT, causing us to cough and wheeze and wake up many times. Each time, I opened my vestibule and gazed into the darkness outside, scanning the blackness for even an imperceptible glow of fire. *Nothing. Wherever it is, it's not nearby.* The next afternoon we reached Crater Lake National Park only to discover that yet another fire was burning close to the trail north of the lake, near Mount Thielsen.

"The PCT will probably close soon," the park ranger informed us.

Again, we pushed ourselves to hike long after dark, and woke before dawn, passing within a mile of the column of smoke as we exited the park and headed up toward the unmistakable pointy volcanic plug waymarking the beginning of central Oregon. Once we were over the shoulder of Mount Thielsen, the air cleared and we encountered patches of snow, lingering reminders of the previous winter somehow still surviving in the intense late July heat.

Nearing Bend a few days later, we entered a wasteland—mile after mile of forest charred by wildfires. The same forests in my memory were cool and deep, smelling of wet earth, and I was overwhelmed with grief at their loss as we walked through nothing but blackened sticks as far as we could see in any direction. The former forest floor was deep soot, pure black with silvery accents. The acrid scent of burnt wood filled my nose and the powdery soot sent me into coughing fits. The destruction was universal.

Ashes formed airborne clouds that swirled around my feet as I walked. *Ashes to ashes . . .*

I THOUGHT OF MY MOM'S arthritis-gnarled hand reaching into the small plastic box and flinging a handful of white ash into the wind.

"I'm sorry I can't go into the woods anymore," she whispered as my dad's ashes floated away. Her legs wobbled and my brother-in-law helped her back to the house.

I looked at my sister Louisa holding the box. With Marie unable to be there, it was up to us. We started down the lane into the woods.

Dust to dust . . .

The scent of pines brought my teary eyes up from the burnt ground of central Oregon. One living tree lingered—bark charred but needles green. Adam was hiking fast, pulling ahead. I paused with one hand on the trunk, disregarding the soot. The living bark felt rough under my palm.

"Spread my ashes here," my dad said, pointing to the knoll of oaks interspersed with small pines he had planted when I was born.

I grabbed his hand. Anytime he spoke of his death, I wanted to grab him and hold on tightly. Even now at age twelve, when I was far too old to do so. His palm was rough, calloused, and strong. *Please don't leave me.*

"This is it," I said, barely above a whisper.

Louisa looked around, her blue eyes inscrutable behind her glasses.

"I'm not touching it like Mom did," she said firmly, opening the box.

"Okay," I assented. *But I want to. I don't want to let go.*

She dumped the contents of the box on the ground beneath the now mature pines. Embarrassed by my emotion in the presence of my sister's seeming lack, I stood stock-still. We paused in silence as the ashes settled, coating the ground in a gray blanket. No words passed as we walked back to Mom's house. When Louisa left, I ran back to the pine grove, rushing through the woods where I'd once carried a hammer to feel safe.

There, I knelt on the ashy pine needles and cried. I scooped up a handful and held it in my hands—silky soft, so unlike my father's Marlboro man toughness. There had been nothing soft about him, even in old age. It felt strange to find him transmuted in such a radical way.

It had been almost thirty years since I'd promised to spread his ashes here. The trees were different, the knoll unseen now. I wasn't even certain it was the right place. *Dust you are and to dust you will return . . .*

"I tried, Dad. I tried to get it right." Tears blinded me. "I've been trying to get it right my whole life. In everything, I wanted to make you proud. I hope at least in this last attempt I made you happy."

The thrumming insects of late summer quieted and only faint whispers in the conifer canopy remained as I sat back on my heels, staring blankly at the forest around me. A few feet away, two blue jay feathers caught my eye. *Dad's favorite bird.* I touched them.

Maybe I finally did something right.

"HEATHER! ARE YOU OKAY?" Adam's voice was clearly worried.

I realized I was kneeling in the ashy soil, one hand still touching the living tree. My eyes were bleary and I wiped them to see his face, depositing charcoal that stung.

"Dead," was all I could manage.

He sighed.

"I know, but it will regrow. C'mon." He reached down and pulled me to my feet.

He was right—nature would regrow, die back, rest, and rejuvenate in a cycle as ancient as the water flowing through the creeks we drank from. She was surely aware of the changes wrought in the landscape by humankind and our carelessness, but she was unwilling to give up.

I trailed after Adam through the burnt trees, the whispers of Michigan white pines still caressing the edges of my mind. Nature seemed to hold infinite space for her traumas without letting them define her. *Show me how. Please.*

In the midst of the decimated forest, we passed "2,000" spelled out with small gray stones on the charcoal soil. I took a deep breath as I stepped over them. *More than four thousand miles on my feet this year . . . more miles this year so far than any other . . . and I'm not even close to being done yet.* The influx of energy from our stay at Scott and Michelle's had been steadily leached away by miles and the necessity of outrunning fires.

Eight hundred miles had passed without a rest day, and I could feel a familiar exhaustion seeping back into my bones, exacerbated by the grief of seeing so much burned land, combined with the knowledge that even more was being engulfed as we walked.

Reaching Santiam Pass was a relief in many ways. A friend from Bend came to get us and took us away from the scorched landscape and my constant need to outrun it, for two days of rest and food—perfectly grilled steaks, loads of vegetables, tubs of ice cream, everything we had been craving. After our rest, we made quick progress across the rolling landscape of northern Oregon. "We're right where I met you in 2013! About five miles from Highway 26," I texted Rachel, a friend I had met on that record-setting PCT hike. "Are you still in the area?"

"Yes! We're at Timothy Lake, must've missed you there. We'll meet you at the road," she texted back.

"Rachel's going to meet us after all," I said, putting my phone away as Adam came up from the trickling spring with fresh water.

"Great! There's not much flow here so I wasn't able to fill up."

We followed the ridge through the thick forest, pausing at a small clearing that revealed towering Mount Hood in the near distance, where we would camp that night. *Please don't let this forest burn.*

The PCT began its descent toward the major highway and I looked forward to seeing my friend and climbing partner for the first time since the previous summer.

At the highway we sat for a few minutes watching vehicles speed by before noticing the blackberries growing on the embankment. Hungry and thirsty, we dove into the bushes, relishing the fruit of the earth, its sweet taste of raw life mixed with the dirt and tang of sweat on our hands. Like bears we silently grazed for ten minutes until two pickups swerved onto the gravel shoulder and eight people from the thru-hiking community—some we knew, including Rachel and her fiancé as well as Cheddar, whom I'd last seen on my AT FKT near Pinkham Notch, and some we didn't—leaped out bearing coolers of drinks and snacks. Best of all was the company.

After an hour of sitting in a circle on the side of the highway in an impromptu hiker gathering, we regretfully stood up and said our goodbyes. Eight miles and several thousand feet of elevation gain still stood between us and our proposed campsite on the flanks of Mount Hood. *And then, the all-you-can-eat breakfast at Timberline Lodge in the morning!* I was beginning to desperately miss nontrail food, even with the recent indulgences in Bend.

The all-you-can-eat breakfast at Timberline Lodge is legendary among PCT thru-hikers. In 2005, my partner and I had hiked fifty miles from Olallie Lake to the lodge in one push and camped beneath stunted krummholz just outside the hotel to be first in line for the unlimited fresh squeezed orange juice and bacon the next morning. Unwittingly, we'd begun a tradition that was now frequently repeated.

Adam and I camped several miles away, unwilling to push a fifty-mile day, but we easily reached the dining room in time to be seated. A few other hikers were sprinkled among the well-dressed hotel guests. We ate until we couldn't handle any more, finally waddling to the lobby and sitting beneath the large plate glass windows to digest.

"Well, we made it!" I announced, cheerful from both satiation and satisfaction. "We're basically out of Oregon, and aside from that small fire we had to detour around at Ashland, we haven't been stopped. Tomorrow it's Washington and clear sailing."

Adam nodded absently, scrolling on his phone, checking the weather and alerts.

"The trail is closed near White Pass."

"What?" I opened my eyes from my blissful rest.

"Looks like a fire started last night in the Goat Rocks Wilderness."

I stared at him, not quite able to comprehend his words. The PCT in Washington was notoriously wet and seldom burned. It was late July and the fires that did start typically wouldn't begin for another month.

"What are we supposed to do? There aren't many ways through there." I leaned over his shoulder to read the closure announcement.

"Looks like it's really close to the highway, so there's a short detour and then on the highway for a mile."

I followed the line on the map with my finger. *As long as that fire doesn't blow up.*

"I guess I jinxed us," I sighed.

"I think the weather has jinxed us, but we definitely shouldn't waste any time."

The next afternoon, we strode across the steel girder bridge spanning the Columbia River, grateful to reach the state of Washington. *Home.* But underlying the relief of having walked five thousand miles in five months and reaching trails I knew by heart was the daunting realization that I still had three thousand miles to go.

CHAPTER 13

WASHINGTON

The Goat Rocks Wilderness was as beautiful as I remembered and blessedly devoid of smoke until after we traversed the knife-edge ridge north of Old Snowy Mountain. From there we could see an unmistakable gray plume billowing high into the sky directly ahead on the PCT near the ski resort. Evening was drawing nigh, advanced by the smoky haze filling the sky, but we pressed forward, intent on reaching the detour before camping.

Every mile brought us lower in elevation and closer to the flames. My eyes watered and my nose burned. I had a momentary panic attack. *What if the fire has spread and we're walking right into it?* The ordinarily busy trail was empty, and the lack of people felt unnerving. *I just want to get to the detour and start hiking away from the fire.*

"We're almost to the junction," Adam assured me, as if he'd read my mind.

I detected the faint sound of voices. Within a couple of minutes, we reached a forested pass with twenty or more tents crammed into every available space. Hikers were everywhere—cooking their dinners, conversing, eating. Obviously, our camping goal was the same as everyone else's.

We were greeted by waves and various shouted instructions about where it was still possible to snuggle a tent in among the ferns. Bright yellow tape barricaded the PCT north of the clearing, and the scent of smoke was thick.

"Thanks, but we're going to go a bit farther," Adam said in a general response, and we veered left down the heavily flagged detour.

The trail immediately deteriorated, its rough tread overhung by ferns and huckleberry bushes. We pushed west, away from the fire, through the overgrowth. Myriad watercourses threaded the forest near the trail, winding through rocks and roots thick with moss. It was the Pacific Northwest forest biome at its finest. However, the thriving PNW understory was not conducive to finding camping.

"It's almost dark," I said, pausing to fill my water bottles at one of the many small streams we splashed through.

"There's nothing here for camping," Adam responded, doing the same. Irritation was evident in his voice.

"We'll have to make do with something. How far is it to the next turn?"

"A mile maybe? I don't have distances on my map, just the trail," he responded, glancing at his phone GPS app.

"Well, it's creepy in here. I feel like Bigfoot is watching. Let's try to get to the junction. Maybe it's wide enough there that we can just sleep on the trail and hope twenty hikers don't step on us at five a.m."

After another fifteen minutes, in the last glimmer of pearly light, I spotted a lumpy clearing alongside the trail. After a cursory inspection, we made it our home for the night. It proved to be a good choice since the tail junction—marked with one small piece of flagging—was almost imperceptible even in the full daylight of the next morning. Had we continued the night before, we might have passed it by.

The second trail of the detour plunged toward the highway following a drainage. The trail was blown out by previous floods in several places and completely overgrown. Massive cedars lay prone across it, slowing our progress dramatically. It was obvious that the trail was essentially unused and unmaintained. However, it did bring us to a small, signed trailhead on the highway. We gladly began our walk uphill on the wide shoulder toward White Pass, where we'd pick up our resupply boxes at the gas station and rejoin the PCT as it traversed the William O. Douglas Wilderness and entered Mount Rainier National Park.

"August 1 . . . five months!" I said, tossing my worn-out shoes into the trash can with a flourish and sliding my feet into the new shoes from my resupply box.

"And you're almost done with the PCT," Adam added, chugging from a carton of chocolate milk.

The Kracker Barrel store at White Pass was thronged with hikers and wilderness firefighters. The staff was harried and it was hard to even make our way through the tiny convenience store to buy what we needed. Outside we sat on a derelict picnic table just to get some peace to eat and sort out our boxes. The fire was visible, burning high on the hillside. Firefighters wandered in and out, unable to fight the fire within the confines of the wilderness boundary. There was an intense feeling of anticipation hanging over the entire area.

"It's moving west now, which is not what we'd hoped," one of the firefighters was saying to a gas station employee on her smoke break a few feet from us. "It's going to breach the PCT today and they're going to have to close the trail even farther back. FS is in there now trying to get hikers out. And we can't do a damn thing until it comes this way."

"I just don't understand," the woman said, extinguishing her cigarette in the sandbox on the trash can.

"Wilderness Act. You can't fight fires in the wilderness areas. They just gotta run their course. Keeping it natural and untouched," the firefighter shrugged, obviously in disagreement with this aspect of the protective act. "But we've got lines ready to stop it if it comes this way, don't worry."

We left the madhouse and hiked past the tent-studded lakes of the William O. Douglas Wilderness and forded the Bumping River, then filled our bottles at dusk from a tiny rill on the steep climb away from it. At the top of the ridge, we spotted a nice campsite and darted into it, relieved to find a stopping place just before headlamps were needed. We pitched the tent in the middle and happily texted friends who would meet us at Snoqualmie Pass in two days.

THE MORNING DAWNED COOL, and the sun dapples playing on the thin material of the tent lulled away the fires of yesterday—and the previous several weeks. We were on the cusp of Mount Rainier National Park, and the air smelled clean for the first time in a thousand miles. We lingered over breakfast and coffee knowing we'd have no problem reaching Snoqualmie Pass on the agreed-upon day. At a luxuriously late start time of seven a.m, we finally got out of the tent.

"What is that?" I cried, pointing at our clear groundsheet while Adam rolled the tent into his pack. A huge brown stain was plastered to the plastic and looked suspiciously like . . .

"Shit," Adam said, leaning back from where he'd made a cautious sniff.

"Oh my God! Are you effing kidding me? Who takes a surface shit in the middle of a campsite?"

Adam was already pulling the tent back out of his backpack. Our groundsheet was well worn and if there had been a hole . . .

"It's clean, don't worry," he assured me after close examination.

I swallowed hard, trying not to vomit.

"What are we going to do with that?" I pointed at the poop-covered plastic.

"Pack it out, I guess."

"Ugh, why are people so disgusting?"

In the backcountry, it was expected that you dig a six-inch-deep hole to defecate in, well away from campsites and water. It was a cardinal sin among backpackers to "surface shit," as some person had done. It was even more horrific because of the location. In our haste to set up in low light without the aid of headlamps, we'd camped right on top of it. The only worse Leave No Trace karma would be to leave a giant piece of poop-stained plastic in the woods.

"Don't touch it!" I worried as Adam carefully wadded the plastic up and secured it in the outside pocket of his pack.

How far to the next trash can? I wondered.

The traumatic discovery of the morning was soon erased by the brilliant day and the joy of being back on home trails. In addition to thru-hiking the PCT twice before, I'd hiked most of Washington's trail miles multiple other times, especially as we drew farther north. I began to recall specific trees, springs, climbs, and campsites. It was a homecoming of another sort. While the AT always generated a *feeling* of home, no matter where on the trail I was, the mountains of Washington had actually *been* home for a decade. I knew the summits as well as the valleys. My mind held a three-dimensional map of the northern Cascades that would make it hard for me to ever be completely lost there.

The next day at noon we crossed over I-90 and walked into the PCT north trailhead at Snoqualmie Pass. Jenni and Kathleen, as well as Kathleen's husband, John, were waiting, cheering at our arrival. They'd brought drinks and food, including an entire pumpkin pie, which Adam and I divided in half and devoured. All of us hiked out together, up the relentless switchback trail to the Kendall Katwalk. A few miles later John turned back, and Jenni and Kathleen continued on with us for the next seventy miles to the highway crossing at Stevens Pass.

It was strange to suddenly have company that wasn't Adam. Jenni and Kathleen were accomplished ultrarunners and alpinists; their fitness was unparalleled. Even so, they struggled at times to keep up with our backpacking-hardened bodies. At other points I brought up the rear, my energy reserves once again flagging, having not rested since Bend. The Alpine Lakes Wilderness was home to deep glacial valleys. The trail led us steeply down to the bottoms and steeply back up to dividing ridges over and over. The oscillations echoed my energy levels—sometimes high, sometimes very low.

We reached US 2 in three days, and Jenni drove us down valley to her home.

"You're welcome to take a zero day," she offered over a hearty dinner on their farm. "A big storm is coming in, and it's going to slam Glacier Peak the day after tomorrow."

Adam looked at me. "That sounds great!"

"But we have to keep going. Maybe just head out midday tomorrow instead?"

Adam and Jenni looked at me, surprise registering on their faces. I'd been talking about a rest day for fifty miles. Though I wanted to stay in a familiar place with a friend and rest, something in my gut told me we had to keep pushing. *It's only two hundred more miles.*

"I'm worried about the Agnes Creek fire spreading," I said somewhat truthfully, but that wasn't the whole of it. My gut told me something else was coming—and we needed to get there before it did.

Jenni and Kathleen had brought the unwelcome news that another section of the PCT was closed due to fire, this time in the heart of the wilderness ahead, near our next resupply point in the isolated mountain town of Stehekin. We would have to detour around it, adding a day of walking and a great deal of elevation. If it spread any more, the only way around might close altogether, barring completion of our continuous footpath to Canada.

After dinner I lay on the bed, catching up on work and communication, when a message from Marie came through.

"Hope all is going well, I hope the wildfires are not hampering your efforts. Good luck!"

I smiled.

"We've had to walk around a few. So far, we're safe!"

"Glad to hear you all are OK. When do you hope to start the CDT?"

"Should be done with the PCT on the 18th! On the CDT by the 22nd going south from Montana!"

"Well, good luck! Hope the fires in Colorado clear out soon and the snow doesn't fly too early this year!"

Me too, sis. Me too. I set my phone aside, drifting toward sleep. The Glacier Peak Wilderness was one of the most difficult sections of the entire Triple Crown, and it lay directly ahead. I felt exhausted just thinking about it.

DEEP BENEATH TOWERING EVERGREENS, we circled the unseen volcano through its eponymous wilderness. I could *feel* the impending storm, even though the sky was hidden from view by the boughs. The stillness of the forest was now being almost imperceptibly infiltrated by a humid breeze. The silence had grown to deafening depths, only our softly padding steps on the earthen trail disturbing it. Perhaps most indicative of all was the brooding darkness beginning to shadow us, hours too early.

"There's not really much in the way of protected camping once we get to the basin below Fire Creek Pass," I said to Adam. "We should probably start looking for a campsite."

A few drops began splattering through the canopy onto our upturned faces.

"A well-draining one," I added.

Within fifteen minutes it was raining steadily and we'd found a marginal spot that was more sloped than we'd like. *But at least it will drain.* We made a hurried effort to set up the tent taut as the rain came down harder. We were nearly soaked by the time we got inside. Having stopped several hours earlier than normal, we sat watching in amazement as water poured from the sky—a deluge of biblical proportions.

"Probably shouldn't have camped on the southwest slopes of the mountain," Adam observed.

I giggled. We hadn't really had a choice.

"Maybe it will put the fire out?" I offered.

"Unlikely, but it might slow it down. But who knows. It might not even be raining over there."

I sighed and spread some nut butter on a gluten-free tortilla. He was right. The fire was on the northwest side of the mountain, many miles away. We were on the brunt side. Glacier Peak itself might be wringing all of the moisture out on us, not allowing any to reach the parched, burning forest that so desperately needed it. The microclimates along the crest in Washington seemed to me even more pronounced now than they'd ever been.

While historically the western slopes were not prone to fires, this year there were multiple conflagrations in these wetter areas. Many of them blazed where pockets of forest had dried out, where soil was porous or rocky, where thick stands of conifers were weakened by beetle kill, hotter summers, and drier winters.

Thank you for your protection. I hope you remain for many more lifetimes. I prayed to the gargantuan cedars swaying gently a hundred feet above us as I drifted into deep sleep.

The next day we followed the deep undulations of the glaciated volcanic landscape, down thousands of feet and back up. Here in the farthest reaches of the wilderness, the trail was thickly overgrown, and we were drenched by rainwater clinging to the leaves. The day was overcast and cold as the inundation of the night before evaporated and billowed up, blocking the sun before gently falling back to float in a mist above our heads. *The breath of the mountain.*

We arrived at the headwaters of Vista Creek as the sun finally broke through the fog, pushing the moisture high into the air, where it dissipated at last. We plopped down in the meadow, drinking volcanic springwater greedily while marmots whistled their alarms from myriad vantages. Adam spread the tent out to dry in the suddenly hot sun, and we reclined with shoes and socks off, eating lunch. There hadn't been many perfect moments on the CYTC, but this was one.

"I'm going to crew you on the CDT." Adam spoke suddenly, firmly. A nearby marmot shrieked and ran for his den.

"What?" I asked, confused. My mind had been roaming through the lupines in front of us and beyond to the distant blue hills.

"I don't want to be apart for another three or four months."

"But you were miserable crewing me," I protested, unsure if I could once again go through the roller coaster of emotion having his help had brought. Only after two thousand miles of backpacking together had our relationship seemed to stabilize. I did not want to set it back.

He shrugged. "I couldn't pretend that I was happy. Telling you how bad I feel is the only way for me to not resent you doing this hike. But I want to see this through with you."

"But your truck is in Pennsylvania!" I grabbed for any limitation that made sense. Sharing his negative feelings might alleviate his resentment, but they were detrimental to my mental state.

"Your car is at Nichole's. I can use that."

I stared back at the field of lupines, watching them bend gently in the breeze and spring back skyward after the zephyr passed. *He was supposed to stay here and use my car to commute to work until I was done, then sell it and meet me in New Mexico. We can't possibly sleep in that sedan together. How on earth is it going to work? It can't drive those Rocky Mountain roads . . .*

"We'll have to take it to a mechanic. It's got almost two hundred thousand miles on it, and I have no idea if it will even handle the roads."

"Of course. We can take a few days at the end of the PCT to get it fixed up and buy supplies before driving to Montana."

I took a deep, slow breath . . . and decided to try embodying the bend and sway of the lupines. Once again, I felt like I was losing control of my hike. I had never meant for anyone to crew me, and I struggled to accept that once again Adam and I would be dancing in these uncomfortable roles. *Maybe after hiking together these last few months we'll be in a better place to work together.*

"Okay, as long as we can afford the repairs we can try it."

Smoke hung thickly in the Lyman Lakes Basin the following afternoon, and I felt my throat grow dry and rasping. The same fears and worries cycled through my mind. *I am so sick of fires. Is this killing me? Will I end up like my dad without ever touching a cigarette?*

I wished for the thousandth time that I had a respirator mask. But whenever I thought about buying one, I told myself the smoke couldn't possibly continue. It had to end at some point. Even as I brooded, I realized that beneath my fears was my grief. *Burning, Washington is burning.* My beloved mountains were on fire and it was heartbreaking.

We reached the tiny religious outpost of Holden in late afternoon. Everything was closed and it was obvious they were struggling to cope with the influx of thru-hikers suddenly infiltrating their "town" now that the Forest Service detour around the Agnes Creek Fire had led us there. Bottles of hand sanitizer and signs requesting it be liberally used were everywhere, and after asking we learned that thru-hikers had already brought—in addition to dollars—a wave of norovirus. I used the sanitizer liberally, and we didn't dally until the restaurant opened in the evening.

Instead, we labored up the rough, steep trail toward the tiny notch of Hilgard Pass. I was exhausted, and here on the east slopes of the crest a previously burnt forest offered us no protection from the fierce setting sun, beating down on us with temps in the nineties. Yet, up we staggered, relentlessly climbing thousands of more feet than we would have on the PCT. *This sucks!*

To take my mind off of the difficulty, I set about mentally mapping this new corner of the Cascades, one of the few places I had never been, marking the peaks towering above us that were on my to-climb list—Devore, Tupshin, Flora, Martin.

"Ugh, finally!" I exclaimed as we reached the narrow, eroded notch. Looking down—nearly vertically—into the Hilgard Creek drainage was dizzying. The narrow, unkempt trail ahead of us spiraled downward in tight switchbacks a thousand feet in a half a mile. My legs were jelly, but we had to keep going. *Miles to go before we sleep . . .*

The trail in the valley below was hardly used, as evidenced by its standard PNW narrowness as well as the overgrowth of vine maple, alder, and thimbleberry bushes. We crashed through the greenery, used to it as Washingtonians, but I felt sorry for the thru-hikers behind us who were accustomed to the wide, clear tread of the PCT.

Unlike the detour near White Pass, this detour meant two full days—at least—of hiking on subpar tread through thick overgrowth. Now on the west side of the crest, we were in shadow and the temperature cooled dramatically as we drew near the playfully tumbling creek. My sweat-drenched clothes dried and I began to feel more comfortable. We replenished ourselves from myriad springs and rivulets sprouting from the hillside—water bound for the creek below and eventually Puget Sound.

"I actually like it back here," Adam said.

I agreed with a grunt. *I'd be enjoying this a lot more if I weren't so tired.*

"I just hope we can find a place to camp. It's hella steep."

The trail traversed high above the creek, contouring along the side of the slope. There was nothing level in sight.

"There's a campsite marked on my map not too far ahead," Adam said.

"Great."

The shadows were lengthening rapidly and I glanced at my phone. *It's going to be dark in an hour.* At that moment an explosion of black burst out of the thimbleberries ahead of us, and we both stopped in surprise. A rotund black bear bolted across the trail, gave us one quick glance, and barreled through the alder toward the creek.

"Uh, let's go," I urged Adam, pushing him slightly. "Before it turns around because it can't go anywhere that way."

My tired legs still found another gear as we surged forward. Sure enough, the narrow valley embankment we'd been hugging suddenly flattened, and within twenty minutes we entered a cathedral of ancient cedars. It was dark enough to need a headlamp, and the thick duff under these giants invited my exhausted body to lie down.

"Think we've gone far enough from the bear?" Adam asked, clearly thinking the same thing.

"No, but I don't care," I said, throwing my pack on the ground. "I'm sleeping here tonight."

TWO DAYS LATER WE STOOD atop Cutthroat Pass surveying the smoky haze blanketing the mountainscape I knew by heart. I turned slowly, my mental map noting where each glacially carved peak should puncture the skyline. Yet, they were all gone, swallowed up by the billows that choked us, made our throats sore, and caused the aching in my lungs that had begun after so many weeks of smoke exposure. Adam slipped his arm around me as tears poured down my cheeks.

"It's all burning," I spluttered, fiercely wiping them away. *I can't bear this turning into a charred skeleton forest like what we walked through in Oregon.*

The next afternoon we sank onto a log in the deep forested gash of Holman Pass and ate lunch. The smell of smoke was stronger than normal, but there was no way to distinguish direction or closeness of it anymore. The air was inundated. We were eighteen miles from the Canadian border and the end of the PCT. If all went well, we'd be done with the trail that night. After our break we climbed high into the alpine basin below Rock Pass. I paused to look back.

"Oh my God!" I pointed to the forest just west of Holman Pass.

"Shit," Adam responded.

An unmistakable black plume rose from the trees near where we'd just taken lunch. It rose fast, growing and spreading rapidly.

"Is it coming this way?" he asked.

"No idea, but now we have to get to Canada tonight. The PCT is going to close right behind us." I surged upward, taking the lead on a climb for the first time in a thousand miles.

What I'd anticipated as a joyful hike with my partner through my favorite landscapes of the Pacific Northwest had become an unrelenting march through burgeoning fires from unknown causes to reach the border. I was grateful we would likely reach the end safely, but my heart ached for the world I knew that was going up in flames all around us.

We reached the terminus monument just before dark after a nearly continuous fifteen-mile push, jubilant as well as melancholy. We walked into the broad clearing hand in hand, brimming with love and accomplishment while behind us fire raged. Ahead, I still had more than twenty-five hundred miles of hiking spread over two trails. We lingered for a few moments cherishing how, despite all of that, in the here and now Adam had become a Triple Crowner and I had just finished my third Pacific Crest Trail thru-hike.

Adam headed into Canada to start setting up our camp at the site a quarter mile away. I tarried in the clear-cut swath, resting my hand on the lowest of the stair-stepped trio of broad wooden pillars marking the end of the trail, one of them bearing the inscription "CANADA TO MEXICO 2627 MILES." My mind replayed the last time I was here, nearly midnight and screaming like a banshee. It was disorienting to be back at a location that represented such a crucial turning point in my life. I'd stood at Monument 78 five times in the last thirteen years. Each journey to reach it had revealed to me new layers of myself. Three of those times I'd arrived after walking there from Mexico. Those hikes had all been unique and full of growth.

I traced my fingers along the smooth edges of the wood, polished from the thousands of hands and feet that had touched it, climbed it. I thought of the thousands behind me somewhere in the smoke. Some of them would reach this marker late in the season, after snow and rain had extinguished the fires blocking access. Others would end their PCT hike less than a hundred miles shy of the long-sought border.

The PCT had changed so much, with the increased erosion, the toilet paper blooms, the campsites carved out of once virgin forest, the shit we'd camped on. But as I stood there in the waning light, I knew I couldn't be upset because change was inevitable, both in the trail and in myself.

In fact, it was my experiences on the PCT that perhaps had the most to do with carving me into the woman I was, standing in the silent clearing.

I never thought I'd hike this trail again when I got here in 2013, yet here I am. It's time to learn to never say never.

I pulled the logbook out of the small metal monument where it lived, wrapped in a plastic bag, and scanned the previous few entries from hikers we hadn't caught up to. Then I clicked the pen and wrote my own words.

"Dear PCT, I will always love you. Your dust and bugs, climbs and forests, your sunsets and mountain vistas. You break my heart and make me fall in love every damn time. For now, though, a trail to the east calls me back to it on a long journey that I'm sometimes not sure I want to complete. No matter the outcome, or whether I walk your path again, I'll hold you in my heart forever. Love, Anish."

THE NEXT FIVE DAYS WERE SPENT resting at a friend's, getting my car repaired to the tune of fifteen hundred dollars, and preparing my supplies. In the midst of the flurry of activity, I retreated to the hammock in Nichole's yard and called my mom.

She was upset. I could tell from the way she talked, more jumbled than usual. While her speech would never return to normal after her massive stroke in 2015, she was usually comprehensible. Now she was talking about Marie, but I couldn't make out what the point was.

"Stop, wait. Mom, take a deep breath. What's going on with Marie?" I asked patiently.

"She was in the yard and got dizzy. So fell down and he had to carry her inside. She's going to the doctor's giving her a skullcap."

I listened carefully, trying to understand exactly what was wrong with my sister.

"But is she going to be okay?"

"Yes, of course."

After we hung up, I lay there staring up into the branches of the massive cedars that held me. Despite my mom's assurance, I felt something inexplicable in my gut, just as I had felt at Jenni's when the Holman Fire was in my unforeseeable future—something that very strongly said Marie was not going to be okay.

I texted her, "Hey, just got off the phone with Mom. She was telling me you are getting treatment for brain lesions and a lump in your lung? Just wanted to check in and see what's going on since I'm never quite sure if I'm getting the details from her right."

I leaned back and waited for a response while my subconscious whispered the unthinkable: *cancer.*

PART III

THE DIVIDE AND CONQUER

CHAPTER 14

MONTANA

Several days of rest felt odd in my body, but I knew it was essential for my mind after more than five months of almost continuous walking—logging thirty-plus miles per day from the late winter cold on the Appalachian Trail into the spring swelter of New Mexico and through the smoky summer heat along the Pacific Crest Trail.

Walking, walking, walking . . . I'd always wanted to walk through all four seasons, the entirety of a year, and now I was finally doing so. Yet, this dream come true was often tainted by the haze of fatigue and the rigorous relentlessness of it. There were days that I hated it, to be completely honest. *It feels like a job.*

Adam piloted my sedan along I-90 as the intermountain desert gave way to the soaring, lush west slopes of the Rocky Mountains. I looked over at him, his tan face watching the road intently as we rode in silence toward the next stage of my fifteen-year-old dream. I'd wanted to hike the Triple Crown in a calendar year since I was twenty-two, when I read about Flyin' Brian Robinson first accomplishing this previously unthinkably difficult feat. Now I was closing in on forty but realizing it's never too late to follow your dreams. I smiled at my partner. While I was nervous that we would fall into the same patterns from the spring, I was also cautiously optimistic that the next few months would be better.

I got out of the car at the southern end of Glacier National Park and charged into the brush beyond the railroad tracks—an ignoble start to hiking one of the premier sections of the CDT. I pushed through the overgrown and gently rolling landscape, making occasional calls for moose and grizzlies. Fully rested and carrying nothing more than a bottle of water and bear spray for the fifteen miles to the next road, I flew rapidly along the trail. I sighed deeply, glad to be back under blue skies and moving toward my goal. Most days, like this one, I was content—content to move through the seasons and the climates one step at a time. *Walking, walking, walking . . .*

I reached the backroads of East Glacier and my phone beeped. I pulled it out, expecting to see an update from Adam. Instead, it was Marie. *Finally, a response to my text!*

"Yeah, felt a little puny went to Dr. Not real good looking at going through a bit. You have your goal ahead, do it!!! Be here when you finish. :)"

I reread it several times. Vaguely reassuring, and yet there was something she wasn't fully disclosing. Her normally perfect grammar and excessive use of emojis were missing. The phrase "Be here when you finish" was a promise that made me worry, because if it needed to be stated, perhaps there was a chance she wouldn't be there when I was done walking.

There's no need to state the obvious. She and mom are hiding something.

My mind was still mulling over her words, attempting to parse subtext, when I reached the main street of East Glacier. Adam called my name from the gravel lot alongside the train tracks. I veered toward him, but before I could voice my concern over my sister he delivered more imminently bad news.

"There's a huge fire burning along the divide in the park. The trail isn't closed right now, but it could close at any minute. It doesn't look good."

I stared at him and then looked west, toward the park. The sky was hazy but not dark.

"Where at?"

"Near Many Glacier."

My mind ranged across its mental map of the park where I had lived and worked for two summers, hiking nearly every trail in the process. If I went in and the trail closed, there were no good options for getting out—at least not without retracing my steps or adding long miles on a road.

Adam held out his phone with the fire map of the region pulled up, and my heart sank. I'd hoped that when I completed the PCT I would finally be free of the fear of fire. Instead, this portion of Montana was lit up like a Lite-Brite. There were fires of varying sizes and levels of containment in all directions.

"Okay, I'll have to come up with a reroute. Let me get to Two Medicine tonight at least."

We slept crammed into the back of the Elantra that night, lowering the back seat and shoving our feet into the trunk. Our sleeping pads overlapped and it was difficult to rearrange all of the gear to fit into the front seats and the foot area of the backseat while we slept, but it was manageable. Fatigued from walking, I slept solidly. Adam did not.

In the morning, I examined paper and digital maps while I drank my coffee, poring over options until I finally determined the most expedient and safest choice. We left the East Glacier train depot and headed for the drop-off point.

Three days later I was back, having connected my way through the park, with a good bit on roads. We reconvened in our trainside sleeping spot, and I sorted through my food supplies to prepare to enter the Bob Marshall Wilderness in the morning. Adam checked the weather, the fire map, alerts, and more while I focused on counting calories. I glanced up when he made a choking noise.

"What now?"

"You're not going to believe this."

My heart sank and I set the box of snack bars down.

"A huge fire is blowing up right in the middle of the Bob. The CDT is closed between here and Benchmark."

I felt like crying. *Will there be no end to fires?* I got out of the car and paced up and down the street, clenching my jaw to keep the tears at bay.

I give up. Seriously. I can't do this. It's aligned against me. All of it. The West is burning and I can't go through. All this time I was worried about the onset of winter, but it's fire that is going to stop me.

I paused at the far end of town across from the post office. The sunset was sublime, painted fuchsia by the particulate matter in the air—all that remained of trees I'd once reclined beneath. I wiped the tears that had made their way onto my cheeks.

"You have your goal ahead, do it!!!"

A cold thought settled in my core. *My sister might be dying and she wants me to do this.* I turned back toward the car. Even if I had to take roads around fires for the rest of the hike, I would finish this.

DAYS LATER, THE SMOKE BEHIND ME, I was thankful to once again be under clear, big, beautiful Montana skies. I walked right along the Continental Divide itself, marveling at the expansiveness of the landscape in clear view. After six weeks of hiking in smoke, experiencing endless headaches and choking on bloody phlegm, I was grateful to be able to take belly-deep inhalations of clean air.

I paused and tilted my face to the brilliant sun, grateful for its warmth on a cold morning. Late August at seven thousand feet in northern Montana was chilly, even with unobstructed sunshine. The trail followed the ridgeline for miles, dropping and rising with the swells of the land. I loved this segment from deep in the Scapegoat Wilderness snaking southward to Stemple Pass. I relished the quiet rhythm of my feet and breath as I moved with the day. I passed some northbound thru-hikers that I'd met in Pie Town so long ago, feeling the circularity of my endeavor.

The trail near Stemple Pass had changed since I'd first come through twelve years before. The new route led away from reliable water sources and added elevation gain and loss. The prior summer when Adam and I had hiked through, I'd felt confused but certain we hadn't gone the way it said on the app. Without my needing to look at maps, my mind accessed its archive of trail memory. I made turns onto less traveled trails, old dirt roads, and newer ones. I drank my fill from several gushing springs in this notoriously dry stretch. *Your old routes may not be traveled much anymore, but don't worry, I remember them.*

I walked leisurely along the dirt roads as evening shadows cooled the edges. I crossed a cattle guard where the rambling official route rejoined my own and soon passed a recently decommissioned fire line. The forest beyond was coated red and I tied my bandana around my face, unwilling to breathe in the flame-retardant dust as I walked. But I was grateful it was here, ensuring this thick forest remained intact.

The trail was clear and twilight was lingering. At last, I decided to pitch my tent along the trail beneath a venerable pine. I set up my gear for the night before lying down to scroll through the app and refresh my memory about the route ahead.

The soft sound of footsteps approaching caught my ear and I sat up, alert. *Grizzly? No, only two feet . . .*

"Hello?" I asked the pitch black.

"Oh, hey!" a man's voice responded as he stopped just outside my tent.

"Sorry, my guy lines are right on the edge of the trail," I apologized. "I didn't think anyone would be coming through after dark." *Or be brave enough to night-hike in grizzly country?*

"No worries. Hey, which way are you going?"

"SoBo."

"Can I ask you a question about water?"

"Sure."

"So, did you drop down the half-mile side trail up ahead here to get water? I'm pretty much out."

"No. This section is really stupidly routed away from water. If you take the old CDT you'll walk by two perennial sources."

He paused. "So, I don't see an alternate on the app . . . "

I laughed. "No, it's not on there. I've just hiked through here a few times."

"Ah."

"If you zoom into the base map I can walk you through it."

Step by step I talked him through the simple alternate and the location of the water sources.

"Wow, thanks. That's so great. Oh, and I'm Passerby," he introduced himself.

"Nice to meet you and glad I can help. I'm Anish."

He began to laugh, deep and resonant. "I should have known."

We bid each other goodnight and good luck and I lay there listening to his quiet footfalls receding northward, knowing that my legend probably just grew a tiny bit more. I smiled and returned to calculating whether I could reach MacDonald Pass the next day. *It's gonna be a long haul, but I can probably make it if I get going early and try to take the old route through there . . .* I trailed my finger along the phone as I calculated. *The road section near the end is flat and fast. I can probably just crank it out.* I snuggled deeper into my bag. I could feel the breath of winter settling over the nights, its frosty exhalations blanketing the meadows in the mornings.

Late the next afternoon, I reached Microwave Hill Road and gazed into the valley that held Elliston far below. *All downhill from here!* I texted Adam as I drew on all my reserve strength to propel myself downhill at four mph. *This is it. Six months on the trail . . . longer than I've ever hiked all at once.* My feet ached from the many miles of dirt road already walked, but my heart soared with excitement as the golden evening light drenched everything. *Five thousand miles!*

My mind was hopeful in this moment, despite all the hardships and fire setbacks. *All I can do is keep eating, drinking, and walking. Either I will succeed or I won't. But I will have to be okay with it either way and trust the process of going until I can't anymore. "You've got your goal ahead of you, do it!"*

Adam was parked at the pass as I popped out of the woods and dashed across the highway. Dusk was falling and I jumped into the car, grateful to sit down for the first time all day.

"I'm so happy to see you!" I said, squeezing his hand.

"Me too." He leaned over and kissed my cheek. "Do you want the good news or the bad news first?"

"What now?" My joy evaporated. I was hungry, thirsty, exhausted, and exhilarated from covering almost forty miles before dark. I didn't want *any* bad news.

"Good news first, then. I got you Wendy's." He handed me a bag of fast food and a Frosty, which I immediately began devouring as he steered the car toward the campground. "Bad news is there is a massive fire in the Anaconda-Pintler and south. You're going to have to hike through Butte. And if it spreads . . ." He trailed off as he pulled into a campsite.

I swallowed the last of the third cheeseburger. "We figure out a plan C."

Perhaps more than anything else on this hike, I was learning that there was no true right or wrong, black or white when it came to making trail decisions. I could only make the best choice I could with the information I had at that time. Adam was a boon with his many hours a day available to research other trails and monitor the fire map and the weather. I took his assessments under advisement, held them in my heart, and made my choices—sometimes in direct opposition to what he wanted me to do. He usually lobbied for the shortest, fastest route to get me done sooner. I had other criteria that I felt were more important, such as sticking to the divide as closely as possible. Ultimately, whether my choice panned out didn't really matter, because in the end I couldn't expect anything more of myself than just to do my best—my best decision making, my best effort.

This was the crux of the difficulty, and the crux of the lesson I sensed I was supposed to learn from this experience. As someone who likes to control every aspect of my life—to run it by spreadsheets, by rules, and by structure—I found this hike to be a nightmare. Accepting and adapting to trail closures was a hard pill to swallow, but I was getting better at it.

UNLIKE THE APPALACHIAN TRAIL, the CDT has large tracts that are inaccessible by car—especially a compact sedan with barely enough clearance to go over a speed bump. If I saw Adam once a day, I considered myself very lucky. Typically, I traveled two to four days between our meetings. He bought my food in towns and brought it to me, switched out gear and clothes, did my laundry and all of the chores that typically take time away from hiking so that I could maximize my walking time. When he wasn't doing that, he roved the region climbing peaks.

His ability to go do things that interested him in between supporting me kept his resentment at bay, although I could still sense his frustration when I would arrive at a trailhead exhausted when he had been waiting for hours and was ready for activity and conversation. Steadily I made my way southward, treading the same path I'd walked with him barely a year prior. The days were still hot, even though the nights kissed freezing. The trail alternated between dense pine forests and magical wide-open places, where the sky stretched to its limit across the rolling landscape below.

These portions of the trail where I felt as though I could touch the far horizon and the sun made me shimmer and shine, a glimmering speck in the vastness, were my favorite. The hillsides looked like soft green pillows inviting me to sink into them. But the horizon was always elusive, calling from unmeasurable distances. The hills—when reached—were rocky, rough, and covered in sage that caught at my skin and clothes, reminding me that I did not shimmer and shine. I sweated and trudged. But therein lay the magic—the juxtaposition of physical reality and the feeling of the moment. Despite the effort and rugged reality, these wide-open skies allowed me to relinquish temporal discomfort and embrace the heavens.

The fires grew larger in the late season heat and dryness. I circled Butte on the official route, rather than the much shorter Anaconda route that most thru-hikers walked. Adam crewed me several times a day as I walked on the fringes of the sprawling city. The trail was mostly dirt roads that were readily accessed by any vehicle. The route was much longer, yet by swinging farther east I avoided the worst of the smoke from the fires. At night we pored over maps and discussed options, all the while referencing the constantly changing fire maps. Eventually the CDT would swing back west—all the way to Idaho—and into the brunt of the smoke and fires. We painstakingly plotted a route that followed the detours combined with obvious alternatives that stayed as close as possible to the divide, knowing that with a shift in wind direction it could all change.

We parted ways for an extended period after I left the city.

"Be careful," Adam said, holding me tight against him. The air was already thick with smoke, the sun obliterated by unnatural gray clouds.

"I will. See you in four days." I hoisted my backpack, heavy with water. Since I would be following a detour rather than the official route, no information was available about sources. I was trusting my instincts to find either natural springs or cattle tanks. "Be careful on Borah." I kissed him on the cheek.

He nodded, getting into the car and heading for the Idaho high point he intended to climb. I turned and headed toward the smoky divide.

Twice before, I had walked this trail with someone else, but there was always a sense deep down that I must brave the CDT solo someday. Traverse these wild mountains alone and unarmed, singing for the grizzlies, wolves, and mountain lions that roamed there—inhabitants that might see me as fellow predator or as prey, which one was completely out of my control. The stream of northbound hikers had run dry, and I was completely alone in the vast wilderness. The days I didn't meet Adam, I saw no one. It was in these periods of solitude that I learned to accept, deep in my bones, the fragility of my thread in the fabric of nature. I walked alone—singing for bears—on a trail that had taught me that until you are lost you cannot know what it is to be found.

CHAPTER 15

YELLOWSTONE

I woke from a sound sleep with an urgent voice in the back of my brain screaming *Bear!*

I pulled out my earplugs and lay there in the dark almost-silence, hearing nothing but the patter of raindrops on my tent and Adam's rhythmic breathing beside me. The prickling hair on my neck relaxed, and I eventually fell back into a fitful sleep for a few more hours, not waking until gray light prodded me. I traded my sleeping clothes for my hiking ones and threw what I needed for the day into my backpack, grateful that Adam would meet me for the night again, reducing my pack weight and the amount of time I would be camping solo in the heart of grizzly country.

The dreamlike bear scare from the night before still lingered in my mind as I unzipped the tent and clambered out. I closed the door and stretched, deeply inhaling the cold, clean air in our remote dispersed campsite on the edge of the park. Glancing down, I noticed a trail of massive paw tracks passing through our campsite within feet of our tent. The now-validated fear cascaded down my spine like ice water as I looked around intently. All was quiet except for a few muzzily chirping birds, reluctant to start their morning.

I knelt to study the tracks. The prints were clearly grizzly and longer than my size eleven feet. As my alarm faded, I noticed something else surfacing—incredible gratitude. Even as a very small part of nature, I knew without a shadow of a doubt that I possess a primitive, instinctual self—one I now knew I could trust to keep me alive. I opened the car, got my food bag out, and began my day of walking.

My mind pondered the experience of the night before, reaffirming my belief that in order to truly find my humanity I needed to embrace my instinctual, animal self. Every day I spent in the backcountry peeled away the layers of separateness between modern culture and nature, bringing me closer to not only my place in the natural world but also the part of me that has evolved over millennia to survive there as a human. The self-centeredness of western culture faded away. Here I was simply part of the whole.

The sun crested the treetops, but it failed to warm me, even as I hiked quickly. I tugged the collar of my lightly insulated jacket up and tried to turtle my chilly face into it. The stained blue garment was worn thin and so was I. The ups and downs of the last six months—both literally and mentally—had exhausted me. I crunched along the frosty trail, alone in one of the most popular national parks. Sometimes I was giddy with the joy of being in the mountains. Other times I wasn't. I thought back to several of my hangry meltdowns on the PCT and cringed. Then there were times—like now—when my emotions were flat. Anxiety about my sister, about the impending winter, about the continued stress on my relationship with Adam overloaded my system to the point that I felt numb.

I wrapped my arms around my chest, even though doing so made it awkward to hike. I could feel the topography of my ribcage through my jacket. *I'm just so cold.*

I thought back to the mirror at Nichole's. It had been shocking to see that I was now almost as thin as I had been after my FKTs—when I'd dropped 6 percent of my body fat, landing me at the bottom edge of the healthy range for a woman. The few pounds of reserve remaining would continue to dwindle as I burned calories at altitude in the cold, logging mile after mile.

What if I am reduced to just the strength of the calories I consume, like I was at the end of my FKTs when I had to eat just to go up a hill?

At least I knew that farther south Adam would be able to access me at more trailheads, and Apple Pie planned to crew me on the final leg of the AT. I would be able to eat more and carry less. *I hope that's enough.*

Remembering that Adam was somewhere behind me with the car sent another pang of worry through me. I was wearing thin financially, too, having spent my entire CDT budget on fixing up my old car. The rest of the CYTC would be funded out of my meager emergency savings.

Was it the right decision to fix the car? I shook my head, trying to clear the ruminations.

There wasn't really a way to know if it was right, but each time I arrived at a trailhead and saw Adam waiting for me, I felt like it was. Being able to see him every few days was a huge morale boost that counteracted the blues that swelled as my blood sugar sank. Not to mention all the ways his support eased the physical effort of the hike itself. *I'm so grateful for him, even if it's been challenging.*

A shaft of sunlight broke through the forest and bathed me in warm autumnal light. I tipped my face up to meet it with gratitude. *I might be wearing out in many ways, but I'm committed to finishing what I started, even if weather drives me off the divide and it becomes a journey of connecting steps. Even if I'm broke at the end. Even if Adam and I will never be the same.*

I exhaled deeply and kept walking.

We spent subsequent nights in campgrounds, the illusion of safety in numbers lulling us until the evening I sat at a picnic table eating canned soup, which felt luxurious after so many freeze-dried meals. A campground host came by to check our registration and go over food storage policies. We listened politely.

"Where you hiking?" he asked.

"Continental Divide Trail," I answered, slurping the last of my soup.

"Hmm," he made a noise that indicated he had something more to add. I looked up expectantly. "Just so you know, a grizzly killed a man and mauled another out there the day before yesterday. Real unheard of. They're looking for the bear now but haven't found it yet. Best be extra careful."

I nodded calmly, but the soup churned in my stomach. Trekking through the greater Yellowstone ecosystem always meant proximity to grizzlies, but I'd not seen one on this hike. My voice was raspy from the amount of singing and yelling I'd been doing. There had certainly been moments that I'd *felt* a bear nearby, but gut feelings—even though I trusted them—weren't always accurate.

Mrs. Parker's third grade science lessons passed through my mind. I remembered my fascination with her deck of food chain flashcards—I borrowed them whenever I could and spent my recesses constructing complex interconnected webs from plant to apex predator. My curiosity was piqued by the vast interrelatedness of flora and fauna, spurring me to find every combination, to see the story of nature mapped out via cards imprinted with line drawings and factoids.

Mrs. Parker encouraged it, but time and again she chastised me for adding a bear or wolf above the man.

"No, humans are always the apex predator. Nothing goes above them," she'd say, pulling the wolf or grizzly card away.

"We don't eat bears or wolves," I protested, resolutely putting them back. "But if they're hungry, they'd eat us."

She paused, then shook her head, reasserting her assessment of the order of nature. She gathered the cards up and eventually stopped letting me play with them. Unwittingly I'd threatened the deeply rooted anthropocentric view of nature that she held—a view I instinctively did *not* hold.

September was a tense time to pass through grizzly habitat. The bears were completely immersed in hyperphagia—eating as much as possible to gain enough fat to last through the winter. I shuddered slightly, remembering a fact I'd learned working for the National Park Service. *A grizzly needs to consume twenty thousand calories a day during hyperphagia. The average human body stores approximately twenty thousand calories.* I slid my hands down my sunken abdomen. I'd be only about fifteen thousand at this point. I smiled morbidly at the thought.

The next section of trail, south of US 26, was remote and generally incomplete. Though lines existed on the maps, there was little in the way of good trail or markings. On each of my previous hikes, I'd taken different routes. Both had resulted in tremendous amounts of heinous bushwhacking. I'd marked a new idea on my phone, utilizing a series of forest roads to bypass the bushwhack sections. I hoped that perhaps this route would be more traveled and decrease my odds of stumbling into a hyperphagic bear ready to assert itself at the top of the food chain.

CHAPTER 16

BRIDGER-TETON

I reluctantly got out of the car the next morning, afraid of what I was about to walk into. In 2006 I'd spent the entirety of a day lost in the upcoming maze of roads and unbroken forest. Last year we'd stumbled into a matrix of baited grizzly traps and fled without running, hearts pounding with adrenaline, legs demanding the opposite. And this time, in addition to the potential for bear encounters, a billowing column of smoke towered. Without internet for the last several days, we didn't know where it was or whether it would impede my progress.

It looks like it's in the Gros Ventre. I guessed the location from where we'd watched it the night before.

Uncertain if Adam would be at the Green River trailhead, I made my way down the dirt road, mentally assessing the food in my backpack. *I can ration to South Pass City if I must, but it would be painful, gnawing. I guess I could go down to the Big Sandy Lodge and beg.*

The sky was barely light, but thankfully dawn came fast here. The cold September air left me longing for the first rays to bathe me and thaw my benumbed fingertips. A rumbling noise brought my head up from studying the myriad footprints in the dust, searching for bear tracks between the tire marks. A silver extended cab pickup slowly bounced toward me. I lifted my fingers slightly in acknowledgment as it drew abreast. To my surprise, the truck stopped. I paused as the driver's window rolled down, revealing a man in his late sixties behind the wheel. A younger man sat beside him, and there was at least one other in the backseat.

I momentarily panicked at the realization that a truck full of men had stopped me in the middle of nowhere. Instinctively my fingers grazed my bear spray, but with the driver's hello I sensed no danger. My hands slid back to my sides, where I tucked them into my hip belt for warmth.

"Good morning," I responded. They were wearing camo and I noted no elk in the back. "No luck?" I waved at the empty truck bed.

"Nope. We're heading home." The driver paused and studied me. "Are you hiking?"

"Yes. The Continental Divide Trail. It goes from Canada to Mexico." His face registered knowledge of the route. "Have you seen any other hikers?"

"No, all we've seen are bears. A lot of bears."

"Oh." I felt the familiar rising tide of adrenaline in my veins. Bears here never meant *Ursus americanus*. It only referred to grizzlies. "Where were you hunting?"

"Pelham Lake."

"That's where I'm headed."

I hadn't meant to say it aloud. *Well, not the lake itself, but the area . . .*

"I've been hunting here for forty-five years. I've never seen this many bears. One killed a hunter two days ago over by Togwotee. It's damn eerie out here this year."

"I heard that." No wonder the people at the camp the night before had all seemed on edge. "I have my bear spray."

He smiled faintly. "You're braver than a truck full of grown men with two weapons apiece."

I shrugged, uncertain what to say. Brave or foolhardy? But then I noticed a new expression dawning on his face, one I'd longed to see on my father's.

Pride.

"Good luck," he said sincerely, touching his hat.

"Thank you," I replied, smiling with more certainty than I felt, buoyed by his expression.

I nodded farewell and headed on into the wilderness, shoulders square and head high, jaw set as though my dad were in the truck watching me resolutely face my fears.

I reached a junction just past the lake. Blue CDT markers glinted at me, beckoning. I pulled out my maps and studied them while chewing on a granola bar. The alternate I'd marked continued on the dirt road for a while longer before crisscrossing through several other roads as it wound toward Fish Lake Mountain. *Once there I should be able to cut cross-country over to the ridgeline proper, thus avoiding the meandering S-curve of the main route and the horrific slog through flooded and unmarked meadows the lower route went through.*

I continued on the road, seeing more cow tracks than anything else. At every junction I cross-referenced my GPS to ensure I was on the right track. The Bridger-Teton National Forest was a labyrinth of unmarked and unmapped roads and trails. Despite my passing through in the height of the hunt, the forest was remarkably untrammeled by humankind.

Everyone has run scared. What am I doing out here?

After several hours, I drew close to an arterial forest road. Blocking my way were two pickups pointed in opposing directions. Their occupants were chatting loudly over the dull growl of the engines. "Bear," "killed," "grizz"—the words drifting to my ears told me that they were engaged in the same conversation I'd had this morning. The same one that every hunter in the area was having. I slowed as I approached, but no one seemed to notice me. So I veered off the road on the right, passing close by the open passenger window of one truck.

"Holy shit," a man yelled, my motion so close by causing him to recoil in terror, hitting his head on the ceiling in the process.

I didn't stop, but I heard nervous laughter trickling out of the windows.

After I crossed a river and started to climb along a secondary road, I began to understand their heightened fear. Cow and vehicle tracks gave way to myriad grizzly tracks in the dust. The pine forest was dry and quiet—not even a bird or squirrel broke the silence—yet a pervasive sense that I was being watched enveloped me. The morning chill had dissipated into rising heat. I was low on water, uncertain where the next creek would be on this exploratory route. My throat, dry and coated with dust, rasped when I tried to call out.

"Hey, bears!"

I had sung for bears over thousands of miles, but here my strangled voice hurt my ears. A preternaturally silent forest set me on edge, the absence of sound nearly always an indication of a predator lurking. Shattering it with a bold announcement of my presence frayed my taut nerves. *I wish I could slink through quietly, unnoticed.* But surprising a bear was considered the most dangerous thing one could do. So I continued my auditory heraldry, even as I identified a tree fifty yards away that was sturdy enough to climb, yet supple enough to eschew the weight of a large bruin. As I drew even with it, I called again . . . and selected the next *Pinus* candidate. *Grizz* can *climb trees, but would I be worth it to them? Only if they're angry—or hungry—enough.*

I stopped my mind's debate with itself; I didn't like the answers. Instead, I focused on syncing my breath with my footfalls.

I kept my eyes on the horizon as I trudged steadily upward, calling out from climbable tree to climbable tree. If there were bears in the forest, I did not want to see them. Without eye contact or weapons, I hoped my intent was clear.

"I'm only passing through," I sang out, the words cut off by a sharp fit of coughing.

Unarmed and intent, I steadily made my way higher in elevation, still not seeing anyone. I passed several hunter camps marked on my maps, each with large, unused fire pits and carcass-hanging crossbeams twenty feet in the air. *All abandoned.* The air cooled and I checked the time—nearly five in the evening. I'd been moving for eleven hours, unwilling to stop, determined to make it to the other side of Fish Lake Mountain and back onto the official route by nightfall. The hairs on my arms and neck prickled. It could have been the now crisp undertone of the breeze at more than eight thousand feet, or something I refused to see lingering outside my periphery.

Only a few nights ago my primitive brain had awakened me, alerting me to danger. Perhaps now it was doing so again. Unable to resist, I stopped, whirling fast. There was nothing in the road. No movement in the trees. Yet, there was a sound. Minute. Nearly imperceptible and moving not far uphill. I resumed walking, my quads tingling, ice and fire pouring from my guts into their fibers. The faint sound was now drowned out by the thudding of my heart in my temples and my unbidden increased respiration. My body was primed to race to the next tree I'd selected.

"Hello bear, I'm only passing through," I called more softly than normal. Reining in my primal somatic response and maintaining composure, I glided up the road, still moving three miles per hour despite my body's desire to run.

A short distance later I turned off of the road onto a trail, the final stretch connecting me back to the CDT. The sudden narrowness felt claustrophobic. *I can't see!* The woods felt like they were closing in on me, hiding something stalking me. The only footprints in the dust were of bears, as they had been on the roads. I began to feel as though I were the only human left in the forest. All of my kind were wise enough to let the hyperphagic animals gorge without disruption.

"Hey, bear!"

Soon the trees began to thin and the trail became faint. I followed its remnants out of the pines and into a vast meadowy expanse. The straw-colored grass was stained rose gold by the sinking sun hovering a few degrees above the western horizon. I exhaled deeply. The farther from the tree line I moved, the more my apprehension and adrenaline ebbed, even though my vertical escape options dwindled. I waded through the knee-high grass along a gentle slope, guided by my GPS and the obvious terrain. Atop the prominent knoll of Fish Lake Mountain, I met a thin dirt path ascending from a verdant valley far below. I recognized it as the junction of the former CDT and the more modern route. I'd been here before.

Leaving the grass for a rock-littered trail, I continued along the thread of pale brown as it grew thicker. Here I could see the looming fire cloud presiding over the entirety of my upcoming path, causing me to momentarily forget my ursine fears. *On toward the next challenge.*

Though the smoke dominated the view, it did not obscure the immense panorama. I paused and gazed eastward toward where the mountains began to flatten into the high desert amid the haze of distance. I turned my face west and took in the blue braided ridges separating me from Jackson Hole and the Tetons. *I am so grateful to be here.*

I strode along the spine of the poorly defined ridge bathed in sunlight, feeling immense relief to have passed through the grizzly gauntlet. Every step took me closer to the fringe of their territory. I'd survived.

"I survived." I spoke the words aloud, manifesting my reality and calming myself at the same time.

I was completely out of water now, my throat sore from calling out without rewetting. My legs trembled violently with the emotion of the day, dissipating all of the pent-up adrenaline in my newly perceived safety.

"I've walked through blizzards and heat. Past hungry bears and through fire. Are you proud of me yet?" I yelled, my throat burning with the outburst.

Tears slid down my cheeks as my whole body began to shake. The encounter with the men in the truck that morning had reminded me that I'd been chasing my father's approval my entire life. My FKTs, my first marriage, my grades in school. Everything I'd done to simply hear him say he was proud of me.

"What did I need to do to prove myself to you, Dad?"

Asking now was irrelevant. I would never know the answer. Why hadn't I asked before? If it was, as I was beginning to understand, the motivation beneath every choice I'd made, why had I waited until it was too late?

"Because deep down I was afraid the answer was no," I answered myself in a whisper that was barely audible above the crunch of my footfalls.

I was not brave enough to ask him for what I needed. His body was ash now; his spirit had gone somewhere else, and the only thing I could do was finally let go.

Tears came in earnest now as my shadow grew long across the golden grass. The ever-closer column of smoke loomed black and ominous, its belly stained pink and orange by the sinking sunlight.

I began to descend off of the ridge, down toward sure water at last, knowing that I needed to let go of my lifelong question. I must accept that I would never have an answer. That I had to instead, bravely ask new questions . . . and bravely answer them myself. Ashes began to fall, softly caressing my skin.

Darkness crept toward me along the dirt road. I hastened my steps, aching to reach Lake of the Woods before a headlamp was necessary. In the violet distance I heard the faint sound of voices and an engine. There were people somewhere nearby, probably car camping. Suddenly I was less afraid of the falling darkness, but now a new consideration was necessary. If I continued, I'd encounter people. I'd need to evaluate whether I felt safe sleeping near them. If not, I'd have to press on into the night until I found a different place to camp.

Aloneness was comfortable, easy. Drained by the day, I didn't feel as though I could muster the intuition needed to make a choice—or the energy to walk farther if my gut instinct told me to. Decision made, I dropped down off the dirt road through scraggly bushes and into a copse of trees.

Without light I established my tent by feel. I crawled inside, zipping the world out with an exhausted sigh. While I was removing my shoes, the sound of an ATV roaring by on the road filled my tent with unwelcome sound. I peered through the mesh door and watched it. I wasn't far from the road, yet I thought I was invisible to anyone on it. They didn't slow down. Satisfied that I was truly hidden, I unpacked the contents of my backpack—sustenance not just for my growling belly but also a few pieces of gear, the things that protected me from the elements. I quickly boiled water for my dehydrated meal. Nighttime silence, unlike the eerie quietude of the day, settled thickly around me as I ate. I could no longer hear the sounds of those I'd sought to avoid by camping here. *Perhaps they weren't camped, just out for the day.*

Full of hot food, I lay back onto my mat, snuggling deeply into the down encasing me. Moonlight illuminated half of the tent, and in its beams I could see my breath spiraling upward, creating delicate frost motifs on the green nylon. I felt my mind drifting toward blankness when a howl crashed through the silver silence. I sat up, heart racing. More howls responded to the first, closer than I'd ever experienced. Over and over, I heard their songs, calling to one another as they drew a wide circle around my tent. The choice to camp alone suddenly seemed less wise.

After I had listened for five minutes, the howls moved away and my heart rate dropped. I sank back again, content that the scent of my humanness was enough to deter the wild hunters.

"Am I brave enough for you, Dad?" I whispered.

The wolves chorused an opaque response in the distance, and I fell asleep while trying to suss out the answer.

CHAPTER 17

WIND RIVER RANGE

I followed wolf and black bear tracks up the indistinct trail from my campsite through a boggy landscape and eventually along a defined drainage to the narrow top of Gunsight Pass. Sitting on a wooden fence, I ate a snack bar and checked my phone. Nothing. *I'm hours late.*

Far below me the Green River Lakes shimmered, looking much closer than eight trail miles away. The fire cloud loomed nearly due west, far off of my route but near the roads accessing the trailhead below. I drank the last of my water, knowing there was plenty more on the descent, and charged down the rough trail. *I hope Adam is down there.*

I made the hairpin turn at the Roaring Fork, my pace quickening into a bit of a jog. I was so far behind schedule I anticipated seeing Adam making his way up toward me at any minute. But, even two miles later, I was still alone in the woods.

What if he couldn't get back here? What if the fire closed the road? What if I'm trapped? Anxious thoughts raced through my head. I had some extra food but not enough to get all the way through the Winds without rationing. *Maybe I can cross the range westward straight to South Pass City? Would that be shorter? Is that even possible?* I forced myself to focus on the here and now after I tripped for the third time, twisting my knee.

I finally halted my somewhat reckless pace to open the large gate across the trail a mile from the trailhead junction. I went through and hurried toward the pedestrian footbridge that veered away from the

CDT to a large dirt parking lot where I could see many cars. I slowed to a walk, relieved that meant the road was not closed due to the fire. If Adam wasn't here, I could still get out.

Halfway across the bridge I saw my car, and Adam rummaging in the trunk.

"Adam!" I called out, relieved and also irrationally annoyed that he was perfectly fine after all my conjured fears.

"Hey!" He hurried over and enveloped me in a huge hug. "I was starting to get worried."

"Me too! I thought I'd see you up by the Roaring Fork."

"I did ten laps out and back to that first switchback already. I was just making something to eat before I did any more."

I dropped my pack on the ground and looked at him hopefully. "Eat?"

"Do you want some pasta?"

I nodded and sat down in the passenger seat while he cooked my dinner. It was only four o'clock. I could easily hike to the nice campsites alongside the second Green River Lake, but I was mentally worn out from the previous day and wanted to stay put. I propped my feet up on the dashboard just as Adam appeared with a pot full of gluten-free pasta. I dug in gratefully.

"So, that fire we saw is on the other side of the highway. I had to drive through the smoke. What a mess. Firefighters everywhere and pace vehicles in place. I ended up going all the way down to Pinedale and hanging out there. I didn't want to go back through that. But you aren't in any danger from it."

I nodded. The acrid scent of smoke tinged the air, but it was nothing compared to the unbearable smoke I'd already hiked through in the past two months.

"And I found out the guy the grizzly killed was hunting. The bear was after the elk carcass, not him."

I sighed, feeling some of the tension melt away. There were not supposed to be grizzlies in the Winds, but telling wild animals where they were allowed to be was a fool's errand. *That detail makes the attack more logical.* I thought of Mrs. Parker and her firm belief that bears didn't eat people. Maybe she was a little right.

"How was the route you took? Better than the one we did last year? I mean, anything had to be better than that," Adam said ruefully. I chuckled, remembering the stench of the baited grizzly traps we'd found while bushwhacking through dense vegetation.

"Oh my God, it was so much better. I mean, I was scared. There was no one out there and I felt like I was being watched all day, but the roads were obvious, marked, and direct. They dumped me right out up top where I rejoined the route. Easiest traverse of the Bridger-Teton I've done. I don't know why the CDT doesn't use it."

I finished my pasta. "Thank you so much. That was delicious. Where are you heading next?"

"I'm going to stay here tonight, then I'll head over to Lander. There's some dispersed camping on the east side of the Winds over there. You heading out soon?"

"I probably should, but I'd rather stay here with you. Is that okay?" I wasn't certain why, but I was suddenly worried that he'd say no to my company.

"Of course! I think we can set a tent up over there." He waved his hand vaguely behind him. "So then, three days to South Pass City?"

"I should be able to do that. It's just over a hundred miles." The truth was that thirty-five miles per day through the steep, rugged, high-elevation Wind River Range didn't sound like something I could do right now, but I also didn't want to carry more than three days' worth of food in addition to the new down coat, warmer sleeping bag, and insulated sleeping pad I was going to lug out of there. "I'm tired." I reclined the seat and tried not to think.

AS I STEADILY CLIMBED into the alpine world of rock, the shrubs and few deciduous trees—aspens mainly—covering the hillsides morphed from emerald to gold. Ruddy huckleberry bushes offered tasty bites that I plucked with my indigo-stained fingers as I walked. Between the beauty and the harvest, I was reminded why September is quite likely my favorite month in the mountains. I reached Cube Rock Pass and drank in the unfettered view of pale gray peaks sprawling across the landscape in front of me. Beyond the vista, the trail became rougher as I hopped boulder to boulder toward the source of the Green River. *This route might be slower even though it's shorter*, I thought as I picked my way across the pure alpine terrain. I made my way over a secondary pass on an old CDT route I remembered. The panoramas were mind blowing, and the terrain—though slightly technical—was familiar. I felt at home in the rocky off-trail world.

I rejoined the official CDT on the Highline Trail, one of the main routes through this part of the range, its tread wider and more worn by the passage of many thousands of feet. The trail wound downhill past several lakes before ascending once again toward Lester Pass. Here the trail was bone dry and dusty. Each of my footfalls sent little puffs into the air, coating my legs as I followed phantom footprints of southbound hikers I would never see. At such perfect mountain moments, it was hard to remember that I'd been walking for most of a year.

I POUNDED ALONG THE DIRT ROADS south of the Winds, anxious that Adam would be wondering where I was. *The mileages are way off on the Big Sandy route.* I tried to dismiss my frustration at the hours lost making my way through mixed meadow and aspens on indistinct trails the afternoon before. For the most part, time didn't exist for me when I was walking, aside from two moments—sunrise and sunset. But when I thought about how things around me had changed—the weather, the fact that there was more gray in my partner's beard than when he had slipped a ring on my finger back in March, as well as my physical changes—it become completely obvious. Now as my stomach growled, reminding me that I had eaten the last of my food many hours ago for breakfast, I was poignantly reminded of the time that had elapsed in an otherwise timeless trek through the Wind River Range.

South Pass City was almost twenty miles away from where I'd camped. I focused on moving quickly, afraid that if I stopped, I wouldn't find the energy to get back up. I felt a bit like Rip Van Winkle. Except that rather than falling asleep for a hundred years, I'd gone into the woods and started walking. *How long have I been out here? Almost seven months?*

It's hard to fathom that I've actually been hiking for this long. It seems like I've only been out for a few weeks. Yet, my connection through texts to the external world provided concrete evidence that family and friends had remarried, birthed babies, remodeled houses, gone back to school—life events that did not happen in a flash.

And what about Marie? Am I missing the last few months I have to truly get to know my sister?

Life had gone on in the other world without me, and I couldn't help but wonder if it had been worth it. *Or should I have done something, anything, else instead?*

On the horizon line a glimmering flash caught my eye, followed by another. Sunlight was glinting off of cars on the highway to Lander. *At last!* I accelerated, my cramping legs complaining in a duet with my stomach. *I hope Adam will be there rather than in South Pass.*

I was slightly dizzy from hunger and thirst. Despite the protests in my legs, I could feel the strength of my body as it rallied to my request—not just to reach food and water, but to fulfill a great dream.

The reality is that I will never know if I should have done something else. I can't know. Because I didn't do anything else. I came out here and I walked. And whether it was worth it for me to hike these three trails all in one year isn't an answerable question. All I know is that I have followed my heart to do something I have always wanted to do—and that has to be enough.

I saw a familiar form jogging along the trail toward me, and I smiled with cracked lips. Accepting where my heart led me without questioning if it was right or wrong was perhaps the truest thing I could learn to do in this life. We embraced, and I vowed to never question this journey again.

CHAPTER 18

GREAT DIVIDE BASIN

"Sunrise waits for no one," I said to myself, dropping my half-packed tent and running to the best vantage on the molten arrival of the daystar.

The world around me slipped from navy to indigo as the horizon lit—seemingly from somewhere inside the planet—with russet, then orange, then gold and saffron layers of light. Lavender clouds couldn't stop the burst of radiation that came upon the morning with such intensity that I had to quickly look away, even as I attempted to take a picture.

I lowered my phone and stood in awestruck silence, ignoring the sound of my tent flapping behind me, mesmerized by the sheer beauty of dawn in the expansive terrain of the Great Divide Basin. The sun melted the inky skies overhead, now blazing bright and warm from horizon to horizon, and I returned to breaking camp. I noted the water levels in my various bottles and bladders and assessed whether rationing would be necessary to get me to the fenced spring ten miles ahead. While there were cow ponds of questionable integrity in between, I was loath to drink from them.

Reassured that I had enough, I set out across the barren, deserted landscape. The basin was home to stunted sage, wild horses, and range cattle. Formed by the unusual aspect of the Continental Divide splitting in two, the Great Divide Basin was a no-man's-land where what little rainwater fell stayed put rather than finding its way to the sea. The CDT skirted along its eastern edge, where perennial springs and cattle tanks were present—albeit few and far between. Beneath the ground lay stores of uranium and other valuable compounds, making this forsaken wasteland highly valuable to modern-day humans. Lands passed over as unsuited to bringing forth crops when the Homestead Act held sway were now being steadily chunked out and sold to those who would lay claim to their buried treasure.

Wild horses approached, snorting and pawing at the ground, whinnying their disapproval of me. I admired them but remained wary. I'd seen an angry horse before, and they were not to be underestimated. After a while they ran away, tails held high, waving like shaggy flags. As I approached the ponds, which were barely mucky puddles, fifty head of cattle rose to their feet from their lounging beds and moved in an uncertain manner. They gauged me as I gauged them. It wasn't unheard of for cows to charge.

I fished in my pocket for the white plastic shopping bag I carried and brandished it in front of me. The wind inflated it and then whipped it into a crinkling spiral that I shook free. The cows bolted away, moving rapidly down into the draw as I circled above. I put the bag back in my pocket, wondering if it would work on a horse should the need arise.

The day grew hotter and I drained my water. *I hope the spring is full.*

Trail life had become my life. Things like scaring cows with plastic bags, sleeping on the ground, and wondering where my next water would come from were normal to me, in the same way that turning on a faucet and operating a microwave were in a different context. Fifteen years of backpacking had blurred the edges of "real life" and "other life" to the point that I wasn't certain which was which. Certainly, this felt more visceral, grounded, and alive than sitting in front of a computer, but which one was an escape from the other?

I reached the fenced enclosure and scrambled over the stile, noticing afterward that the fence had been knocked down nearby. The spring was nothing more than puddles and cow-trampled mud littered with cow pies. I sought farther, looking for the culvert that sometimes held precious protected water.

Finally, I found it—tucked into some sage—and scooped water into my filter bag before sinking down in the small patch of shade the culvert provided. I pulled out my lunch of Lucky Charms and potato chips, and voraciously ate them in alternating bites while the gravity filter dripped clean water into the bottle I held with my knees. Swapping out the partially full bottle for another, I washed down the dry food with muddy-tasting water before leaning my head back against the pipe. I was tired, dirty, and yet oddly content to be in the middle of nowhere, alone.

When I first imagined thru-hiking, I pictured forests, mountains, and pristine water. I could never have imagined that choosing to experience trail life would lead me here, wearing clothes that hadn't been washed in fifteen days. I certainly never imagined I would hike the forests and mountains—as well as the cow-pie-riddled plains—of the Triple Crown trails over and over again. It seemed surreal considering I had had no childhood experiences of hiking or camping. This life I was now living resided in mental juxtaposition with the woman I might have been—the one anticipated by my family and by society, the one who would live indoors, have a child or two, and pursue a career.

Life is a flowchart of decisions—a matrix of interrelated outcomes depending on the answers to myriad questions. Looking back, I wondered where I would be at this moment if I had changed any of my choices, even tiny ones. My choice to spend a summer working at the Grand Canyon, where I unexpectedly fell in love with hiking, had dominoed into my decision to thru-hike the AT upon graduation, which had snowballed into completing the Triple Crown . . . and on and on.

I tucked away the nearly empty cereal and chip bags and squeezed the last of the murky water through my filter. This year was inexorably teaching me to let go of hindsight. I knew I had done my best every step of the way. The Heather that could have been would always exist in my mind. *But I can never be all possible incarnations of myself. So I'll drink the cow water and keep walking through deserts, mountains, and forests as the Heather that is.*

I slung my pack on my back and stepped over the downed fence, thankful for the Heather that existed in real life: trail life.

THE SUN WAS PERCHED ON thin clouds clinging to the western horizon when I reached the electric well at the start of the long, straight road across the desert that the CDT followed for nearly twenty miles until it hit pavement. I drank as much of the gushing cold water as my belly could hold, grateful for it after more than thirty miles in the unrelenting sunshine. I filled my bottles and headed out, walking a line that seemed to demarcate twilight from day.

The air east of me flowed downslope from a lavender sky and blushing hills, chilling bare skin that had been burning only an hour before. I noted glimmering Venus as she emerged like magic from the sky. To the west the sun still blazed, casting a red-gold band along the horizon for as far as the eye could see. The desert in that direction expanded into broad flatness, dyed a saffron tone. It was eerily silent except for my crunching steps.

An inexplicable surge of adrenaline propelled me forward as an irrational thought infiltrated my brain. *I don't want to camp out here tonight. I can just hike all the way to Mineral X Road and have Adam meet me there. It will be a fifty-mile day, but I can walk all night and zero in Rawlins tomorrow.*

I pulled out my phone, searching for service to message him. The sudden desire to push my already tired body beyond the fifty-mile mark bordered on panic. My phone blinked at me. *No service.* I put it back in my pocket. I had no idea where he even was tonight. *He could be camping a hundred miles away.* I wasn't even sure why I was suddenly afraid to sleep in the area.

Night eventually overtook the day, the darkness quelling all sunlight. But I did not have to get out my headlamp to follow the linear dirt road. The abundance of stars sprinkled overhead seemed to multiply with every step, their ambient light revealing a sky that was deep navy rather than black. I stopped my frenetic pace briefly to put on my jacket as the air temperature plummeted rapidly. When I resumed walking, the nearly full moon rose above the hilltops, illuminating my breath as I exhaled.

I was out of caffeinated food and drinks. *Will I be able to walk until the wee hours without them?* The quiet was still unbroken—and for the first time in a very long while I was afraid of hiking in the dark. I took several deep breaths and slowed to a steady pace I could maintain. *You love night-hiking, Heather. It's peaceful and beautiful.* I reminded myself over and over as I walked into the night. Despite my own self-soothing reassurances, I glanced over my shoulder from time to time to dispel the sense that I was not as alone as I felt.

By ten I could feel that I was wobbling as I attempted to stride along. Exhaustion curbed my unease, and I finally stopped without thinking about it and began setting up my tent on the side of the road. The sandy landscape was unremarkable and unprotected. *I hope there's no wind overnight.*

I crawled inside, established the interior setup, made my standard refried bean dinner by rote, and was spooning food into my mouth within twenty minutes. My mind was lost in a haze of fatigue, not processing anything aside from spoon to mouth, when a noise hooked my attention. Instinctively I clicked off my headlamp, preferring to meet any foe in darkness rather than illuminating myself. Every hair on my body stood on end, and I felt the familiar liquid fire of adrenaline course through my whole being, even though I didn't know what I'd heard.

The sound came again. A muffled whirring noise, loud enough to be perceived but eerily quiet, as though intentionally buffered. My mind raced. *A far-off engine?* But then I realized the sound was not coming from the road . . . it was coming from above. I froze.

Suddenly I was flooded with memories of sitting in a dark living room watching *The X-Files* with my dad. He had always been a firm believer in aliens, and I suddenly began to fear he was right.

What is it?

The whirring grew no louder, but still I could tell it was closer. It seemed to hover right above my tent, and I felt the muscles of my legs constricting in preparation to bolt, an evolutionary response useless in the age of flight. *Should I open the tent and see what it is, or just stay still and hope it leaves?* I was motionless—barely even breathing—as my mind tore through potential action steps and scenarios faster than I could register them.

Then the noise was gone, fading into the desert night, and the strange silence reigned once again. My body uncoiled from its frozen position and I flung myself outside into the night, searching in all directions for a glimpse of what had been there. *Nothing.* I crawled back inside, my heart pounding and my breath still coming in shallow gasps as I fumbled for my phone.

10:45. Thank God. I set the phone back down, irrationally calmed by the fact that there was no sizable gap in time. *You really did watch too much* X-Files, I thought. I finished my dinner as the adrenaline faded from my system, and I dropped exhausted onto my sleeping pad. *But I still don't know what that was.*

A FEW HOURS LATER I was treed by six black wolves, all teeth and horror like something from Grimm rather than reality.

Then my dad was there. He pulled out his shotgun and killed them all. He didn't brace the stock against his hip, as he had in his later years after age and injury had stolen the mobility of his arms. Instead, he nestled it into the shoulder pocket just as he had twenty-five years ago when he'd taught me how to shoot. Back when I knocked a row of tin cans off a log with accuracy that made him do a double take.

Unable to hold on any longer, I fell out of the tree and jumped to my feet. The wolves were gone. And so was my dad.

I WOKE UP IN A FROZEN TENT, once again lying in the empty desert. My water bottles were full of slush. *Will I ever hike through my grief? Outwalk it, outrun it, outcry it?*

I lay there in silence, tears seeping from my eyes and rolling down my cheeks. It was three a.m. and still forty-two miles to Rawlins, where a night in a warm bed, a shower, and laundry awaited me—things I hadn't had in more than three weeks of pushing thirty-plus-mile days. Adam would find me on the long road walk.

Getting there sooner would probably do me good. And I really doubt I'm going to sleep any more tonight.

I packed my things haphazardly and started walking through the frigid, pin-drop-silent desert. I noticed the time between times had reversed itself—the faint glow of the setting moon now illuminated the western horizon and the faintest pink tinge cast by the still-hours-away sunrise graced the other.

I made my way southward, sobbing.

CHAPTER 19

NORTHERN COLORADO

The remainder of Wyoming passed in a blur of long days on the many road miles connecting me to Colorado's more verdant landscapes. I left the desert and ascended yet again into forests of aspen, with crowns yellow and shimmering in the brilliant, albeit ever weakening, sunshine. *The only gold I care about.* I ran my fingers along the smooth white bark and raked them through the quaking leaves, drawing the rarefied air deep into my lungs. The equinox had long since passed and October was a whisper away.

Everything was glimmering with the change of seasons—the aspens dancing in the warm sunshine, the whorls of frost that settled across the ground overnight. I reveled in the fragile beauty of autumn while knowing deep in my bones that one day it would fracture, turning from idyll into leaden snow clouds and biting wind.

My flight to New England was in three days. There I would resume the journey I'd begun in March with spring as my mercurial companion. Despite the frequent storms, I remembered spring's warmth burgeoning behind me as it thawed the land. The tiny glimpses of buds and blossoms were a promise of what was to come, even though I walked in snow and rain. An entire season of growth had come and gone, and I hoped autumn would be lingering and be kind to me in those final few hundred miles before I returned to the CDT.

I was grateful not only that I'd found the longed-for summer on the PCT but also that it was complete. The sense that I'd finished something after walking for so long bolstered me when I felt like I couldn't do any more miles. I'd shown up and walked almost every day for eighty-six days on that trail. Those incremental investments of time and mileage had taken me from border to border. There was no other way to complete any long-distance trek but putting one foot in front of the other day in and day out. I just needed to keep doing so until the other two trails were done.

I thought of my sister: *"You have your goal ahead, do it!"*

A few flurries floated down from a dark cloud that temporarily blocked out the sun. Despite the snowflakes' captivating juxtaposition with the yellow aspens, I cringed. Only a couple months before, facing the double-edged sword of summer in the West—great weather and racing fires on the PCT—I would have celebrated any precipitation. But right now, I was in the middle of the CDT with full knowledge that these flurries were harbingers of Mother Nature's inevitable trump card. If she played winter too early, I would fail to complete my quest with only a few hundred miles left unwalked.

The snow ceased as the cloud faltered and disintegrated along the divide. Bright sunlight again penetrated the sparse canopy with shafts of golden light. I was no longer pitted against fire but against its nemesis, water, in frozen form. I could feel the weight of a full circle of seasons settling into my body, both poignant and exquisite in its significance.

With Wyoming fully behind me, I could now push southward as far as possible into the highest part of the Rockies until my plane departed. Chasing the vanishing sparkle of autumn's retreating footsteps, I knew full well that no matter how fast or strong I was, I could never outrun Mother Nature.

I will eventually lose autumn and find myself in the cold embrace of winter.

Whether or not I succeeded now was out of my hands—or rather my feet. Every step would take me closer to both inevitabilities, cessation of the journey and winter's dominion, whichever came first. Yet, somehow that seemed to be the most valuable truth of this entire journey—accepting that I was incapable of escape. Not just from the seasons during almost a year of walking but from the overall ebb and flow of life itself.

My sister might be dying. Oh God, is Marie dying? She can't be. She's too young.

A cold gust smacked me across the face as I emerged from the forest, and I shivered. Forty was not far off. *I am approaching the beginning of my own life's autumn.* For the first time I realized that although I was still strong and golden like the aspens, my body had begun to age and I, too, would pass away like frost in sunlight.

I gazed out at the endless sea of peaks spilling across the vista. Stoic mountains belied their tumultuous past of upthrust, volcanism, tectonic subduction, and glaciation. The ancestral rock beneath my feet was billions of years old—created, destroyed, and reincarnated many times over. *Only the mountains live forever, and even those are melted, molded, and recreated.*

I reached the trailhead and restocked my food and water, exchanging only a few words with Adam. We were both exhausted and looking forward to stopping for the day. *Only a few more miles on a road to our campsite*, I thought to myself as I rummaged in the food tote for peanut butter cups.

"We're going to have to head for Denver by five tomorrow night," Adam said as I pawed through the tote.

"Okay. I guess that's fine. This next section shouldn't be a problem when I get back."

"You're not going to be able to hike any of the high country in Colorado once you get back from the AT. We'll just figure out something."

"You don't know that!" I angrily threw my empty water bottle into the trunk. "It could be fine." His dismissiveness struck the exposed nerve of my deepest fear. I *had* to believe it would be possible to keep hiking later. If I didn't, the hike was already over.

"Heather, be realistic."

"Stop being so negative!"

I stomped away, angry and hurt by his lack of empathy.

A few hours later we sat side by side in the car eating dinner, or rather holding food while fuming silently. Nothing between us seemed easy anymore, even the way we related to one another and situations.

"I'm so sick of hiking," I finally said.

"Now who's being negative?"

"Alright, let's just take turns venting. Because 98 percent of the time I have to stay positive. Otherwise I'll never make it."

It would change nothing about how stressed and tired we both were, but I hoped it would help us find common ground. After thirty minutes of complaining at each other, we were no closer.

IT FELT STRANGE TO SIT in a car and plummet in elevation to Denver, where it was still summer hot. I leaned back in my seat, head aching from the massive shifts in temperature and altitude from that morning's miles on the trail.

We stayed with a friend, and it was bliss to take my first shower in more than a week and eat home-cooked food. Sleeping in a bed was also an indescribable luxury after so many nights in a tent or crammed into the backseat-trunk situation, overlapping pads with Adam.

"I don't think it's going to take you that long to hike the Ouachita," I said, worrying over his itinerary for the thousandth time since he'd told me his plan was to fly to Arkansas while I was on the AT.

"That's okay. I'll just hang out in Little Rock or something," he assured me.

"Are you sure you don't want to just come hike the last four hundred miles of the AT with me instead?" I asked, even though I knew the answer.

Adam sighed and glanced away. "No. I need to do something for myself."

"I know," I whispered. The memory of our fight the night before still hung unresolved between us.

"I'm going to go for a run. You just relax and rest." He kissed me on the forehead and left our cozy guest room.

I listened to him go up the stairs, followed by muffled voices as he chatted with our friend before going out into the bold Denver sunshine. I relaxed into the bed and closed my eyes. I knew he was struggling to keep supporting me, and I knew I could do it without him. But it was much easier to have him with me.

I don't know if I could have gotten this far so fast without him. But I also wouldn't have done things in this order if I hadn't been trying to hike the PCT with him.

Would I be able to make it through the snow solo when I got back? The return loomed in my mind and I immediately shut the thought of it down. Adam was right, it was likely the entire divide in Colorado would be buried under many feet of snow by then, and I knew that I would have to piece together an alternative like most early season northbounders did. *There will always be a way if I am willing to find it.*

Instead, I let my mind wander eastward. October was a beautiful month in New England. Autumn would be prime there and Apple Pie a constant source of support. After so many months with Adam, I needed female friendship. She intuited my needs so much better than he did. *And she doesn't constantly make me feel like I'm ruining her life by doing this.*

I opened Instagram on my phone and scrolled through mindlessly for the first time in many months. It was October 2, seven months and one day from when I started the journey. It was also the fiftieth anniversary of the passing of the National Trails Act, which had created the trails I was currently attempting to hike in one year. I read several posts from friends and trail organizations celebrating the jubilee. I was more worn down than I had ever imagined on March 1 that I would be, but I felt a certainty bubble up. This symbolic occasion was why I had chosen to embark on my Calendar Year Triple Crown attempt, and here I was doing it. It felt good to be reminded of my why.

Why did I want to hike these trails for the third time? Why all in one year? Why keep going when the divide is going to shut you down? Why risk ruining your relationship with Adam to hike these again? Why . . . ?

I closed my phone and let it fall to the bed beside me. The answer was both simple and complex, just like the concept of walking thousands of miles across the country. Complex answers were never easy to formulate.

Now six thousand miles into completing my third Triple Crown, I wondered what epoch of my life I was experiencing. What would I tell myself about this period when I looked back on it? I lay quietly, allowing my mind to fall silent, trusting answers would come.

I am seeing these trails in new seasons, and though there is no longer wondrous surprise, I am noticing the way they have become a part of me. These miles are no longer strangers. Though I'm still growing, changing, and passing into new seasons, I'm no longer a stranger to myself.

I sighed and opened my eyes. There was purpose in it. Deep purpose. These trails were in my blood. The time I had spent with them flowed through my veins, quite literally making me who I was. They were the only constant force throughout my adulthood. If I finished this, others would too. People who perhaps also had doubts and questions that could only be answered by walking. Completing this journey was certainly for myself, but it would also be for them. My hope was that even when I was nothing but ash and memory, my journeys on these trails and the lessons I'd learned along the way would remain. Just as the trails, too, would remain, available for anyone willing to seek themselves on them.

CHAPTER 20

MAINE

It was a bold plan, but Apple Pie assured me that she was game to drive if I could put the legs behind it. And I knew that I could.

Two hard date closure obstacles must be overcome to complete the Maine AT in October. For one, Baxter State Park closes access to Mount Katahdin—the trail's northern terminus—sometime in the last half of the month, depending on the weather. One hundred fifty trail miles south, the canoe ferry across the massive Kennebec River would stop running that year on October 15. There was no way I could walk the more than four hundred miles from Hanover to Katahdin fast enough to beat both of those cutoff dates.

So instead of going to the Connecticut River where I had stopped my hike in April, we drove to the Little Bigelow trailhead about twenty miles south of the Kennebec River, arriving at five p.m. I quickly loaded my pack and hit the trail, hiking as fast as possible over roots and slabby rocks after months away on smoother trails and roads. Despite my stumbling over the impediments, the damp forest was soothing after so much desert. My mind and body soon settled into the pace of hiking. Darkness fell and I continued onward by headlamp. I needed to be on the first ferry at nine a.m.

At 8:45 the next morning, I careened past three groups of hikers all within a mile of the river. My feet remembered the dance of the Appalachians, and despite the chilly early October air I was stripped to my sports bra and moving only a shade slower than a run. I reached the empty beach in time to see the ferryman slip the two-person canoe into the water on the other shore and begin paddling my way.

Release forms signed, life jacket donned, and paddle in hand, I relaxed as the ferryman steered us across the mighty artery of Maine. Apple Pie, clad in bright colors, was visible on the far shore, waving. It took only a few minutes to cross the four-hundred-foot-wide river with the ferryman's strong, practiced strokes. I leaped out, and Apple Pie and I jogged to where her car waited a quarter of a mile away at the highway.

We buckled our belts and looked at each other, laughing.

"We're doing it!" Apple Pie exclaimed, her blue eyes sparkling.

"Yes, we are! Now let's go climb Katahdin!"

By four p.m. I was high on the Hunt Spur, shirtless and slinging my body up the third-class rock. Apple Pie and Greenleaf were far below, moving at a more reasonable pace. My heart was thudding hard with the effort and the joy of the ascent. Katahdin is a sacred mountain and its energy flowed through me as I climbed. The sun-warmed rocks were rough under my hands, but I smiled to touch them. I'd missed the rocks and roots of this wild range.

I reached the Tablelands and resumed a bipedal movement, striding across the protected plateau reminiscent of Arctic tundra. Visible in the distance was the rocky nub of Baxter Peak—the point northbound thru-hikers strived toward for nearly twenty-two hundred miles. A cool breeze lapped my sweaty skin, coaxing it into goosebumps, yet the sunshine's embrace mitigated the chill.

This is how I always want to remember you, I murmured to the AT as several parties came toward me, descending in the late afternoon light. I reached the weathered wooden sign at the summit marking the northern terminus of the Appalachian Trail and stood in silence, resting my hand lightly on it, gasping until I caught my breath. A sunny autumn afternoon on the summit of this sacred mountain all alone was a luxury seldom afforded. But here I was, able to drink into my bones the magic of the journey thus far. My mind fell blank as I reclined on sun-warmed rocks and tilted my face upward for five minutes.

Then I layered back up. The sun would set within two hours—slightly less than it had taken me to get up the mountain. I sat down briefly, gazing across what seemed like the entirety of Maine. Myriad lakes, rivers, and hills were arrayed in all directions. I felt a strong sense of peace pour over me, as though the mountain itself were providing assurance. *Hold tight to the blessing of living. Stay strong in your purpose.* With that hope in mind, and with the two certain limitations of the AT now behind me, I headed back down the mountain to hopscotch southward.

"Thank you," I whispered.

The Hundred-Mile Wilderness south of Baxter State Park was busy with hundreds of straggling northbound hikers pushing to reach the end. The weather deteriorated rapidly after my bluebird afternoon on Mount Katahdin, to the point that I found the open summit of White Cap Mountain covered in snow and rime ice when I reached there one early morning. The air was frigid as it whipped across the summit and lashed my body. The climb had been steep—my heart was still pounding in my temples—and I was sweaty, jacketless, and beyond tired from not sleeping well, but I took a picture anyway.

"Because you never get a do-over of a single minute," I told myself through chattering teeth. I fumbled to put my phone away with cold-stiffened fingers and shrugged my jacket on hurriedly.

Winter was coming, whether I was ready or not. Even though it might stop me, I wanted to remember it—all of it—and appreciate the challenges as well as the successes. I wanted to remember the frozen, silent beauty of early morning on a mountain just as clearly as striking summer sunsets from the Pacific Crest. My fingers were numb by the time I reached the shelter of the spruces on the other side of the slabby peak.

The lower forests were warm, damp, and in the peak of fall foliage. In some places the trail was obscured by thick layers of crimson maple leaves. I smiled. *When Maine rolls out the red carpet . . .*

The weather was surprisingly good and I blazed southward as fast as I could, meeting Apple Pie daily at road crossings. We camped together in her SUV and I'd depart in the still-dark mornings, finding my way by headlamp through the hushed forest until birds and sun enlivened it. All of that changed, however, when I reached the Bigelows.

Torrential rain and high winds racked the subrange of bald peaks in central Maine, and I sat in the car while Apple Pie looked at the weather report. I sipped instant coffee that she'd so generously gone out into the pouring rain to make me, dreading walking into it for the rest of the day.

"It's not going to get any better, unfortunately. But you should have clearing conditions tomorrow for the Crockers and Saddlebacks."

I nodded. "Can't expect perfect weather every day this time of year. I'll see you on the other side."

I dashed into the woods, splashing in puddles as I tucked into the climb. Within only a few miles, I realized I might have made a mistake. What felt like an autumnal rainstorm at the car was a bona fide gale at higher elevations. A rhythmic thumping sound drew my attention up from the slick footing. At first, I thought the enormous conifer was toppling, and I flung myself backward, losing my balance and landing in the mud. Instead, the tree slammed back down into its place with such force I felt the vibration. *Thud! Thud! Thud!*

I got to my feet and cautiously approached the tree. To my astonishment I saw that the force of the wind whipping through its branches was lifting the entire tree as though a giant were yanking it by the crown, pulling its roots up several inches from the sodden soil. At the cessation of the gust the tree slammed back into place as though the giant had dropped it—over and over as the wind rocketed across the ridge I was climbing. I stared in fascinated horror for several minutes. Then I registered that the elasticity of roots may not be infinite and I barreled upward, away from the acrobatic tree. The sound now identified, I discovered that dozens of trees in the forest were also engaged in the same dangerous maneuvers.

"I've got to get out of here," I breathed, pushing harder to climb as fast as the rain-slick ground would allow. In my haste to extricate myself from the risk of plummeting trees, I failed to consider what tree-piledriving winds might do to me when I broke free of the protective forest.

I was sideways on the slab before I could react. The brute force of the wind sent me sprawling and sliding, my feet unable to gain purchase on the wet rock. Luckily my legs careened into a cluster of shrubby pines clinging to the edge of the cliff, and I braced myself for a moment while assessing my situation. I would have to traverse nearly three miles in the wide open, at the mercy of howling wind too strong for me to stand.

What am I going to do now? I rested my forehead on the wet rocks, noting a trickle of blood on my skinned palms.

Even when I was prone, the wind was tugging at my backpack, attempting to rip it from me or use it to lever me off the mountain. I was literally between a rock and a hard place.

It took effort, but I managed to roll over, orienting the weight of my pack downward to pull me toward the ground rather than off the side. Then I heaved up and began crab walking along the trail, my hands sliding on the slimy wet surface.

I had to stop every hundred feet, my underused arms fatigued from sudden employment after months of my legs doing all the work. I rubbed my hands on my rain pants, smearing mud from one surface to the other. *Just don't lose your grip.* Rain poured into my eyes, nose, and mouth as I spluttered my way across the mountain. *This is not the most glamorous hiking I've ever done.* Time became nonexistent. Shuffle, shuffle, squint, shuffle, shuffle . . . There was a different rhythm to the movement and yet it echoed what I had done for almost eight months—forward progress one step at a time, even when the steps were small.

Intermittently, I was able to regain my footing and waddle with a wide-legged stance before dropping down again. Eventually I reached the trees on the other end of the ridge, sliding down muddy, wet roots into their embrace with gratitude. I wobbled when I stood, unfolding from the awkward traverse. Around me came the thudding sound of trees on the brink of succumbing to the ferocity of the wind. But for now they provided me shelter and for that I was endlessly thankful.

I hurried downhill, my arms trembling uncontrollably. I passed the campsite where I'd spent a fateful night in 2015 when I'd begun peeing blood. Recalling that the bladder problem had resolved itself within a couple of days, I gained momentum, eager to leave the Bigelows and this bad memory behind me. Nearing the road crossing I reached a swollen creek, its surface flickering with the heavy patter of rain. Dark movement slipped along the far bank, almost invisible through the chaotic frenzy of the water. But there it was again. My eyes locked on to the weasel and it returned my gaze, each of us knowing that the other was now aware of it.

A mink. I've never seen a mink before!

I smiled slightly and broke the gaze. The mink darted and dove, disappearing in a flash of umber. I splashed through the creek and scurried through the trees toward Apple Pie waiting in the car. Despite warmth and assistance awaiting me, I felt a deep sense of awe once again at the power of nature. Each time I began to feel complacent in my skills, she forced me to push myself beyond comfort, requiring me to find an inner strength I knew would serve me well in my hardest moments—both on and off the trail.

The weather abated for the remainder of my time in Maine, leaving misty, muddy conditions for me to slosh through in knee-high gaiters paired with my hiking skirt. I was much too far south now to see northbounders; anyone with a hope of reaching Katahdin this season had long ago passed through. Instead, I walked in the silence only wilderness brings, the kind that rings in your ears. Over the hills and through the trees, across the rocks and over the rivers. Onward toward the inevitable end of the journey.

I felt almost no doubt now that I would finish both the PCT and the AT in a single hiking season. Nothing stood in my way except Mother Nature.

CHAPTER 21

NEW HAMPSHIRE

I descended from the Wildcats, exhausted after the long traverse of twenty of the White Mountain AT miles. Apple Pie texted me to let me know that some friends were waiting with her and that they'd host us in their cabin that night. Thoughts of a hot shower and a bed danced in my head.

"Hey!" I greeted them, recognizing one as someone I'd run with in the Barkley marathons. "Small world."

We loaded into vehicles and drove to their cabin. Along the way Apple Pie delivered bad news, which always seemed to come alongside the trail magic on this journey.

"There's going to be one-hundred-mile-per-hour winds on Mount Washington tomorrow. It's snowing right now and will keep it up all night." She winced slightly as she spoke, knowing that this setback would feel crushing when I was on a deadline that didn't allow for much wiggle room.

I leaned my head back against the seat and sighed. I was muddy, cold, and massively hungry.

"So, basically death conditions," I said, finally.

"With your gear? Pretty much."

"What's the extended?"

"Not really any better. Lower winds, but still snowing. Ice at middle elevations."

"I just got shut down, didn't I?" I couldn't help but laugh at my own hubris of thinking I might have outpaced Mother Nature.

"Not exactly. I can guide you through the Dry River Wilderness that's just below the tree line on trails that parallel. It's rugged and will be way harder than the AT, but there's a route that will take you all the way to Franconia Notch."

I looked at her, overwhelmed with gratitude at having her support. As a White Mountain guide, she knew the trails here like the back of her hand. Yet again when things seemed over, there was a way through.

"Thank you."

We started early with Greenleaf joining us, carrying our emergency gear. The route would remain mostly below tree line, but we would have to ascend above it and traverse the open slopes for a brief while before going back down on another trail.

The Dry River Wilderness was indeed wild. More than once, I felt like I was in the remote reaches of the Glacier Peak Wilderness in Washington, not on the flanks of some of the most well-traveled mountains in the US. Downed trees were everywhere. The trail tread was almost indistinguishable from the forest floor in many places. *Thank God for Apple Pie*, I repeated over and over to myself as we painstakingly made our way through the jungle and began to climb relentlessly.

We reached the tree line after two thousand feet of climbing and were immediately blasted by wind so fierce that it made the conditions in the Bigelows seem like a gentle breeze. We all stumbled, losing our footing on the rime-coated rocks, clinging with our hands to scale the sometimes vertical rocks. Apple Pie was shouting directions, but they were lost in the shrieking wind. Greenleaf paused to deal with something and I tried to wait—but despite wearing everything I had and a borrowed wool shirt from Apple Pie, I was shivering. I surged forward, following her through the near whiteout conditions, trusting that she and Greenleaf—also an expert in the White Mountains—knew where to go.

My God, no wonder people die up here all the time.

The wind was sideswiping, threatening to send me sliding and tumbling down ice-coated boulders if I didn't crouch and hold on tightly. I sensed movement in the corner of my eye and was relieved to see Greenleaf, bundled up in raingear, right beside me again. His black beard was already coated in ice.

How long do we have to be up here? The air temperature had to be well below freezing, and that would make the windchill unfathomably low. My hands, even inside of thick mittens, and the small amount of my face that was exposed were burning. After what felt like an eternity, we reached the top of the ascent and turned sharply to the left. Apple Pie was moving downhill and I gladly followed, the wind now pushing me in the direction I wanted to go—toward the black outline of the forest vaguely visible through the blowing snow.

Less than ten minutes later, we were back in the embrace of the trees. I felt an extreme sense of relief, even though I was frozen to the core and shivering violently. We were all sweat soaked from the thousands of feet of climbing, and the extreme cold had been like plunging into a flash freezer. Without discussing it we hurried forward—downhill—as fast as we could on the marginal trail. I was so thankful to have them with me, not just today but for nearly all of the northern part of the trail. Apple Pie had truly made my hike so much easier and more efficient. More than that, she had encouraged me from near and far. Her support had been vital to my success. Tears welled up with immense gratitude for her and for everyone who had helped me along the way—especially Adam. Even though we'd fought and it had been stressful, he had given a tremendous part of himself to this trip.

AFTER THE WHITE MOUNTAINS, the Appalachian Trail ranged from snowy peaks to rolling hillsides still enrobed in autumn splendor. Though the days were dreary, the miles were easy—and just like that, the miles reached zero on a bridge over the Connecticut River. I stood there with Apple Pie, Greenleaf, and a friend of a friend in the bitter cold of a mid-October afternoon, bundled against the cutting wind and snow flurries.

I stared at the dark water flowing beneath the bridge for a few moments, remembering when I'd stood there in April on a balmy evening.

Despite everything that had transpired, I'd completed the Appalachian and Pacific Crest Trails in one year. *Is this really possible? Will I succeed after all?* I texted Adam, who had been killing time at a hostel in Little Rock since finishing the Ouachita Trail a week earlier.

"I'm done."

It was an inauspicious place to finish a thru-hike, especially one like this. But hiking itself had long since taught me that it is truly about the journey, not the destination.

And there is still a lot of journey left.

CHAPTER 22

SOUTHERN COLORADO

Wheels up, wheels down . . . in between my feet on the ground. The stunning speed of travel that wasn't ambulatory left me dizzy. The brown landscape below was nothing like the vibrant green, gold, and scarlet autumnal array I'd just been immersed in.

Adam and I found each other easily in the Denver airport. Our flights were both on time and the sun was shining. But I'd seen the snow-covered mountains looming in the distance as we'd circled for landing. I hugged him tightly and wished hard that we were going home and not back out there.

"I'm so happy to see you. I missed you so much," we proclaimed simultaneously, and laughed. In these moments when I wasn't walking, there was so much joy between us. I dreaded the end of that in a matter of hours when we were once again jammed in the back of my Elantra trying to sleep through the frigid night.

"I'm worried about the route," I said as we walked out of the terminal and boarded the light rail. "The mountains look buried, and the other guy doing a CYTC just about died in an avalanche on Hope Pass yesterday. He had to backtrack and go around on a lower route."

"I know, but I had some spare time in between Netflix binges in Little Rock," Adam said, digging into his pack and pulling out a stack of maps. "I worked out a series of connectors and low routes, a lot of Forest Service roads, that will take you to New Mexico. I even have a couple of worst-case scenario options in there, too, that are paved, unfortunately, in case a big storm hits."

I took the packet, including an overview map he'd drawn out, and felt both immense relief and gratitude. I thumbed through them, noting the variations from the trail as I went. He'd been meticulous, which didn't surprise me. He had a master's in GIS and was a cartographer by trade.

"There's a digital version as well, of course, on my phone. I'll see you every day so I can make sure you've got it plotted out on your phone too."

"I don't know what to say except thank you." I set the maps in my lap and hugged him tightly, forgetting our fight about this very topic only a few weeks before. "This would have been so much work for me to figure out on the fly."

"You're welcome, Heather," he murmured as he wrapped his arms around me. We didn't let go of one another until our stop was announced.

We took a Lyft to our friend's house and threw our packs in the backseat of my car. After a stop at a supermarket, Adam steered us away from civilization and toward the home stretch—back to the divide. Ahead of me lay the unknowns of bad weather, low routes, and a race against winter in earnest. Earlier in the year I had wondered if I should have hiked all of New Mexico first, but now I was glad that my favorite portion of the entire CDT remained—the mesas of northern New Mexico.

And then . . . I'd be done.

The thought felt strange in my brain. Though it was of course an inevitable part of this odyssey, the word had been ephemeral throughout the last seven and a half months. *Done.* In the last three, I'd thought that word only in terms of what I was ready to be. But now, speeding along a highway into the purple dusk on an October night, it was almost tangible. *Done.* Something I could finally grasp. With Adam's help—and barring catastrophe—I would be done with this hike soon.

A tear slid down my cheek as I gazed out the window, the world passing far too fast for my liking. I wasn't certain if I was sad, or happy, or something else. Although *done* was powerful in my mind, it was not yet here. Until Grants, hundreds of miles to the south, nothing would be different. I had to keep walking in the same metronomic way I had for almost eight months, thirty-plus miles at a time. *One foot in front of the other.* For the first time I wondered what I would do when there were no more miles to walk. *Who would I be then?*

I WOVE HIGH AND LOW, sometimes in snow and sometimes on the shoulder of a highway. Colorado was barren, beautiful, and cold now. All year, with few exceptions, I'd tempered myself. *Don't do more than thirty-five miles per day. You'll burn out. Keep it consistent. It's a marathon, not a sprint.* But now, pacing seemed irrelevant—it had become a sprint. Thick clouds pelted me with sleet and snow flurries daily. It was only a matter of time before even lower route options were buried in snow too deep to safely traverse. So I allowed myself to push, tipping past forty day after day. *If I gotta hike on the road, I might as well crush miles.*

This was a different style of hiking, one of expedience to reach safety—the safety of New Mexico sunshine. Adam met me as often as he could, offering encouragement, direction, food, and coffee. In between he looked for accommodations and supplies, all while keeping an eagle eye on the weather. *Where would we sleep on long road walks?* It was a question I'd answered any number of ways over the years when fire or weather or the trail itself had demanded it.

I'd slept in ditches and down by rivers. I'd slept on highway embankments and in the backyards of kind strangers whose homes I'd walked past, and in other places that weren't quite legal, slithering under fences and leaving nothing but matted grass that could as easily have been left by a transient animal that bedded down for a few cold hours, which indeed is what I felt like. I'd slept in hostels and in cemeteries, in closed-up campgrounds and in city parks.

With Adam the camping wasn't quite as adventurous, usually a pull-off or trailhead. But after a week of it, he'd begun to secure us nights in the warm beds of cheap motels that lay on our path. Normally fussy about lodgings, I was now too tired to care. My arrival at dark was followed by a shower, plowing food into my mouth, and then collapsing between sheets I hoped were clean, contemplating how I'd ended up in that moment.

The pondering wouldn't last long, my need for sleep tabling the ongoing existential discussion until the next day's long walk. In the mornings, I filled my belly with acidic coffee from the front desk and rolled out into the cold predawn light to walk once again—another day of relentless forward progress.

As I walked along a straight dirt road, I texted Marie, having heard nothing since early August.

"Heya! Just wanted to let you know that some boxes are heading your way. It's full-on winter in the Rockies now so I'm mailing my summer gear back. I hope to be back in FL by Thanksgiving! Miss and love you!"

I walked steadily, my ears attuned for the tiny beep of my phone. I wanted to hear something good. Reassurances that all was well. That no news was good news. When the ding came, I stopped to read the reply.

"Two boxes have arrived. Looking forward to seeing you. If all goes well, we will have some sort of Thanksgiving besides giving thanks. I am still around and feeling good, having you back safe and sound. so keep warm. Go girl."

Still around and feeling good. I sighed with relief. She was doing better. I felt like a weight had been lifted from my shoulders, and I walked even faster toward the heart of Colorado's southern mountains and highest point.

THE LAKE WAS FROZEN SOLID, much to my dismay. I slammed my heel down hard on the gray surface. Nothing happened. Again, harder. I heard the slight snapping of frozen bonds uncoupling, reminding me of breaking the ice in the horse's water trough on dark mornings when my father was hospitalized.

I was in eighth grade when my dad had his first heart attack. My mom and I arrived home from church to a house gone cold, when normally he would have been tending the fire. His absence was glaring, and I felt an eeriness clutch my gut.

"Heather, go to the barn and see if your dad is out there," my mom said, obviously worried as she called up the stairs. "Andy!"

I stared at her.

"What?" she asked, turning back to me after there was no answer.

"What if . . . ?" I paused, uncertain how to say the fear that was coursing through my veins. "I don't want to find his body," I whispered.

My mom made a strange noise and went out the back door. I walked to the blinking answering machine and hit play. Fifteen messages from my sister played back, all saying the same thing: "Call me at work."

My mom reappeared, stomping snow off her dress shoes as the final message played.

We looked at each other. My sister worked at the local hospital.

By the time we came back that evening, the house was fifty degrees. My mom fought with the woodstove, finally igniting a small fire, which I patiently fed while she went outside to take care of the horses and made us dinner. We didn't speak, but I felt the fear in her—the same fear that filled me too.

At five the next morning I dragged myself from the warm cocoon of my bed, down the stairs, and into the kitchen. My dad's desk looked oddly empty. The house was cold without him there to start a fire at four thirty, when he normally woke up. I opened the desk drawer and took out his giant Maglite.

The dark horse pasture was winter silent. The trough was completely frozen. I stomped the ice over and over, the horses whickering from their loafing barn.

"I know I'm late," I called to them, grabbing hold of the barbed wire fence, careful to put my hand between the rusty barbs. I brought my foot down with all the force I could muster and a sharp crack rang out a millisecond before my foot broke through, submerging my boot in three feet of water.

A swooshing beside me drew my attention away from the water pouring into my boot. Linda pushed her nose into the hole, widening it as she drank greedily. I grabbed her neck and hoisted my overflowing boot out. Lucky nuzzled me aside, joining his mother. I tipped my boot out, the water instantly turning to ice on the snow-covered ground.

The horses were occupied with slurping water as I made my way to the haymow, my foot squishing in my sodden boot. I slid the door open while holding my breath. I'd always been afraid of the darkness and of what lived outside in our woods—and occasionally in our barns.

Ever since my dad had found the threadbare coat of someone who'd fled the haymow at his approach a few months before, I was also afraid of *who* might be in there. I shined the Maglite rapidly around the hay bales. A rustling made me shriek and jump backward. A fat raccoon lumbered past me and disappeared into the darkness. My heart banged dangerously in my chest as I hurried to grab the battered aluminum saucepan scoop and measure the grain and pellets into a bucket. Grabbing five flakes of hay, I limped across the pasture in a now-frozen boot, struggling to keep the horses' noses out of the bucket until I reached their feed boxes, even as they snagged tufts of hay.

Inside the house I crouched in front of the woodstove with a pile of kindling I'd snapped across my knees, just as I'd seen my dad do hundreds of times. I wadded newspapers and arranged layers of kindling and small wood. With one match the fire caught, its merry crackling a welcome sound in the cold house. I sat back with my white-cold foot propped up to receive the heat it offered. Behind me the upstairs door opened and my mom emerged.

"Oh, you're up," she said muzzily. Like me, she was not a morning person. "And you started a fire."

"I did," I said, feeling proud. Without my dad lurking over my shoulder, I hadn't messed it up. Real heat was emanating now, and I put a medium piece of firewood in.

"Okay, well I guess I need to go take care of the horses."

"I already did."

She blinked at me, owl eyed. Then she came over and gave me a hug.

"Oh, thank you, honey. Thank you for taking care of me."

"It's gonna be okay, Mom." I patted her back, feeling her tears on my neck. "I'm going to get ready for school."

Unlike the ice in the horse trough, the lake ice in Colorado refused to give way. I dropped down to my knees and pounded the fractured spot with a large rock until it disappeared with a *gloomph* into the blackness of the cold water. I dipped my bottle and drank the untreated contents greedily, thirst overcoming caution. After drinking my fill, I sank back to the ground and dug in my backpack pockets for a snack.

Who? Who cooks for you? an owl inquired from the snowy evergreens nearby, no doubt uncertain about the unnaturally dark day.

I finished my snack, noticing that the hole in the lake ice was filled with slush. I got to my feet, thankful they hadn't gotten wet but aware that so much icy water in my stomach had lowered my core temperature. I shivered as I glanced around the forest-fringed lake but didn't see the owl. I checked my phone. Three p.m. *Gotta get going.*

"**YOU'RE GOING TO HAVE** to take the highway from Salida," Adam said the next night, after my manic consumption of dinner in the passenger seat of my car.

I looked up at him, somewhat mollified by food. "Why?"

Adam sighed and held out his phone for me to see. A giant blob of blue and pink was over Utah.

"I take it that's coming here next?" I handed it back to him.

"Yep. Day after tomorrow. Right now, they're forecasting three to five feet of snow. It's the first real winter storm."

"Well, we made a damn good run beforehand at least. How much is going to fall down lower?"

"Nine inches."

"That's not much better," I laughed ruefully. "So, I'll have to drop all the way down to Alamosa and then back up to the Creede route on the highway and then down into Chama?"

Adam nodded, pulling out the corresponding maps and drawing his finger along the pink highlighted "worst-case-scenario" route he'd created from a hostel bunk in Arkansas.

"You're going to have to do as many miles as possible tomorrow. You'll only have until about two p.m. the next day before the storm hits, and you've got about a hundred miles to get to Alamosa."

"Better get some sleep then," I said.

I lay down in the cozy bed, so grateful for the comfort. *It was worth driving here after my hike today.* I closed my eyes and tried to release the tension in my body. I was oddly calm about what lay ahead. *I can do fifty. Maybe even sixty if I start early.* I sank into the dark.

FIFTY-FIVE MILES LATER, AFTER WALKING mostly on roads, I reached a dirt track leading into BLM land. A hundred yards up, in a small copse of trees, I could just make out my car in the last rays of daylight. I whooped and Adam called back. I stumbled into the campsite and flopped into the tent, kicking my shoes off and lying flat on my back. It had taken every last ounce of energy I'd had left to get here . . . and I still had forty miles to go in order to reach Alamosa tomorrow.

"I can't do it by two p.m.," I said piteously, exhaustion and a burgeoning sense of failure creeping into my voice.

Adam reached into the tent with a hot pot of something cheesy and delicious. "You get as far as you can and I will drive you into town. You can always walk backward after the storm goes through."

I shoveled food into my mouth. I hated the thought of nonlinear progress. Outside the tent, the full moon rose in a crystal-clear sky. A riot of coyote howls shattered the almost unbearable silence. I handed the empty pan back to him. *All progress is progress.*

The moon was still illuminating the tent when my alarm went off. Adam pulled me close to him, and I relished the extra warmth and moments of rest. After a few minutes he relinquished me to the not-yet-day and I crawled out of my bag into the frigid air. The frozen grass snapped as I walked back to the dirt two-track and followed it out to the deserted blacktop. The moon's visage was no longer keen. Gauzy clouds blurred its glow—nearly imperceptible portents of what was to come.

I pushed all day to stay ahead of the impending winter storm, desperate to drop below the elevation line where multiple feet were expected to where *only* nine inches were. I hiked as hard as I could, despite the protests of aching feet, burgeoning shin splints, and nagging IT band syndrome from the many road miles. Yesterday's nearly fourteen-hour push had left me hobbling.

Adam passed by me at ten a.m., as snow began to fall softly, lightly. *Early.* I forced myself to keep to the strong four-mph pace I'd established, determined to crush miles just as hard as I did when the sun was shining. *More storms will come, and I don't want to be here to see them.*

The snow thickened and a glance back revealed nothing but a gray wall in the higher elevations where I'd slept. *If only I hadn't needed to sleep.* Unlike me, Mother Nature needed no rest. She was the ultimate persistent huntress, overtaking me and drenching my world in white. Thirteen miles from Alamosa I met Adam waiting on the roadside, four inches of snow already piled around the tires. I got inside.

The next morning, I put on every layer of clothing I had and topped it with a reflective vest. I left the motel room despite everything inside me saying to go back to bed. A foot of snow was piled on top of my car; the streets were unplowed. Skid marks led to deserted cars all along the roads. The world was silent, draped like a house abandoned. I plodded through the deep snow, back on the highway and heading north. *If they don't plow before I get to my connection point, what will I do? Adam can't drive in this.*

I pushed the thought away, letting the piercing wind carry it eastward. It would take me hours to get there. I walked at a much more moderate pace, slowed by the snow and crippled from covering almost seventy miles in thirty-six hours. Slowly the sounds of reviving humanity began echoing across the empty world outside of town, carried by the wind and muffled by the snow.

A plow passed me at mile seven and again in the other direction an hour later. The sun broke free from the bonds of thick stratus clouds and beat down with such ferocity I had to stop and peel off most of my layers. It was still only twenty degrees, but the UV made it seem twice that. I heard a familiar engine as I passed the twelve-mile mark. Adam slowed as he pulled alongside, and I could see the sense of relief on his face.

"Do you need anything?"

"No, but can you take this?" I shoved my backpack full of extra clothes through the open window.

"I'll be up at the turnaround!" he called, pulling away slowly. I watched as the car slid slightly in the slush before finding grip and disappearing into the distance. *One more mile today. Then you get to rest.*

CHAPTER 23

NORTHERN NEW MEXICO

It took several days for me to regain all the lost elevation, climbing back up to the divide. The snow piled along the road was deeper than my shoulders. I walked steadily to stay warm, thankful that the highway was maintained in winter and grateful that Colorado was almost behind me. New Mexico beckoned, and I could feel that it was the "almost end." I knew this headspace well. I'd been there so many times before.

Though very little remained, it seemed unachievable—as though not enough was left of me to quite reach the terminus. But I also knew that it would take only a fraction of what I'd already done to get there. The marriage of exhaustion and rationale was fraught.

"We can camp here," Adam said as I scarfed my second lunch. "I found a pull-off that will work right there where the trail crosses the highway."

I shook my head. "No. I'm not stopping until I get to New Mexico."

"That's going to take you until after dark."

"I don't care. I just need to be done with this part of the hike."

"You're so stubborn, you know that?"

I gave a dismissive shrug and headed down the road again. *If only you had met my dad, you'd understand.* My dad always did things his way—against all advice. Retrospectively, I could see, too, that he often had to prove something to himself—just as I did.

Did grandfather forget to tell you he was proud of you too?

MY DAD'S SECOND HEART ATTACK came a decade after the first, this time requiring open heart surgery. Living at home after my first thru-hike—working at a Subway restaurant—I was glad to feel like I could give something in return by helping them out while he was hospitalized and with aftercare.

I stumbled downstairs at five a.m. to feed the horses, just as I had at thirteen. This time, however, I was surprised to find my dad already awake. I stopped short in the doorway of the living room and stared, my sleep-blurred eyes not quite comprehending the sixty-eight-year-old shirtless man on the floor cranking out one-arm push-ups.

"Dad?"

"Oh," he said, jumping to his feet. His face was barely flushed, although he was panting slightly. The sutured gash on his chest stood out stark and ugly in the dim light of a lamp.

"What on earth are you doing? You'll blow out your stitches! And also, I'm pretty sure that's not what the doctor meant by 'light exercise'!"

To his credit, he managed to look slightly chagrined. He waved his hand, dismissing my misgivings.

"I just needed to know I could still do it."

AS OCTOBER DREW TO A CLOSE, I stepped aside as a car whizzed by me in the growing dusk a few miles before the state border.

I just need to know I can do this.

Only the faintest light lingered in the sky as I reached the bold yellow New Mexico sign and my car where Adam waited for me. Instead of collapsing into the seat and eating, I hobbled to the sign and leaned against it, crying. *Only about two hundred miles left. Only two hundred miles. Heather, you're really doing this. You can do this.* I kissed the cold metal. "Done" was becoming so much more than a nebulous concept.

New Mexico was so much warmer, and I was happy and relieved to leave the snowy landscapes behind for the final time. The next afternoon, I happily threw all my cold weather layers into a tote in the trunk of the car and returned to hiking in my skirt and short-sleeved shirt. As I chipped away at the final two hundred miles, we returned to finding campsites near trailheads, where we basked in the luxury of being inside a tent rather than crammed into the car. I drank in the golds, roses, and muted tones that had enthralled Georgia O'Keeffe.

There was no sign of any other hikers, although I knew some southbounders must be only a few weeks ahead of me. Instead, I followed signs of the other forest residents—bear tracks were common, as were the winding lines of snakes and the tiny heart-shaped hoofprints of antelope. I felt like yet another member of the herd.

I'm doing this—just keep walking was a constant refrain in my head. Though this hike was three times longer than any other I'd done, the way I accomplished it was exactly the same. Start walking and don't quit.

That was the only thing driving me when I set out on my first thru-hike fifteen years earlier. I was overweight and had never before backpacked for longer than two days. Still, I believed with all my heart that as long as I didn't stop walking, I would make it to Maine—*and I did.*

In the dark winter months that followed, I lived with my parents and applied for jobs with the National Park Service. Then I waited, making sandwiches at Subway, helping my mom and dad, and dreaming of the trail.

"Did you put your hike on your résumé?" my dad asked me one bright afternoon while I dried and put away dishes.

I glanced up at him, surprised at the question.

"Why?"

"Well," he looked away from me, then back with a little shrug, "it shows you've got stick-to-it-ism!"

I smiled, and he looked slightly embarrassed that he had spelled out a compliment.

"Yes, I did put it on there."

My dad nodded, satisfied, and walked away grinning. My AT thru-hike would end up being the reason Glacier National Park called to offer me a seasonal job as a visitor use assistant.

IN CUBA, NEW MEXICO, I packed up my backpack for an overnight out in the mesa country south of town.

"I'll see you at Torreon Road tomorrow evening," I said, kissing Adam goodbye. "Then only one more night, hopefully!"

He smiled, the most authentic one I'd seen in many months. "Just two more days!"

I followed the highway out of town before eventually turning onto a dirt track leading toward the first of several mesas. The afternoon was perfectly golden, and the foliage matched, seeming effervescent as the reds and golds danced in the warm light. I sweated as the trail climbed, weaving between sandy tread and slickrock. I gazed down dramatic pour-offs that were cavernous enough to create their own landscapes.

Dipping into a cool canyon, I walked a short distance up a sandy wash to where Jones Canyon Spring gushed from a black pipe. It was serenely quiet in the lush grotto as I knelt to gather water, but my senses were still keenly observing everything around me. My uncanny ability to detect even the slightest disturbance had become nearly superhuman over the course of the hike. After so many days out-of-doors, I no longer felt like a displaced human but more like a transient animal seeking some uncertain refuge. Now when I wandered the aisles of a grocery store or slept in a bed, I felt displaced, like a feral cat brought inside.

I glanced over my shoulder. *Something isn't quite right.* I stood up, turning fully around. Nothing was obviously amiss. *Mountain lion?* I stood still, tensely listening. There was no better place for an ambush than at a water source at dusk. I crouched down again and grabbed my water bottles without taking my eyes away from scanning the landscape. A breeze cooled my sweaty skin, and with it my body relaxed. Trusting my senses, I knelt back down to finish filling the last bottle.

Back at the trail I made the sharp left and pushed up the steep grade out of the arroyo. At my feet, distinct and unmarred by time, were fresh bear tracks. I looked around the open vista and seeing nothing, continued southward. After a hundred yards the bear's tracks veered off of the trail, and I continued onward toward La Ventana Mesa.

The miles remaining ebbed to double digits as I watched the sun kiss the horizon. I had walked for so many days, it was impossible to conceive that soon I would not walk anymore. As with all of the thru-hikes I'd hiked before, what came at this point were thoughts of the miles that were behind me and those that remained ahead. My mind vacillated between two questions. *Is this more of an ending—or is it a beginning?*

The only true answer was: both. Bubbling up from beneath those unanswerable questions came a response to a completely separate query.

The sky flamed orange as I threw my tent out on the ground, setting it up just like I had thousands of times before. I remembered the moment in our sunny kitchen when my dad had declared the one thing I'd always been looking for and I had somehow missed until now. I'd missed it for so many years because it hadn't come in the words I expected.

A flash of blue feathers darted through the trees, barely discernible in the waning light. *"You've got stick-to-it-ism!"* What my father had left unspoken was suddenly clear to me: *and I'm proud of you for it.* Tears began to pour down my cheeks.

"I'm going to do this, Dad," I whispered. "I stuck to it."

THE NEXT NIGHT, DESPITE HAVING walked the CDT twice before, I got lost. While most CDT hikers consider this inevitable, I was proud of the fact that I hadn't once wandered astray this time around—that is, until this very last night of my hike. Somewhere in the patchwork of roads and trees on the flanks of Mount Taylor, I wandered off the route. It was nearly ten p.m. when I came crashing through vegetation on a dead-reckoning line back on to the CDT.

I was cut up and exhausted from fighting my way through the brush, and I set up the tent haphazardly. The ground was frosty already and I shivered as I readied myself for sleep. Although I knew it was the last night of the hike, my body reminded me of the hardship by complaining more loudly than normal. I sat at the open door of my tent and stripped my shoes and socks off my filthy, taped-up feet. I stared at them by headlamp light, feeling almost as though they were strangers. My feet had long since stopped feeling like my feet and had become more like the hardened hooves of an unshod land mammal, one that had logged thousands of transcontinental miles. *I wonder how long it will take for them to feel like human feet again.*

I pulled clean-ish socks onto them and lay down, groaning as my back and legs unfurled from their working shape where they spent most of their time. *How long before my body unwinds from its locked position of nothing but forward motion?*

The night was so clear and cold, it felt as though it could shatter. I crawled out of my tent to pee before sleep and gazed up at the myriad pinpoints of light freckling the indigo sky. The dipper pointed downward, a reminder of where and when I was—back in the aptly named land of enchantment with winter close at hand. I nestled back into my warm bag beneath juniper and pinyon pine and quickly fell asleep to a coyote lullaby.

I was a third of the way down Mount Taylor the next day when I spotted Adam coming up toward me accompanied by a tall, rangy man. When they drew close and greeted me, I was blown away to discover it was Flyin' Brian Robinson, the first person to complete a Calendar Year Triple Crown. He explained that he had guessed my itinerary from my online posts and had driven out from California, then slept in his car at the trailhead for two nights hoping to intercept me in order to show his support.

Brian's presence brought me new energy, which I needed for the final miles, a seven-mile highway walk to and through Grants to where a tree growing in a diamond-shaped median awaited me. Adam took my pack, and Brian and I flew along the road, falling into deep conversation of the kind that comes rapidly when strangers meet on the trail. New friends that immediately know their time together is limited by the very thing that has brought them together.

Our time would consist of a few hours as we walked down a highway and wove through city streets, our words distracting us from our path. I repeatedly checked my phone and guided us back to the route after yet another missed turn. It was a relief to talk to someone who understood what I was going through. What I had *been* through. Someone who was excited for my achievement.

Finally, we emerged into the open outskirts, and I could see the crown of a lonely tree in the distance. Adam was standing beside the median waiting for us, relief evident on his face. I wondered if our relationship would ever recover.

I'd finished many epic treks, and always something broke free in me at this point when the end was in sight. Usually tears, sometimes howling, but this time nothing except the conversation with someone who understood everything I had been through in a way that few others could. To be the first is a difficult role. You have to take on the unknown with confidence built on internal strength rather than the foundation of example.

We made the final turn, and Brian held back as I surged forward and embraced the tree with fervor. In that moment, at this otherwise innocuous tree, my fifteen-year-old dream came to fruition. Despite my face-aching smile, tears slid out of my eyes. Two years of planning and commitment had paid off.

A bone-deep fatigue flooded my body, mixing with joy that eight months of walking had ended. Under the branches of this insignificant tree, I became the first female Calendar Year Triple Crowner and the first female Triple Triple Crowner. It was the culmination—the terminus. But I knew that each of the millions of footsteps I'd taken in the last 251 days added up to so much more than these titles could convey—everything I had walked through and learned, and who I had become along the way.

I turned away to see Adam and Brian standing there, beaming. The next moments were a blur of hugs and cheers. Then they raised their phones, and I touched the tree symbolically for them but also to steady myself with the strength that only the earth can give. I smiled broadly as the photos were taken. As I leaned against the rough bark, my gaze traveled beyond Adam and Brian to Route 66.

Perhaps I saw it, or perhaps it was only in my imagination, but there it was nonetheless—a brown classic Buick cruising by, windows down. I glimpsed the man driving, jet black hair and a white T-shirt, emanating James Dean vibes. *I did this for you, Dad.* The warm November sun embraced me as I stepped away from the tree. *I did this for us.*

We walked away from the inauspicious end point of a long-sought-after dream, my fingers entwined with Adam's. I had conquered my doubts, my fears. I glanced back over my shoulder for one last look.

I did this for myself.

ACKNOWLEDGMENTS

Thank you to the thousands of volunteers who ensure that our National Scenic Trails remain accessible footpaths for everyone to enjoy.

Thank you to Adam. This hike was hard on us in the greatest of ways, but I couldn't have done it without you. I will be forever grateful.

Thank you to Apple Pie for always being my cheerleader and a tremendous support in my CYTC quest and everything else. You made all the difference.

Thank you to Greenleaf and all of my friends and the strangers who helped me out along the way. There are far too many to list here, but you know who you are.

Thank you, Dad, for everything you taught me. I know you did your best. I love you.

Thank you to my oldest sister for cheering me on, even as your own life was drawing to a close. I wish we'd had more time together, but I am so grateful for the moments we shared.

And of course, thank you to Mountaineers Books for continuing to work with a nomad who has a story to tell.

ABOUT THE AUTHOR

A National Geographic Adventurer of the Year, Heather Anderson is the first woman to complete the Appalachian, Pacific Crest, and Continental Divide National Scenic Trails three times each. This includes her historic 2018 Calendar Year Triple Crown hike when she became the first woman to hike all three in one March-to-November season.

She has set self-supported Fastest Known Times (FKTs) on the Pacific Crest Trail (2013) and the Appalachian Trail (2015). She has logged more than fifty thousand miles on foot since 2003, including numerous thru-hikes. She is also an avid mountaineer and trail runner.

As a professional speaker, Anderson regularly recounts her adventures and the lessons learned on trail. She is the author of *Thirst: 2600 Miles to Home*, chronicling her PCT record, and *Mud, Rocks, Blazes: Letting Go on the Appalachian Trail* about her 2015 AT record. With Katie Gerber, she coauthored *Adventure Ready: A Hiker's Guide to Planning, Training, and Resiliency*, a guide to preparing for long-distance hiking.

You can learn more about Heather at wordsfromthewild.net or follow her on Instagram, YouTube, and Facebook @_wordsfromthewild_.

recreation • lifestyle • conservation

MOUNTAINEERS BOOKS, including its two imprints, Skipstone and Braided River, is a leading publisher of quality outdoor recreation, sustainability, and conservation titles. As a 501(c)(3) nonprofit, we are committed to supporting the environmental and educational goals of our organization by providing expert information on human-powered adventure, sustainable practices at home and on the trail, and preservation of wilderness.

Our publications are made possible through the generosity of donors, and through sales of more than 700 titles on outdoor recreation, sustainable lifestyle, and conservation. To donate, purchase books, or learn more, visit us online:

MOUNTAINEERS BOOKS
1001 SW Klickitat Way, Suite 201 • Seattle, WA 98134
800-553-4453 • mbooks@mountaineersbooks.org
www.mountaineersbooks.org

An independent nonprofit publisher since 1960